Because God Walked with Them

...Holy Experiences Shared

Clyde H. Embling (Rev. Dr.)

PublishAmerica
Baltimore

First printing

ISBN: 1-4137-5818-5
PUBLISHED BY PUBLISHAMERICA, LLLP
www.publishamerica.com
Baltimore

Printed in the United States of America

To
Cindy and Mary,
two beautiful
daughters,
and
their delightful husbands,
Stephen Hadley and Thomas Reagan

and

Audrey,
my dear wife
of fifty-three years

in
loving memory
of our beloved parents:
Arnold and MaryAnn Baker
and
Harold and Marion Embling

In Appreciation

To my family, who has been so supportive and helpful in this endeavor, I give a sincere thank you. And to all who took the time to share an experience or two for this book, I want to do the same. This kind of sharing is so vital for our continued "reaching out" to all sorts and conditions of people; so important in our effort to help others come to know God's presence and to grow in the faith.

I also give a special thank you to Larry and Ellen LaCroix, who not only proofread my first book, but did some early reading of this one as well. For their frequent encouragement to complete this book, which proved so helpful (albeit almost annoying at times)!

Finally, I owe a big note of appreciation to all who wrote, phoned, or spoke to me with such positive words after reading my first book. Your part in my writing this book has played a most positive role. Thanks and may God's blessing continue to be with YOU and with ALL.

Table of Contents

CHAPTER FIVE

CHAPTER SIX

CHAPTER SEVEN

CHAPTER EIGHT

Introduction

In the movie *Contact*, based on the novel by Carl Sagan, there are some lines that speak to the Holy Experiences that people have encountered. Jodie Foster played a woman of science who was in a nationally financed program to listen for sounds and noises from outer space. During one specific endeavor, she made "contact" with her father who had died when she was a child. Being a nationally known scientist, working in a federally funded program, she was highly criticized when she shared her experience with the public. There was eventually a hearing, which was designed to interrogate her, and to hopefully get her to deny her experience.

(I suspect most readers of this book know that when one has what she/he considers to be a personal religious experience, two things happen. First, they soon find out that it is a blessing to share the experience. Secondly, one quickly realizes that to deny such an experience is next to impossible.)

At the hearing, the scientist was asked if she could prove her story. She answered, "No." Then in utter disgust she was asked, "Why don't you just admit that it was hoax and move on?" After a time of thoughtful introspection the dear and humble scientist responded, "BECAUSE I CAN'T."

She then goes on to say what you and I might utter ourselves and I suspect the contributors to this book would readily concur. She affirms what we know. "I had an experience I can't prove; I can't even explain it. But I know as a human being, everything that I am tells me that it was real. I was given something wonderful, something that changed me forever."

That is what happens when anyone experiences the presence of the Holy in their midst.

The scientist then says, "I had a vision that tells us we belong to something that is greater than ourselves; that we are not alone—that none of us are alone. I wish I could share that vision with you, that everyone, if even for one moment, could feel that awe, that humility, that hope! ...That continues to be my wish." (*Contact* has been called "One of the best movies of the decade." It is available on video and I recommend it to you.)

With that same measure of humble honesty, this book has five score and more personal experiences of people who want you to know of their experiences with the Holy. After writing the book, *Because God Walked With Me...Life Experiences with the Holy*, I began receiving letters and notes from readers, many of whom I did not know, from places where I had never been. They were thanking me for writing the book and sharing my experiences.

I never dreamed that I would receive such uplifting responses. But equally surprising, and totally unexpected, was that a lot of letters, phone calls, and casual meetings found many readers sharing their personal experiences with me. They shared experiences that truly had affected their lives. The experiences shared a time when God and/or God's Son, Jesus, was so close to them that they could never again doubt the Presence of God with them. For me, this was incredibly exciting and also very humbling.

Eventually, after reading and hearing many heart-warming experiences, the thought came to me that I should write a book, sharing what others had shared with me. I was encouraged by family and friends to pursue the idea. With that, I personally contacted each person who had shared with me and told him or her what I was considering. Each one, without exception, was supportive and ready to participate. Once the decision was made, I asked them to send me their experiences in writing.

I assured each contributor that I would edit each of their offerings prior to including them in this book. Many conceded that this gave their writing-out of the experience more freedom to just tell their stories, without literary concerns. My editing only consisted of spelling changes and/or words to clarify portions of their script.

As my family, friends and others learned of my effort, I gained many additional experiences that are now part of the whole. I personally know most of those included herein, but a few I have only met by e-mail, letters or phone calls. They are all beautiful people who want to share how God spoke to them, gave them direction, support and/or healing of physical and emotional difficulties. In each case, they share how God is still speaking to them, and has "touched" the very core of their lives.

Writing this book has been a rich experience for me. As I read and re-read each offering, I tried to put myself in the reader's chair; reading, questioning, and then corresponding with those from whom I needed more understanding or clarification.

The experiences shared run the gamut. Some of them made me sit in awe, as I read of what cannot happen but did! I personally think this book is especially important for our so-called main-line churches. We have done a creditable job in teaching ABOUT Jesus. But as Pastor Jason Fairbanks, Pastor of the Fort Pierce United Church of Christ, in Florida, said from the pulpit on Easter Sunday of 2006: "To know Jesus is not simply to know about Jesus—anyone can go to a library or bookstore for that information. BUT TO KNOW JESUS IS TO EXPERIENCE JESUS."

I could not concur more positively with that statement than I already do. We can hear a thousand stories about Jesus and still not know Jesus! Do not forget the importance of the biblical stories. They are extremely important and helpful. Hopefully they lead us to discover Jesus in the main stream of our lives. But, too often we are amiss in not sharing with children or adults that Jesus is real to us. Our sharing the Good News of Jesus needs to include not only the historical reality, but also a present actuality of our Lord's intimate presence with us.

The Jerusalem Bible expresses the words of Deuteronomy 9:4 with these words: "Take care of what you do and be on guard. Do not forget the things your eyes have seen, nor let them slip from your heart all the days of your life; rather tell them to your children and to your children's children." And like the Old Testament, the New Testament also tells us about numerous things that the eyes of believers had seen. Those stories give us a vast variety of experiences that had assured followers of Jesus that the crucified Jesus was with them in very real ways.

And guess what? We know of those Holy experiences today, because the early Christians did what the book of Deuteronomy asks of us all. Rather than letting their faith experiences be lost, they shared those experiences with others.

The New Testament contains most of what we know about Jesus, as shared by His disciples and other early Christians. Thankfully, they shared their experiences, whether they realized they were following Deuteronomy's directive or not! Their sharing continues to "teach their children and their children's children." If I had to give one reason for writing this book or my previous book—it would be to share the Good News of Jesus the Christ, to keep it dynamically alive and real in today's world.

How we do that will, by our very nature, vary from church to church, and from person to person. For example: For some, personal testimonies during worship are very affective; for others that manner of sharing may seem all but inappropriate. In any case, we will do well to "unlock" our sharing skills. Whether we gather to discuss theology or play cards, we can let our children, neighbors, and friends know that God is known and still speaking in our day as in days past.

Our sharing should help us all to open our eyes to God's presence. This short, but powerful piece of poetry by Elizabeth Reagan speaks to an almost universal concern when it comes to our being truly aware of God's presence in our lives:

A New Dawn

A new dawn is born
When pale fingers of pink
Spread across the night sky
Taking away the black
While making a beautiful veil for the stars
Turning out street lights with
A soft gentle hand
Changing from pink to gold
Like a colorful parade
While everyone misses it
Snoring in their
Beds.

This book is an effort to share the very Presence of God in our lives. The experiences are as personal as if God were tapping them on the shoulder, saying, "Here I am, I will be with you always." As you read these experiences, keep in mind that those sharing are people just like you and me, and may YOU be blessed!

CHAPTER ONE

God Called Them into Service

As a way of introducing this aspect of God's presence, I want to remind you that God has always called people into service. For example, the Old Testament gives us numerous accounts of people being "called" by God. The New Testament is also filled with a wealth of like examples. The experiences continue to this day.

An illustration of this "being called" was shared in the *Living Faith*, a daily Roman Catholic devotional. The shared experience was authored by Elizabeth-Anne Steward, and can be found in the January edition for the year 2003, page 47.

She tells a beautiful story about a young man who sensed that God had plans for him. She writes that she just happened to come upon this young man, whom she had not seen for some time. He was in his mid-twenties. They had become acquainted a few years earlier when the two of them had been in a postgraduate class together. Seeing him again proved to be a most interesting encounter.

When Elizabeth-Anne asked him what he was doing now, he said that he owned his own company and that it was very successful. But, he then added that he wanted to go back to graduate school to study philosophy. Following a brief discussion of his desires for going back to school, she asked a very big question, one that often puts a snag in our willingness to venture out into unknown waters. And that is true whether one believes it is God's Will or not!

Referring to his overwhelming success, owning his own business and all the perks he admittedly had been enjoying, these words blurted out from her lips: **"Can you give all this up?"** His response was heartwarming; it is the reason for my including his experience. He said, "Money has not made me happy and the work is no longer challenging. The company takes up all my time and I'm working around the clock. There must be more to life than this."

His friend then used a follow-up question: "So what are you looking for?" Robert answered in a serious and humble manner, **"I THINK GOD IS LOOKING FOR ME."**

As I pondered those words it seemed to me that we could all take something home from that story. God is forever doing that same thing to you and me. God is looking for us, desiring a response to His presence among us. Why? Because God desires that we be in close relationship with Him so He might comfort us in our times of fear; guide us when we are lost; give us strength when we are weak; challenge, inspire, and call us as we live our everyday lives. Yes, God, in Eternal love, is always seeking our closer attention, encouraging us to be in a closer relationship with Him and with His Son, Jesus.

As a retired clergyman, I realized very early on that God was still calling me. We are never too young nor too old, in fact, we are never too *anything* for God not to be calling us. Like you, I thank God repeatedly for that truth and the comfort it gives me.

That embrace of God seeks to call us into ministry; all sorts of ministry as we are called to discipleship. That discipleship ideally finds us striving to put God first in our lives and seeking to "do unto others as we would have them do unto us." And it hopefully finds us walking where and doing what Jesus would have us do. Yes, we are all called to share the Good News of Christ, in word and by example, in all of life. That is our call; everyone's call to the discipleship of Jesus Christ, our Lord.

The embrace of God also leads some into what we know as the professional ministry, as we clergy are often identified. (We often refer to this as a call to full-time ministry. I hesitate to say "full-time" ministry, because we are all called to full-time discipleship.) We have witnessed this call to "Professional Ministry" throughout biblical history and ever since.

We have seen this call to ministry in the life of Moses when he was enticed to climb the mountain to check out a shining light. It was there on the mountain that God spoke to him from the Burning Bush that did not burn (Exodus 3:1 and following).

How Moses received his call from God is a marvelous and miraculous story. **What happened, what took place, seems impossible**. Although it "could not happen," it did. From that holy experience, Moses became a changed person. Throughout his ministry we find that the God of Love who had called Moses, also guided Moses. Repeatedly, Moses called upon God and consistently God was with him.

Look, if you will, at Proverbs 3:5-6, where it reads: "Trust in the Lord with all your heart and lean not on your own understanding; in all your ways acknowledge God, and God will direct your paths (or God will make your paths straight)." It's really great; God's call promises a guide for your life and God's Presence in your effort to fulfill your call to discipleship. God offers to be your "mentor."

As Jesus spoke to his disciples, asking them to go and make disciples of all nations, to baptize them and teach them, he also said, "And surely, I am with you always" (Mathew 28:20). That is a promise that he also speaks to you and to me.

We are also familiar with the call of Jeremiah, the prophet. In Jeremiah l: 4-9, we find how Jeremiah described his Call. "The word of the Lord came to me, saying, before I formed you in the womb I knew you, before you were born I set you apart; I appointed you as a prophet to the nations."

Here now is a response that Jeremiah made upon receiving his call. It is, to this day, so typical of people who sense the call of God. And the reason is consistently the same, *we feel so inadequate*! **Jeremiah said, "Ah, Sovereign Lord, I do not know how to speak; I am only a child."** But the Lord said to him, "Do not say, 'I am only a child.' You must go to everyone I send you to and say whatever I command you. Do not be afraid of them, for I am with you and will rescue you." Then the Lord reached out His hand and touched Jeremiah's mouth and said to him, **"Now, I have put my words in your mouth."**

Jeremiah became a great servant for God. He followed God's call and was led into a ministry that was extremely meaningful to him and helpful to God's people ever since.

Ezekiel, the prophet, also described his call from God. He speaks of seeing a great storm: "I looked, and I saw a windstorm coming out of the north—an immense cloud with flashing lightning and surrounded by brilliant light" (Ezekiel 1:4). He then describes what he saw in the storm. He concludes by saying that the image was like that of a man. "It was like the appearance of a rainbow in the clouds on a rainy day, so was the radiance on him. This was the appearance of the likeness of the glory of the Lord" (1:26).

Now again, I want to assure you that if you have the thought that **that experience might seem to be impossible,** you are not alone! But guess what? It happened just like the experiences happened to those who will be sharing with you throughout this book.

For me, Ezekiel's experience becomes authentic when I see what it meant to him, and what he did because of it! To Ezekiel, that experience was so meaningful and powerfully real, that look what the prophet did. He tells us, "When I saw it, I fell facedown, and I heard the voice of one speaking" (1:28).

As Ezekiel lay in this position, his mind must have been swirling with bewildering thoughts until he heard the response God made to him. Ezekiel writes, "And he said to me, 'Son of man, stand up on your feet and I will speak to you.' As he spoke, the Spirit came into me and raised me to my feet, and I heard him speaking to me" (Ezekiel 2:1-2). Indeed, our Holy Scriptures frequently describe how intensely meaningful the call of God was to the individual prophets of old. That "call of God" changed the direction of their lives and gave them the strength and courage to persevere against all odds.

Amos, the prophet, is also a vivid example of one being called by God. At one point in his following God's Will for his life, Amos was confronted by Amaziah, the priest of Bethel.

He asked, or rather he told Amos to go back home and stop prophesying in Bethel because Bethel was the king's sanctuary. But Amos did not then turn back nor did he stop speaking where and what God had directed him. He answered Amaziah, with these words found in Amos 7:14-16: "'I was neither a prophet nor a prophet's son, but I was a shepherd, and I also took care of sycamore-fig trees. But the Lord took me from tending the flock and said to me, "Go, and prophesy to my people Israel." He then said to Amaziah, 'Now then, hear the word of the Lord.'"

Without question, the call from God is serious stuff. Just imagine how courageous Amos was to stand there and point blank deny Amaziah, the priest of Bethel. No, a person cannot back down when he knows that he is in fact doing as God has called and directed. Or perhaps I should say, "No, a person cannot back down and still know he/she is doing God's Will."

People from all walks of life have received very meaningful and personal calls into ministry. I shared my own call in my first book. I now want to share some calls to ministry from people I know and love. In each case, those who have shared with me have readily agreed to have me share them with you, the readers of this book.

The Reverend Doctor Paul Hammer

One of the many joys of my ministry was getting to know and to work with the Reverend Doctor Paul L. Hammer. He is now retired from his position as Professor of New Testament Studies at Colgate Rochester Crozer Divinity School. Paul is well known throughout the United Church of Christ, his denomination, as well as in wider circles of the Church. He is known for his brilliant Bible Study presentations as well as for being a superbly outstanding preacher of the Gospel.

It was at an association gathering of some sort that Dr. Hammer "made my day." During a social time he told me he had just finished reading my book, *Because God Walked with Me.* He had not only read it, which itself was an honor for me, but like the infamous breakfast cereal advertisement he told me "He liked it!" He remarked that it was "beautifully written and inspirational." Let me tell you, it doesn't get any better than that!

Well, it did not take me very long after that to ask him, as I have asked others, to think about sharing a personal experience wherein he felt God's presence in a very real way. His response was powerful. He sent it to me with a note thanking me for "the invitation to participate in another of your inspiring books." What a nice thing to say; it is so typical of this scholarly, yet humble and compassionate man who is loved by all who know him. He is retired from being a New Testament professor, but not from his discipleship.

Dr. Paul Hammer wrote me about his experience wherein he sensed God's presence calling him to the Christian ministry. He appropriately chose to title this sharing of his call:

CHANGING SHIPS

After being active a year in the Naval Reserve toward the end of World War II as an aviation electrician mate, I received a fleet appointment to the U. S Naval Academy.

About a fifth of each class received such "fleet appointments," compared with the four-fifths of congressional appointments. I was on my way to be a career officer in the United States Navy.

I liked the Academy and was happy there for the next two years, including summers aboard respectively the battleship *Washington* and the aircraft carrier *Kearsarge*. On the *Kearsarge* we sailed the Atlantic and had stops at South Hampton in England and at Gothenburg in Sweden. The latter was especially interesting for me, since my father was born in Sweden, as were also my mother's grandparents.

I really enjoyed the Navy and loved the sea, but during my second year I found myself thinking about the Christian ministry. Yet, liking the Navy, I did not want to go in that direction. I shared my thoughts with Chaplain Scholl aboard the *Kearsarge*, and he was a great help in helping me to sort out my thoughts and feelings.

Then one day I was up on the forward deck, high above the water with the wind blowing in my face as the ship cut its wake on a beautiful sea-green ocean of rolling waves. Somehow God's Spirit was breathing and blowing in that wind and I felt that I had to answer "yes" to that call of the Spirit to ordained ministry. (I learned later that the Greek ***pneuma*** could be translated "spirit" or "breath.")

I resigned from the Navy aboard ship. My resignation was telegraphed back to the Academy, and when we arrived back, my resignation having been processed, I left the Navy.

God called the Prophet Amos from following the sheep. God called me from following the ships and put me into the ship of the Church. (The main part of church buildings is called the ***nave.***)

That same Spirit, blowing in my call, has breathed in my life through more than 50 years of ministry, initially as a pastor and then for nearly forty years as a seminary New Testament teacher. In retirement from academic teaching, that Spirit continues to breathe and blow in opportunities to teach and preach in churches and conferences, and even in writing these words at the invitation of my colleagues and friends, Audrey and Clyde Embling. Thanks be to God!

What a beautiful sequence of events. God calls us from all walks of life and from any place where we might find ourselves. Dr. Hammer is so right. Yes, that same Spirit blows upon us as we go about our daily lives. Thankfully, Paul Hammer "changed ships," for not only has he, himself, admittedly been blessed and guided by God's presence—he has also been an inspiration to his seminary students, his colleagues and to countless thousands.

We thank Dr. Hammer for sharing this personal and beautiful Call of God with us. Indeed, knowing this adds a whole new dimension to our appreciation of this man. Thankfully, he continues to be a strong shining light for the Gospel in the sea of life on this planet Earth.

Marjorie and Robert Dix

I grew up in a family of eight children. Marjorie is just a bit older than I am. As I look back at our childhood, one of the joys and privileges I treasure dearly was for me getting to know my seven siblings, meeting their friends, and getting to know those whom they dated. I had five brothers-in-law and two sisters-in-law. I love them all like I do my brothers and sisters. Marjorie was next to me in age; we have two beautiful sisters younger than we are. Marge was an outstanding cheerleader all four years in high school and she played the violin in the school orchestra.

Knowing how close we are in age, I suspect you can better appreciate the fact that when she started to date Bob (who later became her husband), I quickly related to him. More than that, actually, I was fascinated by his interest in cars. He and I had a similar interest and he was good at repairing and modifying them.

I remember when he had a Pontiac convertible. He changed the gear ratio in the differential so that the engine could run slower and the car could go faster. It was like our present cars with overdrive, except his was always in overdrive! I never really knew whether he did it to save gas or to enable the car to go faster. I suspect the latter. Going down the highway, if he wanted to pass someone, he would shift into second and go around that car like a rabbit passing a turtle.

Bob graduated from Morrisville Institute, where he specialized in auto mechanics. He was "the best" in my book and that thinking proved it when he soon became a mechanic in a large Chrysler-Plymouth dealership in Rochester, New York. But all too soon after Bob and Marge were married they moved to Florida. There he worked at another Chrysler-Plymouth dealership in Sarasota. In giving me a reason for making the move, he would say, "I'm going where snow doesn't fall and cars are not coated with ice, snow and salt, all of which drips on anyone working beneath them!"

Marge and Bob were always involved in the life of the Church. Guess what happened to them? God called. A scripture that became very dear and special to them is from Proverbs 4:5-6 "Trust in the Lord with all your heart and lean not unto your own understanding. In all your ways acknowledge him and he will direct your path."

Marge and Bob lived in Bradenton, Florida, when they received their call to ministry. They now reside in Waxhaw, North Carolina. They sent me their experience with God.

God Calls Us to Full-time Ministry

Bob had dreamed for many years of getting his pilot's license. He had only thought about this becoming a hobby. He had no idea that God would use him as a pilot on the mission field. We both read Christian books and enjoyed reading books on missions. *Jungle Pilot*, the story of Nate Saint, a pilot who worked with Missionary Aviation Fellowship, was a favorite book for both of us. The Auca Indians of Ecuador killed Nate, along with four other missionaries, while they were trying to reach that group for Jesus. **Upon reading this book, God laid it on Bob's heart that he should become a missionary pilot.**

During and after reading this same book, God stirred my heart in a similar way. For about three weeks I continued to be quite certain that God wanted us to do something fulltime for him. One morning as I was washing dishes and talking to God, as I often did throughout the day, I asked God to either take this thought out of my mind, or let me know that day, if He had other plans for us. I was open to God's answer, either way.

I continued on that day as I normally would. THEN IT HAPPENED. I was rocking my little girl, Barbara, and singing familiar tunes and hymns. The rocking chair was near a bookcase, so I reached over and picked up a hymnal. After singing a few hymns I came across one I had never heard before. The words penetrated my heart. They went like this: "I'm on the Battlefield for my Lord. I will leave my kinfolk and my friends and travel into distant lands with my Bible in my hands."

The most wonderful peace came into my heart. I knew, without question, that God used those words for me. I joyfully, peacefully and sincerely praised the Lord as I remembered that I had prayed for an answer to the persistent thoughts in my mind. Remember, I had asked God to let me know that day what His desire was for our future."

Wow, God does work in surprising ways. My sister, Marjorie, must have been "on cloud nine" so to speak, after all those happenings. She never did say whether her little girl went to sleep or not!

But, her side of the story was only one side of this whole remarkable faith building experience. Somehow Marge had to find the words and the right time to tell her husband what had been going on in her life. She pondered questions like: How was she going to tell Bob that he should quit his work? And how would he feel about all of the kinds of concerns that intermix with such a life-altering experience? Well, read on, God is so good at preparing the way for our doing what he asks of us.

> We were in the habit of doing most of our serious talking and planning each night in bed. While praying before going to bed that night, I asked God to give me the words to tell Bob that I thought he should give up his job, leave our new home, and that he should prepare to become a pastor. When we both got up from being on our knees in prayer and got into bed, Bob almost immediately asked me if I would be willing to move! He proceeded to tell me what was happening to him and that he wanted to become a missionary pilot.
>
> I had not thought about him becoming a missionary pilot but that didn't bother me. I thought of that hymn again—I WOULD TRAVEL INTO DISTANT LANDS. Distant lands, I pondered, I guess that is what missionaries do! I then found that another prayer had been answered, for it was very easy to share with my dear husband what had been on my mind and what had happened to me that very day. With that we were both encouraged and excited as we realized God was dealing with us both, in the same way, at the same time.

As I read and thought about Bob and Marge Dix's experiences, I thought of Isaiah the prophet. Do you remember God's call to Isaiah? In Isaiah 6, we find the experience that changed Isaiah's life.

Isaiah tells of being in the Temple and seeing the Lord sitting on a throne, high and exalted, "and the train of his robe filled the temple" (Isaiah 6:1). He also speaks of seeing seraphs (or angels) around God and they were singing, 'Holy, holy, holy is the Lord Almighty; the whole earth is full of his glory.' At the sound of their voices the door posts and thresholds shook and the temple filled with smoke" (Isaiah 6: 3-4).

At that point in his vision, Isaiah felt very sinful, because he had seen God, but he was a man of unclean lips and lived among people of unclean lips. Then Isaiah 6:6-8 reads: "Then one of the seraphs flew to me with a live coal in his hand, which he had taken with tongs from the altar. With it he touched my mouth and said, 'See, this has touched your lips; your guilt is taken away and your sin atoned for.' Then I heard the voice of the Lord saying, 'Whom shall I send? And who will go for us?' And I said, HERE AM I, SEND ME!"

I am sure the Dixs felt unworthy of their call, as did Isaiah and many thousands since. The experience they had enabled them to humbly accept their call to ministry. Then, not unlike another prophet, namely Abraham, Bob and Marge picked up their belongings and followed the Lord. In Genesis 12 it says: "The Lord had said to Abram, 'Leave your country, your people and your father's household and go to the land I will show you.'"

I am not sure just how Abraham was able to make the proper response to the Spirit of God that called him. Perhaps he just did it. But in my case, I was helped tremendously as I was reassured by my wife and then my family and friends. In Bob and Marge's case, the good Lord gave them encouragement through the many almost unbelievable experiences that they had.

They wrote about a couple of these happenings.

Reassurance in Knowing God's Will

Soon after Bob and I were convinced that God wanted us to be missionaries, God gave us several events to reassure our decision. One such example included my mother, who came from her home in Churchville, New York, to visit us in Florida. She arrived on a Saturday. On Monday, Bob's mother and his uncle Cecil were coming from St. Petersburg, Florida, to spend the day. It was our intention to tell them all about our experiences and plans at that time.

God had other plans. On Sunday evening we went to church as usual and took Mother Embling with us. Bob led the welcome, singing and announcements for the service and our pastor preached the evening devotional message.

After we were back home and had the children in bed, Mother said, 'Bob, I know you like your job, but you are not in the right profession. You should be a pastor.' What an exciting moment of reassurance that was for us! What made it more impressive for us was that Mother was not one to give unsolicited advice; telling Bob or anyone else any such thing so bluntly was foreign to her. She was a very religious person, as were Bob's family, and we knew they would stand behind us all the way—but for her to even suggest he was in the wrong profession was mind-boggling. God was truly working through her to help us.

After hearing her comment we proceeded to tell Mother Embling about our decision to begin working full-time for the Lord, not as a pastor but as a missionary. She was very excited and gave us her blessing, even though she was not overly joyful about the thought of us leaving the United States.

God called them and God continues to call people from all walks of life, from all stages in life, and from all races to "Go into all the world." Bob and Marge followed their call from God and it is hard to find anyone who has been any happier in their effort to serve the Lord.

They have three children. Each of those children, one by one, became involved in the missionary work of Wycliffe Bible Translators and the Summer Institute of Linguistics. In a variety of ways, they are endeavoring to give the Word of God to people of all tongues and dialects.

Their older daughter, Barbara Grimes, who Marge was rocking and singing to when she found that new hymn, is now married. She has her doctorate, as does her husband, Chuck. They both translate the Scriptures into native tongues.

Bob and Marge also have a son, Clinton, who is married to Diane. They are in administration and have served in Brazil and elsewhere in following their call to serve. Clinton is presently project coordinator for the Brazil Branch of Wycliffe Bible Translators and ALEM, the national Brazilian Translation Organization. He also coordinates the startup of Bible translation efforts in Guinea-Bissau, West Africa, and does translation of materials into Portuguese for Portuguese-speaking Bible translators to use.

Janet is the youngest of three children. She is married to Carmen Frith, and like her sister and brother, she has joined the missionary team at Wycliffe, following the call of God upon their lives.

It is also a great tribute to Bob and Marge and family, that now their grandson, Ben, who is Barbara and Chuck's son, is going into mission work as a linguist, which is what his dad and his dad's dad have done.

The Dix family is a living testimony that God calls us, regardless of age or where we may have been born or happen to live. Thanks be to God for the call He gives us all, some for a life's work, others for discipleship in everyday life.

Ted Warner

Ted Warner is a member of the Castile United Church of Christ in Castile, New York. He is an involved lay person; being superintendent of Sunday School, serving on the Board of Elders which also finds him being one of the regular lay leaders in the worship services of the church. I have known Ted most of his life, albeit I've gotten to know him much better over the last few years.

Ted grew up in a Christian home. His parents worked on the farm and taught their children the farm ethic of hard work, honesty, and a certain dependence upon God. In his mid-teens or thereabout, he began attending worship services. His faith grew as he continued to worship and grow in knowledge and understanding of the faith.

Upon graduation from high school, Ted attended and graduated from the State University of New York at Geneseo. There he naturally studied a variety of subjects and, not unlike other college students, he began to question his faith. He will share some of that with us.

The well-learned lesson of the importance of hard work found him not only attending college but also working about thirty hours a week on a farm. Ted Warner will now share with us his story of how he came to be called by God into the ministry of Jesus Christ.

> At age twenty-two, I learned an important lesson: when in doubt, pray. It may be the most powerful act a human being can perform. I grew up in a Christian family. My faith was strong, even though I rarely attended church before I was eighteen and had my own car.
>
> Prior to entering college, my faith had become important to me. However, like so many students with a history major, I began to question my faith. By the time I began my student teaching experience, I had come to realize that I had accepted Jesus as my Savior out of cultural tradition rather than belief.
>
> I rarely had leisure time during my college days because I also worked on a dairy farm throughout those years. Interestingly, with only a couple weeks before the end of my student teaching experience, in December 2001, I found myself with some free time! I had my work done and about four hours before I had to attend a class later that day. I decided to eat lunch away from school for

a welcome change. I went downtown. After I picked up lunch, I decided to pick up a cold dessert at McDonald's.

I recall it was a very warm day for December in New York State. Just as I finished my lunch in the parking lot, my salvation experience and call to ministry began. I was casually listening to the radio in my car. All of a sudden, the guitar riffs of the AC/DC classic, "Highway to Hell" rumbled through my speakers. I tended to think about religion whenever I heard that song. This time was no exception.

I had just recently received Christmas cards from a few of my students that said things like, "Jesus Loves You." With my doubts about faith dominating my mind, I thought that perhaps God could give me some answers. I began to pray as that song began. I told God that my faith was weakened by the confusion of my studies. With that knowledge, I still wanted to follow Jesus, but I needed a sign to show me that He is for real.

I continued in prayer, telling God that I would do anything in return, even if it meant I had to be a minister. Having said that, I said to God that this song playing on the radio makes light of hell. If Jesus is really who the Bible says he is, please find a way to shut this song off. I then added, "If possible, please do not break my car down, I need to get back to those kids who believe in You."

Quite honestly, with the "Amen" ending that prayer, I never thought God would send an answer! I was then singing along with that song and as the chorus came up, a minute or so after I had prayed, a woman came out of McDonald's and headed straight for my car. "Excuse me sir," she said, ""May I talk to you for a minute?" **Without thinking about my prayer, I shut the song off!**

When I did that, of course, God had unbeknownst to me already answered my prayer. I did not think about it then. God also knew I was stubborn, so God did not stop with that act. The woman introduced herself as Helen, and then she restated my question (although I do not think she was aware of it). She said, "It's around Christmas time right now and a lot of people are wondering **who Jesus really is.** I just want to tell you who He is and to make sure that you are reading the Bible. Jesus is the Son of God and He was sent to us to die for our sins so that we can have eternal life. I have found happiness with Him and so can you."

She then went on to give me a lesson on reading the Bible. When she left, I started my car and realized that a different song was on! **God used my own hand to turn off the song in answer to my prayer!** Not only did God respond to my request, but also God found a way through that woman to restate my question and respond to it! **Unbelievable! What a moment that was for me**.

I was stopped in my tracks and I humbly and joyfully prayed, asking forgiveness for my sins and accepting Jesus as my Lord and Savior.

I will long remember the day Ted came to see me about entering the Christian ministry. I was not surprised, because he is a serious young man who impressed me with his demeanor, compassion and love for all. He was seeking direction and answers and he received them. Yes, he had ears to hear and he heard; eyes to see and he saw! Ted Warner has been accepted at Colgate Rochester Crozer Divinity School in Rochester, New York. His starting time has been temporarily put on hold, due to an addition to his family and the financial needs of both home and school.

The Reverend Larry Brodie

Within minutes of his birth, I knew he had been born. You see, Larry was my parents' first grandchild. What a thrill it was to have him come into the world; he made me "Uncle Clyde" without even trying! Larry was a lovable child and I remember how we all tried to "spoil" him, but he just would not be spoiled.

I do remember one story that was so funny and yet appeared to be embarrassing to his mother and father. I had just graduated from Rochester Business Institute and was employed at a large department store in downtown Rochester. I was the assistant shoe buyer and manager of their shoe department. That Christmas I purchased a pair of cowboy boots for Larry from our shoe department (employee discounts helped greatly). When I gave them to him, he was genuinely pleased. I doubt that he would treasure them nearly as much today. It was a year and half later that his cowboy boots were quite worn and getting tight on his feet. At some sort of a family gathering, of which we had many, Larry came to me and said loudly enough for all to hear, "Uncle Clyde, it's time for you to get me another pair of cowboy boots."

We all roared with laughter, including Larry. During the merry making laughter, Larry's mom and dad tried to tell him that just because I gave him his cowboy boots, it did not mean that I should get him another pair. I think he enjoyed the laughter too much to be paying any attention to his parents, because after all quieted down, that little guy came over to me and said, "Uncle Clyde, I really do need new cowboy boots!"

As a child, and unto this day, Larry has always been a super-polite person, a positive-thinking person, and a person full of love for all people, even his Uncle Clyde.

Larry graduated from high school and then went to the Rochester Institute of Technology in Rochester, New York. At that great school, he majored in their Industrial Technology and Electromechanical Program. In 1972, he received a Nuclear Regulatory Commission Operator License. In 1978, Larry received Nuclear Regulatory Commission Senior Operator License. The details of his work included becoming a Senior Engineer-Field Technical Service and from there to become Senior Instructor—Nuclear Training Services.

Now let me tell you, I did not know anymore about all those titles and the nuclear work he was doing than I know about being a dentist! But I do know that Larry advanced quickly and was very good at what he was doing. When he left that employ, he was Senior Site Outage Manager. This meant that he was responsible for detailed day-to-day management of the company's projects to assure maximum utilization of time and resources. Need I say more?

The now Reverend Larry Brodie, had a wealth of experiences in the secular workplace. His ability to take "care of details," his experience in giving instruction, his teaching and overseeing employees and projects all played a valuable training ground. These experiences have helped him to further develop and refine his natural abilities and skills, all of which are very evident in his Christian ministry, as he serves his Lord and Savior, Jesus the Christ.

Larry writes about growing up in the Church and his lack of serious involvement in it, especially in his late teens and early twenties.

> I did not attend worship services from eighteen to twenty-six years of age. During this period, I married and fathered two children. A man at work kept witnessing to me. I kept telling him I was all right and had been saved. One night, in October of 1976, another man, after he had shared his testimony with me, asked if I had ever received Christ. I said, "Yes, once I was saved, but I'm not now."
>
> He explained to me that I either was or was not saved, but had not lost my salvation if I ever had been saved. He showed me how being saved transforms one into a new creation in Christ. I couldn't see any transformation in my life, only sin and rejection of God. **That night I went home and kneeled alone by my bed and gave my life totally and completely to the Lordship of Christ.**
>
> I believe that's when I was truly born again. I've never since knowingly been able to sin without guilt. Since that day I can look back and see how God is daily making me a new person in Christ. Shortly after that time, my wife, son and daughter also received Christ. I was baptized on May 3, 1982, at the Calvary Baptist Church in Midland, Michigan.

Larry Brodie has had quite a journey in the faith. It is very obvious that once he became a renewed Christian, he took it very seriously and consistently sought God's direction for his life. As well, he read and studied God's Holy Word and he prayed regularly and often. All that is to say, that he sought a close relationship with his Lord and endeavored to do as he believed God would have him do, and to be whom God would have him be.

Larry now shares his Call from God to the professional ministry.

> In early 1982 and 1984, God seemed to place in me a daily growing desire to be used by Him. I remember often sitting in a service and just weeping because I was so overcome with the love of God and the desire to share that love with others so they might experience what I was experiencing. It was during this time that I committed myself to a time of daily prayer and Bible study.
>
> The Lord impressed upon me the need to read and study the Bible and to comment in written form what I was learning. Following the principal of Mark 14, I began to watch and pray more each day as I studied to understand God's way for my family and me. The desire to be a preacher grew and grew until the early morning hours of January 16, 1985.
>
> That morning I wrote out the following verses in order, then placed a space for "Date Requested" and "Date Answered." The verses were Psalm 37:4-5: "Delight thyself also in the Lord; and He shall give thee

the desires of thine heart. Commit thy way unto the Lord; trust also in Him; and He shall bring it to pass."

It was my desire to be in the pastoral ministry, if God would allow me the privilege. It was my intent to delight daily in Him and ask Him for the privilege. Another verse that I wrote down was I Timothy 3:1: "This is a true saying, if a man desire the office of a bishop, he desires a good work." This was my desire. It was not yet my wife's desire and I wanted God's Will, not mine. I knew my relationship with Judy (my wife) was important to God and He'd have to give her the same desire I had. Matthew 26:39b reads: "Nevertheless not as I will, but as thou wilt."

After that I wrote out this prayer in my devotional book: "Prepare the Brodie team, O Lord, I pray thee, if this be your will, there must be unity in Spirit, which only You can give. Lord let us prove what is acceptable unto you, submitting ourselves one to another in the fear [awe] of the God. Nevertheless, let me in particular so love Judy even as myself; and be with Judy my wife and helpmate, so that she shall reverence her husband in obedience to God. As we do this, give us unity in these things because we have obeyed you, and the two of us are one."

DATE REQUESTED: January 16, 1985

God answered the first part of this prayer later that same year. I was on a business trip to Knoxville, Tennessee. Judy was with me. While I was out on business, Judy was in our hotel room reading the Bible and praying. God dealt with Judy about our being in the ministry. Upon arriving back at the room that evening she shared with me, in tears, how she knew God wanted us in the ministry, how that scared her, but how she was more afraid of disobeying God. Thus, she had committed to God in prayer, and was now committing to me; completely surrendering to be my helpmate, wherever and whenever God wanted me in the ministry or any place else. This happened in April of 1985.

DATE ANSWERED: May 1, 1985

This prayer was completed on May 1, 1987 when, without application or inquiry of any kind, I became the Assistant Pastor of Timberlake Baptist Church in Lynchburg, Virginia.

Wow! Here in Larry's experience we see once again that God calls us into the ministry of his Son Jesus in a variety of ways. Each call is not only different, it is personal and it alters one's life forever. In all that I have heard about my nephew, Larry, he was skillful, knowledgeable and effective in his nuclear work in the secular world. It is no different in his pastoral ministry. Thank God for that call and for both Larry and Judy responding in a way that continues to give glory to God and to God's Son, Jesus.

The Reverend David Huels

David Huels is presently the chaplain at the Road Runner Travel Resort in Fort Pierce, Florida. He is there from mid-October through April. He then travels with his lovely wife, Ellen, to the area where they lived for most of his pastoral ministry. Around that area in Buffalo, New York, today, he is often to be found doing interim pastoral work or supply preaching as needed for pastors' vacation, sickness, or any other reason the local pastor may be away.

Needless to say, David is not retired, although he may claim to be if he were asked. His work at the travel resort in Florida finds him visiting not only those who are involved in the worship and service of the Fellowship there, but any one of the five hundred plus camp sites and park model homes in that place. Along with that, he is kept busy visiting those in hospitals, ill at home and people otherwise in need of pastoral care. No, he is not retired, for more evidence on the subject I heard him say just this past Sunday, "Since I've retired I am busier than ever."

I first met Dave and Ellen at Bangor Theological Seminary in Bangor, Maine. We were both students there at the time. Although he was a couple years behind me, our paths crossed frequently and we got to know each other quite well.

We both had children about the same age. Thankfully, we somehow managed to have apartments in the same seminary-housing complex. This meant, among other things, that our children could play together. In addition to that sort of acquaintance, seminary students also had individual study areas on the third story of that beautiful old mansion where we lived. This afforded us the opportunity to get away from the everyday distractions of normal family living. It also gave us the privilege of personal discussions with one another.

We have always enjoyed each other's company, (at least I have!) over the last forty years or so. Like most friends there have been picnics, parties, celebrations, weddings, grandchildren, illnesses and deaths, and for them the rich blessing of a great-grandchild as well.

In my wife's and my eyes, David and Ellen Huels are two beautiful people who love and serve our Lord faithfully and joyfully. They have had some amazing experiences with the Holy; experiences that continue to call them and direct them in their ministry for the Glory of God, in the name of God's Son, Jesus.

Dave and Ellen shared these personal-holy experiences with me for including in this book.

> Back in 1956, Ellen and I were just two and a half years into our marriage, which at this writing has continued for fifty-three years. We had two beautiful children, a lovely apartment in which to live, and most of the material things we needed in life. I had a good paying, secure job and Ellen was at her happiest, being a mommy and a homemaker.
>
> We were active in our church; being a lay reader and doing volunteer work at the Crippled Children's Guild in Buffalo, New York. Ellen would even push our babies in a buggy to attend the Woman Fellowship meetings and activities.
>
> One evening after dinner I took a walk with a good friend of ours, Ray Whitehead. He was already studying for the ministry. As we strolled along, I shared with him the empty feeling I had in my life. I wanted to do more for God and for mankind. We spoke of many way of doing that and then Ray startled me with his question: **"Why don't you study for the ministry?"**

My reaction was one of shock and I unbelievably replied, "Who me, be a minister?"

Listen to Dave's words of response. He sounds like Moses on the mountaintop, and thousands of others since. To accept a call into ordained ministry is not a simple, thoughtless, or easy decision.

I said to my friend of whom I had great respect, "I'm afraid to talk in front of people. I stutter when I get nervous. And I just plainly do not feel that God could, or even would use me." To my response, Ray calmly, understandingly and seriously said, "Dave, you have to trust more in God and not so much in yourself."

When we got back to our apartment, and Ray had left us, I shared our "ministry" conversation with Ellen. She was not as shocked about it all as I had been! With a lot of uncertainty, a great deal of hesitation and a large bagful of questions, we prayed and continued to pray about it. Simply put, we put it in God's hands.

God's Spirit kept tugging me! The more we prayed, the more assured we became. Eventually, I followed my good friend's advice of putting more trust in God. Accordingly, I considered the ordained ministry as a possibility. With Ellen solidly behind me in this decision, I applied to Elmhurst College in Illinois and was accepted.

A year later I left my employment. Then Ray, Ellen and I drove to Elmhurst to secure our pre-made housing arrangements and check out a part-time job opportunity. Upon arrival we found out they had no campus housing saved for us. It seems that one of the college deans had taken our names off the housing list. On campus living quarters for married students would have been only $49.50 a month. Rental apartments in the town paper were much more costly and beyond our financial capability at that time.

Back to Buffalo we went. Indeed the thought that perhaps "God does not want me for the ordained ministry" came to my mind. Back in Buffalo without a job, I searched and found a job at a dairy. I became a retail route salesman in an effort to get ourselves back on our feet financially.

During the following year, I heard about Bangor Theological Seminary in Bangor, Maine. They were geared up to accept older students and their families. Their "Open Door Policy" accepted students with or without a four-year college degree. Students without their college degree take two years of college classes and then their three years of seminary work. Following that, once they received their other two years college, they would be given their seminary degree. All this meant that students could begin their ministry earlier. A part-time ministry would help defray the cost of the seven years of school required.

It sounded good, so I applied there and was accepted. But again, I did not have the finances needed to start at that time. By the year 1959, we were just getting ourselves financially able to begin school at Bangor. THEN I was lifting a case of glass-bottled milk when I slipped a disc in my back and was laid up for a month. The good doctors advised me not to do that type of work anymore unless I could have some help. Following their advice and needing the income, I hired a young boy to do the lifting. I did the selling. This went well except that I had to share half of my income with him! After several months of this, I found that we were going financially backwards once again.

I let the young man go and set out to try it again by myself. Not smart! Just three weeks later I was flat on my back once again. This time I had a ruptured disc. It was so bad that I was put on disability, which made we think the pastoral ministry was not going to be for me. In fact, it became the furthest thing from my mind.

Little did I know that God had something else in mind for me. After many months of pestering the people at the unemployment office, one of the workers (probably tired of seeing me there so often) asked me, "How would you like to go to school?" I could not believe my ears! I was so elated that I shared with him how many years I had been trying to go but could never quite afford it. I talked with him about Bangor Theological Seminary and his response was, "Go for it." I was ecstatic and overcome with thanksgiving to God. It was that day in August of 1960, that I called Ellen from the Unemployment Office and said, "Honey, start packing, we're off to Bangor!"

God opened the door for me to go to school. My back injury turned out to be a blessing in disguise. The New York State Rehabilitation program helped with my finances through those years of schooling. All of this taught my wife and me a tremendous lesson. God does not call us to do something that cannot be done. Rather, God provides help, enables, and shows us the way to do what He asks of us.

So many times different situations would arise and seemingly a door would shut. But then, God would open it again. It has been that way all through life for us. One such example that I remember so vividly is that time when we had no money to pay for the premium on our car insurance. But, when we went to the mailbox, there was a bank check for the exact amount of the car insurance premium. It was signed, "Anonymous" but no one knew what the amount was except the insurance company, Ellen, myself, and GOD! To this day, we do not know who was God's angel on that occasion. But we do know that was real Christian giving. It was a beautiful gift that we cannot explain, nor understand. We can only thank God for enabling and directing His servants, to touch us.

Here is another time when God somehow caused a needed miracle to happen. Our food cupboards were empty, except for a single can of enchiladas that was on the back top shelf. It was Sunday and we were looking to prepare Sunday night supper for five. Ellen in a positive way said, "Okay Lord, if this is what you want for us, we'll eat it." I knew she was not happy about it, but she meant it!

Just then we heard a knock on our apartment door. When we opened the door, there sat three boxes of food.

There was no one in sight. What a faith-building experience that was for us!

In our third year of school, Ellen and I were summoned to the Dean's Office. We were having a tough time financially. The dean looked at us and said, "I think it's time for you to get out until you are better off financially." Wow, those words stunned us and actually hurt us.

But Ellen, lead by the Spirit, spoke up before I could say a word. She looked the dean in the eye and said, "No Dean, God paved the way for us to be here and we're staying."

And so it was and so it is, all through our 53 years of marriage and 48 years of Christian Ministry, we have been blessed and enabled to carry out the ministry that God has called us to be engaged in. God has provided for us time and time again for which we will be eternally grateful. What a life we have had, but more importantly, what an awesome God has been our strength, our joy, our peace, and our promise for life today and forevermore.

Dave and Ellen have given so much of themselves in the service of Jesus Christ. From their story, we are indeed reminded that the way may not always be smooth, but God calls us, and does provide the wherewithal to respond to the call that is given. David and Ellen Huels have experienced that truth over and over again. Yes, these dear friends and dedicated servants of Jesus Christ, like all of us called into the

Christian Ministry, appreciate that close supporting relationship with God.

Thankfully, Dave followed through on God's Call to him. Because of it, he and his wife have "touched" countless numbers of people with the Good News of the Gospel of Jesus Christ. Concurrently, he continues to be following his call from God to do Christian Ministry, whenever and wherever they find themselves.

The Reverend Leland Booker

My children call him Uncle Leland and they know his wife as Aunt Bertha. That should give you some idea of the close relationship we have with them. Not only that, but we feel deeply loved each time one of their two daughters call us Uncle and Aunt! I have known Leland for some forty-eight years. We think a lot alike and though we may have different opinions now and then, we enjoy the discussion of our dissimilar thoughts.

Leland and I have grown in the faith and work of the Church together. Our ability to be candidly open and honest with each other has been a blessing to us both. The basis of our relationship has always been a mutual desire to serve the God who has called us and to grow in our relationship with God's Son, our Lord and Savior. I think that makes us brothers!

Leland has had a very interesting life as a Servant of Christ. He, his wife Bertha, and their two beautiful daughters have been a part of our extended family and there, they will always be.

[It was a few months after Leland and Bertha shared the following experience that my dear friend Leland was ushered in to God's Eternal Kingdom. We miss him sorely, but we rejoice that he is no longer confined to a body that caused him to suffer and also was increasingly granting him the inability to be the gregarious outgoing disciple of God's Son that gave him the predominance of his identity.]

The Reverend Lee Booker and Bertha share with us now under a title she has chosen.

Leland's Story

Leland Eugene Booker was born on October 11, 1926, to Sarah Laveda Almeda Besecker on the Hog Path Road in Clay Township, Clark County, Ohio. His family consisted of Mother, Grandfather and Great Grandmother and Almeda's sister, Olive. (An Aunt Idella lived with the Smith family.)

It is said that little Leland could never do anything that Great Grandmother ever thought was wrong. Needless to say, he was a "spoiled child." Leland attended a one-room schoolhouse for the first four years of his formal education. It is known that he would frequently play in the side ditches along the half-mile road to the school, making him late for class. He would then "be switched" by the teacher but that never deterred his ditch adventures. Of course, Grandpa took him to school in a horse-drawn buggy if it was raining, or in a sleigh, when the winter's snowy weather made it necessary.

The family moved to Phillipsburg when Leland was ten years old. His sister Anna was born on January 5, 1936, and brothers Jay in October 1938 and Steven on January 27, 1942.

When Leland was sixteen years old he began working on weekends and during summer months at the Dayton Tire and Rubber Plant. He was ambitious and liked the work and enjoyed getting to know the others employees. Of course, the income was not all that bad either.

During Leland's senior year in high school, he was drafted into the United States Army. He was stationed at Camp Croft in South Carolina for basic and military police training. He then served two and a half years in Austria. He was honorably discharged in 1953, after three years of service.

Leland volunteered for the regular Army at Camp Croft. After that, while others were sent to the Pacific, he was given new uniforms and sent home for two weeks, after which he was to report to Indianapolis, Indiana. From there he boarded a military railroad coach for Spartanburg, South Carolina. He ended up in Georgia in the middle of the night. The train was pulled by a steam engine, and by the next morning when embarking, all the recruits looked like coal miners!

It was not a pleasant ride; there was no water on the train and they became very thirsty. By the time they arrived at Spartanburg, not only their arms and faces were covered with soot from the steam engine, but also their summer uniforms blackened and soiled. A shuttle steam engine took them into Spartanburg. Leland remembers that he went to sleep in the baggage netting, covering himself with his overcoat and using his duffel bag as a pillow.

From his basic training, after two weeks at home, he again went by military train to New Jersey Port. He then, with a whole group of other soldiers, was loaded on the Henry Kaiser Ship and traveled for nine days. They landed and docked in Bremmer Hofer, Germany."

From Bremmer Hofer, Germany we traveled by an electric train until we reached the German-Austria border. A diesel train took us into Austria. Six carloads of the soldiers, including myself, went to Lyns Austria and the others, went on to Vienna.

Lyns was the home of a German Air force Base. Upon arrival in Lyns, it was so foggy that I literally could not see my hand in front of my face. We found our way onto an Army truck and I remember that the driver stood on the running board in order to see the double white lines that guided him where he was going. He, somehow, got us to the Lyns Yards, which was a huge place. We were encouraged when we saw a flagpole made from a debarked pine tree that once grew in the Austrian Alps. It was set in concrete but the most beautiful thing about it all was that on it flew our United States flag.

My duty there was Post Guard, which meant I was part of the group that guarded the railroad cars. That was interesting duty, once I found out why we had four guards on each of four cars. The railroad cars were hauling potatoes. But actually, the potatoes were only a foot and a half deep; beyond that depth was Austrian gold. We were guarding secret shipments of gold going into Vienna.

Another happening that sticks in my mind is an example of how serious and demanding things were during World War II. A Master Sergeant was on duty guarding personal passenger trains. I remember that he was only five feet eight inches tall or so and he wore many ribbons on his uniform. It was a most unusual sight because at that point and place we did not wear ribbons. One day a Russian soldier appeared and the sergeant ask him to stop. The soldier did not stop, the sergeant shouted at him a second time but he kept on walking. At that point the guard took aim, shot, and killed him. The Russians came and picked up the body but made no trouble over what happened, and no charges were filed.

Among all these kinds of activities, there was a situation over there that really troubled me. I realize the tensions of the war were very real, but the military chaplains often became a source of tension themselves! The military chaplains stationed there were often drunk!

I still remember seeing them; one was the Lt. Colonel who was an Episcopalian Priest, and the other was a Major who was a Roman Catholic Priest. **It haunted me. It seemed to be as if God were speaking to me; or giving me vivid examples of how badly responsible clergy were needed**. Whenever I encountered them, I had these thoughts. I then decided that the military needed spiritual guidance better than what those two were giving. **In response to that experience, I**

committed myself to the ordained ministry with the words, "I will go to seminary when I get out."

At that time I had no idea where I would go nor did I have the knowledge that I would marry a beautiful girl named Bertha. She has been a companion, par excellence for me in my private life as well as in my professional life in the Pastoral Ministry.

With that experience I was far from being "out." In the remaining years in the military, I had some interesting assignments. At one point I was working in the place of relaxation for ladies. There they could play games, read, and drink coffee. On one occasion I taught one of them to drive a vehicle. I took her in a jeep to the former German Air Force Base. The big wide and long runways were ideal.

In the middle of a runway, we changed seats and she began to drive. Because it was a standard shift, she spent most of the time driving as she looked at her feet! Finally, we drove those runways enough so that she got "the hang of it." I was happy to find out that she did get her license.

Another unforgettable experience was the result of having gout in my left big toe! I did not go for help until it was so swollen that I could not get my shoe on. The doctor was a lady. When I walked into her office carrying one boot she asked me, "Why are you carrying one boot?" When she saw my toe, she had me transported to the hospital by ambulance. When I got to the hospital I was questioned what I was doing there. I looked perfectly healthy—except for my toe, which they had not yet noticed.

They made me take off my clothes and put on pajamas. I was then given a bunch of pills and they soon ran out of them. They then started giving me shots. When a male nurse told me to bend over, he admitted he had never given a shot before. I encouraged him to go ahead and finally he did. I remained in the hospital in a ten-bed ward for six weeks.

Once I got out of the hospital I was assigned to work in a movie house. I ran the projector, showing movies for the military personnel's relaxation. I also worked on the ham radio.

Once I did get out of the Army, I completed my high school work and graduated in 1952. I worked for local restaurants, where I became quite a chef; at least I received many compliments on the meals I prepared for customers.

I also worked for the Faulkner Hardware Company delivering bottled gas, driving truck and clerking in the store. During this time, I was active in the local fire department, became Sunday School Superintendent and was a lay preacher in the local Christian Church.

By the summer of 1954 I was employed at the Fort Wayne YMCA summer camp in Kendallville, Indiana. At that same time while visiting Defiance College campus, I met Bertha. She was wearing a yellow dress with red flowers, which remains in the family to this day!

We dated during that fall and winter and when Bertha graduated from Defiance College in 1955, we became engaged. We were married in Bertha's home church on

May 12, 1956. I continued to work at the hardware store and Bertha taught school.

In January of 1957, my brother Jay was killed in a tragic traffic accident. A month later, I finally answered God in the affirmative, setting sights on beginning my seminary education. It was a scary time in that there were few funds available and not many worldly belongings.

After one year of marriage, deeply in love, we left our apartment, our family and friends in Ohio. We departed for the great State of Maine and The Bangor Theological Seminary.

It was during the first "get together" of new students at the seminary that we met and fell in love with the Embling family of Clyde, Audrey and little Cindy. It was their constant love and encouragement that kept Leland in Seminary! We became one family and to this day they are very precious friends. Our families have so much in common, sometimes it does not seem real.

The Reverend Norman Dubie

Norman presently lives in New Hampshire with his dear wife, Doris. They have been married for over sixty years. I became acquainted with the Dubies when Norm and I were both students at Bangor Theological Seminary in Bangor, Maine.

We have kept in touch all these years. Both he and his wife are very dear friends of ours. They have three beautiful children. Their youngest, Rebecca, lives in Massachusetts where she cares for an elderly lady who cannot be left alone. Becky was married but has become a widow at too young an age. Their middle child, Robert, owned and ran a bookstore in New York City prior to his untimely death. Norm Jr. is a college professor and is known worldwide for his gifted writing of poetry; he has published a number of books.

Here now is Norman Dubie's sharing of his becoming an ordained clergyman. He begins at a time when his sister was gravely ill.

> "Lord, if you'll let my sister live I'll do anything you want." My sister lived and I went on with my life, not thinking very often about the promise I had made. God didn't seize to call it in a hurry. In fact, God left me free for a varied work life that in later years enabled me to feel and understand how people felt right where they were at.
>
> I did such things as working on a farm one summer; while in college, I worked on construction building houses. I worked for a boat company; a wholesale fruit company; a bowling alley setting up pins; in a laboratory; a granite quarry; as an insurance adjuster; an aircraft factory, and I served in the Medical Corps during World War II. I share those workplaces because in retrospect I marvel at the varied work experience God let me have before calling me out.
>
> My childhood was a happy one. My parents allowed us to go to any church, so I often went with my friends to different churches. For Sunday school I attended the Presbyterian Church that was next door to where I lived. I also went with friends to a Baptist Church, an Episcopal

Church and a Roman Catholic Church. I had a rather varied church experience, which proved helpful in my adult years.

After high school I attended the University of Vermont on a football scholarship, a scholarship for an essay I had written, and a scholarship for my grades. With all that put together it didn't nearly pay the cost, so my father had to sign six–month notes to pay for what I was lacking for school. There was no way he was going to be able to pay those notes if they were called in. After one and a half years, my conscience would not let me go any longer.

After leaving college I worked at a number of places. I was enjoying life and free living at home with my folks, but something was nagging at me to do better. In an effort to find a better job, I went to Springfield with my aunt. Then in a short while my cousin told me that I was crazy working where I was and that I should go home with him and get a job in Hartford, Connecticut.

There the Crattonwood Aircraft employed me and I stayed there for about three years before I went home and claimed my wife and she came back to Hartford with me. We lived in a small apartment. While at work one day, the boss called me into his office and said, "Now it's your turn. We are going to let you go and you will be drafted."

He was right. I ended up in the Medical Corp in the 300th General Hospital. I had to go for training to Fort Benjamin Harrison, Indianapolis – Billings General Hospital. But first I had to go through Basic Training. Finally I was sent back to my 300th General Hospital.

From there I went to England and on to France. I was sent to Marseille to work and from there I was released and sent home.

At last I was again joined with my wife, Doris, and for the first time able to see my son, Norman Jr., who was thirteen months old. After a couple small jobs in Barre we decided to go back to school. In pre-med the class was told that if we stayed on and went to medical school, we would have to neglect our families! I said I could not do that; I had already neglected them enough serving overseas during the war.

Doris felt that I should stay in school, so I continued and got my Masters in Education. Upon interviewing for a teaching position I decided teaching was not my thing. About then, my sister-in-law suggested that I go back to the insurance office in which I once worked. I did and I came home with a job. I was, in fact, offered two jobs. I chose the claim's adjustment position. After some training in the claim's department I began working.

We started going to the Presbyterian Church in Manchester where we became well acquainted with Homer, the minister. He was a good guy. Both Doris and I were very active in the church and of course, Norm Jr. was involved in the Sunday School.

One day as I sat in the back pew during worship, I felt a tap on my shoulder. And then I heard a voice that said, "Come follow me." I immediately knew that God was calling in my promise that I'd do anything He wanted.

The next morning at 9:00 I started out to do my claim's adjusting work but instead I pulled into the church parking lot just in time to help my minister open his office door! I told him that my wife and I had discussed my call and had decided that we'd like to serve in missions. My minister said that with my education I should go to Seminary and then go into missions if that was what you still feel called to do.

I followed his advice and guidance. I did not know much about the Presbyterian Church but I attended a meeting and was taken "In Care" of the Association. I met a minister at that meeting, who worked for Bangor Theological Seminary. He invited me up to visit, assuring me that we would have a good experience with them. In the fall of that year, we sold our house and moved to Bangor, Maine, where I began four years of seminary education.

Norman Dubie is now retired after serving a number of churches in New England. That "tap on the shoulder" is another example of the wonderful mystery of our Creator. God's calling, Norman Dubie became a very rich blessing to the Church all inclusive, but especially to the denomination in which he served—the United Church of Christ.

Before we leave Rev. Dubie's sharing, I want to tell you what Norman also wrote in regard to his ministry. He writes, "There was never a day that God hasn't supported us, guided us, and helped us to continue being the disciples we were called to be."

In his first pastorate, Norm spoke of a tragic event that took place. One of his dear woman parishioners went from her house to her mailbox at the end of the short driveway and during that time her stove blew up, engulfing the house with flames and she could not get back into it, nor even close to it but could only watch as her baby was burned to death. He wrote, "Clyde helped me through that one" although I was not aware of it until I read his words.

He also spoke of the time a young parishioner parked her car in her driveway and as she walked on her driveway she was hit by a speeding car and pinned against a telephone pole. The driver was drunk. He made mention of these events to say that he had to deal with many sorrows in his ministry as well as experiencing many joyful and inspirational times. In all such moments, including the very serious illness that almost took his wife's life, he confesses that the God who tapped him on the shoulder was there to hold his hand and somehow enable him to carry on in the work for which God had called. Praise be to God.

The Reverend Alan Dailey

It seems like I have known Alan Dailey and his lovely and supportive wife for years. Actually, I guess it has been about five or six years since we became acquainted. Also interesting is the fact that I have no recollection of when we met for the first time. It may have been at one of our area Association meetings or when he presented a very interesting and helpful seminar at a New York Conference meeting. Alan has done a great deal of work on how we share the Gospel of our Lord.

And his presentation on "Reframing Evangelism; Witnessing Jesus' Way" at our state conference proved that point. It was a "shot in the arm" for all of us who sat at his feet on that occasion.

We have become close friends, I am thankful to be able to have you read his experiences that have become the driving force behind his life and his service of our Lord, Jesus the Christ.

I am a recently ordained pastor in the United Church of Christ (UCC). I originally heard God's call when I was a youth, but I said "No." My call to ordained ministry is about faith. It is about my faith, my recognition of how God has worked in my life and how this has changed me. It is about a call to witness through my lifestyle and to live, preach, teach and communicate the Word of God in such a way that others' faith in God can be built up too.

Bill Cosby once said, "I started out as a child." I too, started out as a child. My parents, Rowena and Earl Dailey, raised me during the postwar 1940s and '50s in Rochester, New York. I was the older of two children (my sister is five years younger than I). My first recollections of my spiritual journey go back to my youth. The Church had been a cornerstone in the lives of those I admired as a child and continued to be so for me throughout my youth.

While my family attended worship regularly, I do not recall ever feeling any pressure to attend, but rather I went because it was something I enjoyed. As a teen, church became a safe place for me as I struggled for peer acceptance in other areas of my life. It was a place where I had many friends and was encouraged to assume a leadership role. Throughout high school, I was involved in youth activities; retreats, singing in the choir and taking advantage of participating in worship as often as possible.

The summer between my junior and senior years, I attended a week-long youth retreat. That week was a pretty profound one for me. Over the next year, with the help of my pastor, I began seriously exploring the ministry as a career option. My spiritual interest continued through college. As part of my Social Science major, I took several religion courses, which I found very stimulating, and in which I earned good grades. However, I also realized there were many stereotypic aspects of the ministry with which I was uncomfortable. As a result, during 1962 I shifted gears and elected to pursue a career in marketing and sales.

Following graduation from Michigan State in 1964, I married, moved to the New York City suburbs, started my career, joined a church, and began my life as an adult. While I do not think it was a conscious decision at the time, I saw my church involvement ebb and wane during the 25-30 year period following the death of my wife in 1967. During that time, I attended worship sporadically and had limited formal church affiliations. However, in reflecting back over my life during that period, my faith connections were always a source of hope for me. The Church seemed to remain a safe and positive place to which I returned when I was in some level of emotional turmoil. In spite of an erratic pattern of worship attendance and spiritual involvement, I frequently found myself revisiting my previous interest in the ministry.

Through the 35+ years between when I decided not to pursue the ministry, while an undergraduate, and the time I began seminary, I found myself wondering how I might be able to combine my experience and skills with that recurring interest. However, each time I was able to find sufficient strength to create, yet another excuse to procrastinate as the time just never seemed right. It was during that period, that I now realize there were several instances when I felt the presence of the Holy Spirit in my life.

About nine years ago, I found myself in that place yet again. This time the catalyst was Nancy. She was a friend, a ballroom dance partner, and someone I had known for several months. Somehow our conversations never got around to what we did professionally, until one evening she asked me what I did. It was then that she shared with me that she was a pastor. She had been seeking a call for several months and had just received a call to pastor a church east of Rochester.

Well, I have to say that that revelation had a profound impact on me. I had known her for quite some time and I still did not have a clue that she was a pastor. She certainly had dispelled many of the stereotypic images I had of the ministry. I could not get that thought out of my mind. I knew it was something I needed to follow up on.

At that point I elected to pursue the tug that I had tried to ignore for so long. Since Colgate Rochester Crozer

Divinity School (CRCDS) was practically in my back yard, I decided to start there.

It just so happened they were holding an orientation session the following week for prospective students. I decided to go and listen and basically be the proverbial "fly on the wall."

However, at lunch one of the administrators, knowing that I was doing behavioral medicine research with a couple of local psychologists, asked me about a friend of his. And wouldn't you know, it was the guy with whom I was trying to start a business. Then, as I was leaving, I spotted a friend from my home church. At the same time we both exclaimed, "What are you doing here?" After lunch, I attended a class with her. I was surprised to find the students engaging, and the material not overwhelming.

I then found myself thinking, "Perhaps this was something I could handle." Well, so much for being a fly on the wall! During that day I learned that I could enroll as a special student and audit courses and not be enrolled in a degree program. That seemed like a prudent safe approach for someone who was "just exploring."

However, that too was not to be. Once again, if it wasn't one excuse, it was another. After an additional eighteen months of dragging my feet, **it became very clear that "not now" was *not* going to be acceptable this time.** The new business opportunities had all but dried up; there were no jobs on the horizon and I had had virtually no income for over twelve months. My savings were running out. I was in debt, and felt as if my life was aimlessly floundering without a rudder.

It was then that I saw the headline of a recruiting ad for CRCDS. It read: *"I believe faith is spread each time one life touches another. I believe I can spread faith."* The whole idea of "faith being spread every time one life touches another" touched me. It certainly was not the in-your-face domineering approach I expected. Then one evening a few weeks later, I found myself in prayer and that ended in one of my "Jephthah moments" (one of those times when you commit yourself to something in the heat of the moment, only to realize that maybe you just might have stuck your neck out too far!) What had happened was that I had told God that if I were shown a way to make it happen, I would apply to the MDiv degree program and attend seminary full-time. And so eight weeks later, at fifty-six, with God's help, I was officially enrolled in CRCDS, as a full-time student, still not really knowing where it all might end.

So where was God while I was in seminary? Everywhere! I went to CRCDS expecting to be "put in a box" and told where the walls were. Instead, what happened was that I was put into that box and then all the walls were knocked down. Then as I reconstructed my walls, I was then encouraged to look through lenses or perspectives other than just the one I walked in with. This certainly helped me peel away the layers of stereotypic barriers that I had toward religion, the ministry, and my going to seminary. As it turned out, the barriers surrounding the subject of evangelism were also peeled away.

As that became apparent, many of my friends like to remind me of another of my "Jephthah moments." When we were in the student orientation session during my first week at seminary, we were asked to share some aspects of our journey and some idea of how we perceived our call at the time. I said, 'I am not really sure what is drawing me here nor what my call might be but I do know one thing it is not. **It is not evangelism!'** Within weeks, I found myself with an overwhelming desire to share everything I was experiencing. This was all very new to me. Over time, I sensed an awareness of incredible new levels of energy around many things in my life.

It was during this time, that one evening, after reading the *Prayer of Jabez* that I found myself motivated to pray asking God to "Fill my plate to overflowing, to enlarge my territory." (Then I wondered, is that another "Jephthah moment?") Along with that, came an increased willingness to risk trying new things, which included: accepting a field education assignment. Where in addition to participating in worship and pastoral care, my focus was to help in the development and implementation of an evangelism program. My overflowing plate also included opportunities to lead several small groups including developing a workshop on helping churches re-frame evangelism into something they might consider. It also prompted an invitation for me to join the United Church of Christ, New York

Conference Commission on Revitalization, Evangelism and Church Development, a group that I was ultimately asked to chair.

God certainly does speak to us in many strange and surprising ways. It was also during this time that I was given a plaque that read, *"Faith is not just believing that God can, but rather it is in knowing that God will."* It is through understanding faith in those terms that has helped me realize that seeking God's Will for my life is the key to reaching God's heart and it has been that understanding which has helped form the shape of much of my personal theology and outreach ministries.

What I have now come to realize, is that, **throughout my whole life, God has been preparing me for the journey ahead.** And while it was that advertisement, which appeared in the Rochester Democrat and Chronicle in 1997, that became the catalyst in finally drawing me to seminary, it was God who knew me and of my gifts for evangelism. **It has been that "piece" which would encapsulate much of what my journey has been about over the past eight years.**

Ironically enough, while I certainly did not see evangelism as part of my call at the time, in looking back, it was that which finally drew me to seminary. Thank you God for knowing!

Alan's call has been a step-by-step walk with God. As he looked back over years of experiences, he has more intently seen the divine guidance and enabling presence. That divine presence not only guided him to commit him to attend seminary but all through those years of study, Alan was excitedly aware that God was "walking" with him on his journey.

Alan Dailey now shares how experiences in his life have given him and his call to ministry support and encouragement.

Jeremiah 29:11 reads, "*For I know the plans I have for you,' declares the Lord, 'Plans to prosper you and not harm you, plans to give you hope and a future."* That text was certainly one that sustained me during the three years following my graduation from seminary in 2003 and my being called to my first pastorate at the First Congregational Church of Riga UCC in 2006. It was three years to get a call and to be ordained; three years of watching what seemed like all my seminary colleagues get calls and be ordained; three years of meeting with multiple search committees and each time only to receive a polite rejection letter.

Every time my plans seemed set they were derailed and I experienced another roadblock on my journey. Each time I reread that verse from Jeremiah, and carried on with the faith that God did have a plan for me. BUT, I would find out in God's time, not my own!

The result of this wait was my being called to a congregation where there was a direct "fit" in matching my gifts and interests with their needs. In fact, I once read that if you want to make God laugh, just share with God what your plans are for life! So, I suspect there was much 'heavenly humor' at my expense.

One of the clearest times that I have recognized God's presence or God speaking to me since seminary was following the unexpected death of my fifteen-year-old nephew, Christian. He was my son Mac's cousin. They had been born three day's apart and their mothers were sisters. In spite of living about three hundred miles apart, the boys were like soul brothers. It was about 7:00 p.m. on a Sunday evening, just as a small group meeting was to begin. When I got the call from my ex-wife, she was hysterical as she told me of Christian's death.

Without hesitating, I immediately left to be with them. My wife, Sue, joined us a short time later, after she had sent the members of the group home.

While there, I told Barbara, my ex, that while she might be leaving for Pennsylvania early the next day, she was in no condition to drive down alone with Mac. I told her I was going to drive them down. (That was probably the most assertive I ever was with her.) I spent two days there with her sister and her family before returning home.

Just before I left for home, I had some time alone with Paula, Christian's mother. She told me that I had been a tremendous help to her and everyone else in the family. Then she said that she thought I was going to make a tremendous pastor. The impact of that conversation did not hit me until about one hour into the trip home. When I arrived home, I sent her this e-mail:

Paula, first I need to tell you that in spite of knowing you were in good hands it was hard for me to leave.... Unbeknown to you, that afternoon I had received a call from a church to tell me that I was not still among the candidates for their position as pastor. That news had really blindsided me…While this was not the first time I had gotten this far only to get rejected, it was the one, which seemed to have the most sting. Especially since obtaining a call from a church is considered by the United Church of Christ denomination as God's affirmation of an individual's call to ministry. That is the final step in the preparation process for the ordination and becoming a pastor. As such, I found myself beginning to question whether I really did have the ability or gifts to be a pastor or whether this was even God's Will for me….

All that pondering dropped off the radar screen when I received Barb's call. It remained there until somewhere between Harrisburg and Williamsport this afternoon. That is when I realized that without my ever asking, God in the midst of your grief, used you as an instrument to reinforce me (very clearly and directly I might add) that I, in fact do possess the gifts to be a pastor and that I am truly called but the time has not yet come.

It is rare that God's messages are so blatant and clear (I guess for some of us it has to be). I also expect that it is still more rare that we have a chance to tell someone that they have been used for that purpose. But you, my dear, were! For that I am eternally grateful and I felt compelled to share it with you.

I had an opportunity to draw on that experience about one week into my pastorate at Riga church. I received a phone call that the 28-year-old daughter of one of the church families was unexpectedly found dead in her apartment. During the twenty-five-minute trip to see the family for the first time, I found my thoughts flooded with memories of my own grief baggage. So fortunately, I knew one of the first questions that I would be confronted with would be, "Just where was God in all this?"

the exact same question I had faced almost one year earlier. God was there for me the previous year and God was with me that morning with my new friends. And God was with me the following morning when I changed my sermon to address that same question for the grieving congregation at large.

While I had not received a call to pastor a church, this was the period between completing seminary and receiving the call to the Riga Church that God had answered my prayer, "to fill my plate to overflowing." Yet, God did not answer my prayer to be called to pastor a church. It was a time when I served several churches in extended supply situations, including a Lutheran church that would eventually provide me with a Praise Band that would play for my ordination. It would be a time when I would participate or lead several small groups. It was also a time when I started listening to my own sermons, and realizing that if I was going to preach it, I'd better be trying to live it too. I began looking for and inviting God into the valleys of my life, rather than just on the mountain tops, and in this way I continued my preparation to receive a call to pastor a church community of my own.

It was also during this time that I was introduced to a prayer by my spiritual director that would ultimately become yet another Jephthah moment in my life. It is called "The Radical Prayer" and it comes with a warning from the author, Flora Slosson Wuellner. She says that one should not pray this prayer unless he/she means it, for it is always heard and answered in definite and surprising ways: habits begin losing their grip, relationships can change, neglected parts of our souls begin to grow; surprising abilities and gifts appear while some old comfortable tendencies become unattractive to us. Something always happens when we pray it in honesty. It certainly has for me and I can see why, for it very directly linked me to seeking God's Will and showing a willingness to accept and embrace that Will no matter what.

The Radical Prayer is: "*Holy Spirit, if this is right for me, let it become more firmly rooted and established in my life. If it is wrong for me, let it become less important to me and let it be increasingly removed from my life.*"

Alan's journey has been long but it has also been a growing relationship between him and God. In his sharing we have seen how important it is to keep ourselves open to God's presence. As in the enriching experience with Paula we had demonstrated before us just how important our expressed words and thoughts of encouragement can mean to others.

Alan's shared experiences were not only faith-building for him, but if we look at them carefully, we will find that his experiences can also be stimulating to our own faith. His journey has been exciting for many of us to watch, as he moved along the pathway hewn out for him. For the next part of his journey, Reverend Dailey drew on the wisdom of Paul Harvey. He writes more of his journey, which he has entitled:

Now Here Is, the Rest of the Story.

While I have shared a significant piece of my journey, I do not want to overlook God's most significant gift to me during this period. It was New Year's Eve, 1996. I attended a party given by a friend where I met Sue, a nurse who had recently found herself single, following a thirty-year marriage. Our friends have told us separately that we monopolized much of each other's time that evening, even though neither of us was aware of it. Over the next couple years we ran into each other several times socially, but never dated.

Then on Thanksgiving, during my initial semester at seminary, we had both been invited to a post Thanksgiving" dessert party. The party was given for people who were seeking a reason to leave a family gathering. We both showed up having left family gatherings, something neither one of us had done before. On my way to the party I wondered if Sue would be there. I had not seen her in six to eight months and she was unaware that I had started seminary. To my surprise and pleasure she showed up. Once again, we monopolized each other's time but this time much of our conversation was spent sharing something neither of us knew we had in common, a strong spiritual component in our lives.

Neither of us was involved in any relationship with anyone else at the time, but neither of us was interested in any serious relationship. I was going to school full-time, working full-time, coaching my son's sports teams and sleeping once in a while! Sue was interested in having fun and not being in any kind of involved relationship. We both thought it might be safe for us to go out once in a while, so we agreed to meet for coffee a few days later.

Well, as we got to know each other better over the next eight or ten months, those coffee breaks became dinner dates and were much more frequent. We were amazed at how much we had in common, how easy it was to share and we were constantly amazed how we had indirectly stayed connected during the two years between when we first met and when we reconnected that Thanksgiving afternoon. We often said to each other that it must have been God watching over us and working in our separate lives.

Sue became an important counterbalance for the chaos in my life, always there, but never overbearing. More importantly, we always found time to squeeze in time for each other. Our relationship continued to grow. Sue continued to insist that she was not going to let it get serious. Sue still had scars from one long relationship and did not want that to happen again. Two years later, in 2000, after much thought and many conversations lasting well into the night, we decided to get married.

When we married, Sue had four adult children and three grandchildren, I had an eleven-year-old. Now six years later, Sue has become my soul mate, my best friend, my proofreader and critic, my prayer partner, my son's "other mother" and a grandmother of ten. She has been there almost every step of the way and is more supportive now of this journey we are on than ever.

Sue is now excited about assuming the role of the "pastor's wife" and exploring what that might mean for her. The congregation of Riga Church is just as excited having her, as she is in being there. In many ways, we as a couple were just what they were seeking. The truly amazing piece of this story is that over the past sixty years it took so many pieces. And God orchestrated, putting this puzzle together so it worked out as it did and **God did it**. Again, thank you Lord.

Bruce Wilkinson, author of *Prayer for Jabez,* once said, "The most exhilarating miracles in my life have always started with a bold request to expand God's Kingdom a lot. When you take little steps, you don't need God (as intently). But when you jump into the rushing river of God's plans and ask for more ministry, God goes to work all around you." His words certainly have been true for me, whether it has been in one of my Jephthah moments or on other parts of my journey. However, in understanding that truth, I've also come to realize that it is about God's plan, not mine. It's about God's timetable, not mine and it's about God's 'to do list,' not mine. Once I realized that and was willing to let my own agenda go, I found myself experiencing God's presence throughout my day, every day of the week. It was then that I realized the value of knowing and emulating how incredible faith drove this man called Jephthah to seek God and do

God's Will. And in keeping with the Jephthah theme, I've asked Sue not to be the first one through the gate when I return home, in the event I have found it necessary to have another "Jephthah moment.""

Thank you, Rev. Alan, for sharing with us. Your journey has so much to say to all of us. As I bring this chapter to a close, I will sum up by saying that God's call to ordination is given to all sorts and conditions of people. That Call comes when, where, and how God so Wills it to come and to whomever God Wills it to be received.

Yes, the sacred call to serve as an ordained clergyperson comes to people of all ages, and in any place that one might find her/him self. We have had this truth demonstrated in the experiences shared in this chapter. We have seen that God's call to ordination is given to many people just like you and me and many people unlike us.

As a very small sample, we have seen in this chapter how that Call of God was received by a man who was the owner of a very successful business; by a young man in the U.S. Navy aboard a Naval Ship, with the breeze and wind blowing in his face; by a young couple settled in their new home and having a promising career; by a student in college, questioning his faith; by a family man with a top echelon position in America's Nuclear Power; by a man searching for a more meaningful life and opportunity to be helpful to others; and a soldier serving in the U.S. Army in Austria where he saw the need for Christ' ministry; by a young man who was a football player, a draftee, who served in the Medical Corps and who was also an insurance appraiser. All sorts and capabilities of people are called into the professional ministry.

Jesus' gave his first disciples what is called "The Great Commission." It is found in Matthew's Gospel account and it is the same commission he has given to people ever since.

To all who have shared their PERSONAL, VERY PERSONAL CALLS FROM GOD TO GO INTO THE CHRISTIAN MINISTRY, I extend a very sincere THANK YOU! May God's Love and Presence continue to be their strength, their wisdom, and their life for evermore. And may we all be cognizant that what Jesus said to his disciples, and what he said to those who have just shared with us— He has said to hundreds and thousands of others.

Yes, God is still speaking, AND TO ALL PEOPLE OUR LORD STILL CALLS: "Go and make disciples of all nations, baptizing them in the name of the Father and of the Son and of the Holy Spirit, and teaching them to obey everything I have commanded you. And surely, I am with you always…"(Matthew 28:19-20).

CHAPTER TWO

The Presence of God Touched Them During WWII

In this chapter I want to share some experiences of people who were in World War Two or had loved ones in that war. It was a horrendous war and most of us who were alive and old enough to comprehend anything, still remember that day when President Franklin Roosevelt spoke on national radio. He shared with the country that Japan had attacked Pearl Harbor. He soberly did his best to share the seriousness of the attack, how numerous people were killed, and that our Naval fleet had been vastly destroyed.

I was only nine years old then, and it remains etched in my mind how we gathered around our radio, stunned by the dreadfully appalling news. My wife, Audrey, who was only six years old, remembers so vividly how her father took her on his lap. He then proceeded to explain to her that we were at war and that it was a terrible, terrible thing.

I share this, and more, to remind you of the horror "gifts" of war. World War II was an extremely difficult time for all of us who lived in that era. Loved ones were separated from each other for one, two, three, four or five years! Think of it. They were not only separated, but also confronted with the nightmarish reality of not knowing where their loved ones were, if they were safe, injured, or even still alive.

I remember that two of my sisters had friends and/or loved ones in that war. Helen's friend, Charles, who later became her husband, was in the U.S. Army. He saw so much carnage, killing, bloodshed and massacre that it nearly destroyed his emotions. How he lived through it all remained a mystery to him. He received all kinds of medals, including the Bronze Star and others that I was not aware of until after his recent death.

My sister, Julia, was married to Gordon Brodie in the very early stages of our country's involvement in WWII. You see, Gordon had by then completed college and was commissioned as an Ensign in the U.S. Navy. Julia and Gordon had been high school sweethearts and had planned their wedding and set the date. That all had to be changed because Gordon was not going to be around home by then!

I can recall the beautiful wedding at the Union Congregational Church in Churchville, New York. I must admit, however, that I more keenly remember the splendiferous reception held at our homestead. When they were in high school, both Julia and Helen played in the high school band.

Julia was great on the trumpet. I borrowed her trumpet years later and absolutely failed as I tried to follow in her footsteps. Helen played a beautiful trombone. I just loved to hear her play that instrument. It was not surprising, therefore, to find the high school band set up on our newly built front porch. As we ate and chatted and danced on the front lawn, the band played on! Our driveway was outlined with freshly painted white stones and the bushes were trimmed just right. Oh, yes, the flowers were even weeded and the lawn neatly manicured. That old and familiar song, "Everything is Beautiful" expressed what seemed to be the fact.

But it was not the fact. There was a very definite other side. The side we tried to push into oblivion for a few hours on that wedding day. Regardless of how beautiful everything seemed, we all knew that Gordon was soon to leave for the war. Without question, with our joyful celebration there was also a dance of agony churning within us.

We were fully aware that the young man in the sharp looking naval officer's uniform had already been assigned to a ship. He was to board a Naval L S M. That, we learned, was a landing ship that took machinery and personnel to the shores of battles. Many years later, Gordon told me that the L S M Ship was like a shoebox on the ocean. It was 208 feet long and to be called a ship it had to be at least 204 feet! That ship had double two thousand horsepower engines in it. The ship also had another significant attribute that helped him and Julia during those long years of roaming the seas.

It was L S M Ship number twenty-nine. It happened that that number had become "their special number." They were married on June twenty-ninth; on their honeymoon their room number was twenty-nine; thus when he was assigned to ship twenty-nine they both smiled at each other and found a sort of comfort in that reality.

All during the war we had a world map on which we tried to plot his whereabouts. It was a most difficult and futile task. For obvious reason, the actual location of his and all the ships and troops were not known. The crew on board the ship would not know themselves where they were going until they were well out to sea. Letters were "censored" to protect the troops from unwittingly disclosing their locations.

War costs more than dollars and cents. It comes with a bundle of pain and agony for those in uniform and for those who remain at home. That played out from shore to shore in this great land we call the United States of America.

It seems that whatever peace and hope we had was rooted in our faith. It was supported by the prayers and shared concerns during worship in our churches. And our faith was also strengthened as we prayed together as a family and in the individual prayers we spoke in the closets of our own lives.

When we would see pictures of our ships being blown up at sea and photos of the fierce battles that were taking place day after day, it was a sorrowfully agonizing time. The *Life* magazine was famous for its graphic pictures of the war. I can still remember how we would fight back tears as we peered over those magazines, listened to the news on the radio and read the daily newspapers.

It is no wonder that when the war ended we (our whole family) went into the village that evening to celebrate. Hundreds of us from all around the countryside gathered and shared our common jubilation and delight. The men of the village and I do not know who else,started an enormous bonfire in the four corners of town. It was massive.

They burned logs and railroad ties and I do not know what else. The fire burned for hours as we sang and danced in the streets like fools! We were so thankful that the hellish killing war was over; we were so overcome with a sense of joy that it was all a spontaneous event. It happened all across America.

War is always painful. It is a lot like hatred between races, or neighbors or between individuals. The only real answer to such hatred and war is love. To love one another as God in Jesus Christ loves us is to find, not war, but a peace that passes all understanding.

I previously mentioned that a few of our contributors to this book shared experiences with me of a Divine Presence with them during the war and /or because of the war.

Avis Theis

Avis Theis has been a dear friend of mine for as long as I can remember. She lives in Churchville, New York. She wrote me of her experience when she truly felt God's Presence. This particular experience came about some time after the war was over. Avis knew the agony and painful reality of War. Her husband was in WWII, braving the battles and fighting for peace. In fact, Avis wrote me a note that included these words, "My husband landed on the Normandy Beach on June 6, 1944. He was a part of the first wave with the First Infantry Division. Not very many of those in his division lived to tell the story of that invasion."

It is not at all surprising that as I talked with Avis, she shared with me the anguish of not knowing where her husband was, or in what condition he was in, during that heartrending time of war. But her sharing for this book is about what she experienced some twenty-five years later, when she and her husband visited the battle site.

Twenty-five years after the end of World War II, the First Infantry Division had a Battlefield Tour and we were a part of that group. Those who had fought in the battle traveled so they could in some way relive the experience. I think most of us, who were their wives, traveled so we could accompany our husbands and gain a greater appreciation of what our dear ones had gone though. At any rate, I not only accompanied my husband but I learned so much more about the experiences of those fighting in the war, and the impact it had upon them. During this tour, I felt the Presence of God in our midst.

We traveled from London to the English Channel, so that on the tour we could cross into Normandy by boat as they had done in 1944. Guess what happened? There were many in our tour group who became very sick, incredibly so. The waves beating on the boat and the continued rolling of the boat caused unbelievable misery along with upset stomachs galore.

As this happened on our tour boat, we were told for the first time, a terrible fact of which our war heroes had not spoken. During the time of the infamous Normandy invasion, many of the men became so violently seasick that they literally could not get off the landing crafts. As a result, many of our soldiers were killed right there, helplessly unable to protect themselves, or be of any help to one another.

I cannot imagine what it meant to my husband and the others who relived that horrendous day. They were now middle-aged men. I watched them as they walked the beach trying to remember where they landed and how it was back then. They looked for parts of foxholes and spoke of the agony of seeing their friends blown to pieces or shot and killed by enemy fire.

From the beach, we walked to the Normandy Cemetery. There we viewed the gravesites of three thousand of their comrades buried in that place. We walked among the Crosses and the Stars of David to see if any of the former soldiers and officers could find the marker of special friends who gave their lives for our country and for peace in the world.

It was at that time and in that place that I was invaded by the Holy Spirit. I felt as if that place was the most holy place I had ever been. Yes, God's Presence "touched" me and I have not been the same since.

I am sure others had like experiences. My whole outlook on life changed after that experience. I am now much more aware of God's Love and God's Presence with me. I now find more genuine peace and enduring comfort in the beauty of each new day that the Lord gives me to live on this good earth.

As the days went by, our tour visited many other American cemeteries. In each of these, the veterans seemed to find a deep sense of peace. They, like all of us there, were humbled as we considered the pain of battle; the suffering of loved ones, the horror of war and the cost of so many men and women whose lives were sacrificed for us.

I truly wish that more American people could visit these hallowed places. I can't think of this experience without shedding a tear for our men and women who gave their blood for our great country.

In the face of battle, in the battle, and in the results of battle, God spoke and continues to speak to all who will listen. Don't think for one moment that God speaks to only one side of a two-sided battle. God speaks to all his children to comfort them in all the trials and tribulations of life. God loves all whom he has created and it must "wound" God when the only way we can see to end strife is to deliberately and overtly seek to harm, kill, and/or otherwise trounce and prevail over one another.

There is a true story that should help to demonstrate what I have been trying to say here with considerable effort. During the Civil War in our country on Christmas Eve a lonely, probably scared soldier began to sing a Christmas carol. He came out of his hiding and put his weapons down and sang with all his heart. Pretty soon others in his unit put their weapons down and joined him in singing. The "enemy" across the dividing river heard them singing. They were mystified. Soon, they put down their weapons and began singing along with the voices of their opponents on the other bank. It was a "holy experience" for all as they set aside their human differences and sang to the glory of God together.

God loves all people and seeks to be to one and to all what He must have meant to the Psalmist who wrote these beautiful and well-known words of Psalm twenty-three. Yes, these words become ever more endeared when one experiences God's Presence in and around them. Avis did, and we thank her for sharing that beautiful life-altering experience with us. I am certain that all who have shared with us, their personal experiences with the Almighty, have founds these words to have a deeper more meaningful message. The Psalmist wrote:

The Lord is my shepherd; I shall not be in need.
He makes me lie down in green pastures,
He leads me beside quiet waters,
He restores my soul.
He guides me in paths of righteousness
For His name's sake.
Even though I walk
Through the valley of the shadow of death,
I will fear no evil,
for You are with me;
Your rod and your staff,
they comfort me.
You prepare a table before me
in the presence of my enemies,
You anoint my head with oil;
my cup overflows,
Surely goodness and love will follow me
all the days of my life,
and I will dwell in the house of the Lord
forever.' (Psalm 23 (NIV)

Dallas F. Embling

The Second World War had a tremendous effect upon the whole world. It touched individual people as well as nations. My brother, Dallas, was one of those people. He wrote me about a number of specific events in his life that proved to him to be God's way of preparing him for what was to come.

There are three boys in our family. Dallas is the eldest, William next and I am the youngest. I love them both. I have always looked at or thought of Dallas as being physically very strong and fun to be with. William and I spent a lot more time together. We worked on our small farm together. Perhaps more importantly, we played together. We played basketball in our large barn; we played baseball and soccer on our front lawn. Willie was fast and he could kick a soccer ball like a bullet from a machine gun. In fact, I still remember him kicking a ball clean through the glass window on our front porch!

These two brothers are the best of brothers. Dallas was so good in shooting a basketball that I could never beat him. Willie was so fast that I could never catch him. I share all that with you just to be sure you could appreciate the words of brother Dallas when he shares with us. You see, it was almost a surprise to me when I read some of his words; even though we were, and are very close.

In my brother's sharing, I found an example of my reason for writing this book! Really. I had never heard my brother express, nor had I ever thought of his experiences as a way in which God was guiding and blessing him. I say this, reminding you that we lived together; worked and played together, without my ever getting to really know him! His story truly touched me as I learned for the first time that he was cognizant of the fact that God was walking with him.

At the age of ten, when I was at our church one Sunday, I was pushed by another boy as we played during the short time between Sunday School and the Worship Service. I fell from the upper edge of the lawn and landed on my head eight feet below. You won't be surprised to learn that when I crash-landed headfirst on the cement sidewalk, it gave me a rather serious concussion. (My brother says it is the only time he can remember our worship service starting late!)

As a result of that concussion, I had to spend the summer in bed or at least inside the house where I had to be slow-moving, quiet and cautious so as not to trip, fall or bang my head again. When school started in the fall that year, I was not allowed to play the active games for several months.

I was not happy about all that; it was not fun, but now I understand why. Somehow, God had a hand in it all. You see, I now realize that that incident and the elongated recuperating time help prepare me for the next six years of my life. **With the advent of World War II, I was no longer able to have carefree summer vacations from school, as did other children.**

What happened was that at the young age of eleven, I had to begin working for my dad. Due to the war, my father could not find enough men to hire and help him with his busy schedule as a Custom Thresher. He threshed grain always beginning by July fifteenth each year. We worked seven days a week from six in the morning to about nine at night. In addition to that, when I was twelve I began working as the mechanic at one of the Curtis Burns pea vineries. That job began the day after school was dismissed for the summer. After three or four weeks of this, the peas were all harvested. Then dad and I began threshing grain.

As you can see, I had no summer vacations. In fact, I often missed the beginning of school in the fall, in order to help finish threshing for the farmers and ultimately for the country at war. "Today, I thank God for those experiences in the early years of my life. I know the Lord works in countless ways. Yes, for seven years I worked summers instead of playing, but this prepared me for my life's work. It gave me a work ethic that led to success. It also provided me with other lessons for my future; it became almost a tutorial for life.

I watched my dad get the most out of each new day. I watched him talk to people; I saw how he was able to get along, with all kinds of people, in a wide range of situations. I proudly observed how my dad believed in charity, giving what he could to help others. I was blessed by God as I was not just told how to act, dad showed me by being a living example himself. All these things have been a very real part of who I became, and who I have been ever since.

Reading my brother Dallas' words brought about the thought expressed on the book jacket of Rick Warren's book, *The Purpose Driven Life*. The words are, "You are not an accident. Even before the universe was created, God had you in mind, and he planned you for his purposes" (Zondervan, Grand Rapids, Michigan). In juxtaposition, I remember the words that God spoke to Jeremiah. "The word of the Lord came to me saying, 'Before I formed you in the womb, I knew you'" (Jeremiah 1:4-5).

Dallas goes on now as he shares some specific events in his life where he knew God's intimate presence was with him.

> In July of 1993, I had a kidney stone that was so painful it put me in the Highland Hospital in Rochester, New York. While I was in the hospital because of the kidney stone, guess what? I had a heart attack. This prompted my medical team to want further evaluation. I was accordingly transferred to the Strong Memorial Hospital, which is just a few blocks away.
>
> At Strong Memorial I first had an angioplasty to get my blood flowing as it should. After several tests, they found that I needed a quadruple bypass. On the tenth of July this surgery was done. I spent the next few months recuperating and the balance of the summer healing. It slowed me down so that I could not do nearly what I was accustomed to doing.
>
> This whole experience reinforced what I already knew; we do not always have control of ourselves, what we will do, when or how. I cannot help but thank God for that truth. Think about it. The kidney stone attack sent me to the hospital, which is perhaps the last place I would have been otherwise. Being in the hospital for my painful kidney stone meant that when I had my heart attack, I was

already there. I was only "a stone's throw" from some of the most qualified physicians, nurses and staff to be found in our area. Accordingly, the very minute I had the first sign of a heart attack, I received medical attention. Thank God, my heart attack did nowhere the damage it could have done had I been at home or elsewhere and did not know what was happening to me.

Then again in March of 2003, because of pain in my chest and left arm, I spent three days in the hospital. Thankfully, it was only a muscle strain. But guess what? Because of all the testing that I went through during that stay in the hospital, the medical staff found out that one of my arteries was closing and causing the flow of blood to be restricted. For that reason, whenever I did any extra hard work and strenuous activities, I had pain to contend with. As a result of all that, I now know that I need to limit my activities, and why pain is present when I don't.

Today, I am so thankful that the Lord has been watching over me; actually helping me when I was unaware I needed help. God gave those warning signs in sufficient degree and at the particular time that prevented major damage that could have had tremendously adverse effects on my life.

As I read and pondered the words Dallas sent me for this book, I could not help but think of the Prophet, Habakkuk. He is one of my favorite Old Testament prophets. He saw the destruction and chaos all around him. He used the following words to share his address to God. "Why do you make me look at injustice? Destruction and violence are before me; there is strife, and conflict abounds. Therefore the law is paralyzed and justice never prevails" (Habakkuk 1:3).

Like the prophet of old, Dallas was keenly aware of the toll of World War II and how it affected his life, especially as a young person. Yet, it seems to me that his outlook was so much more than the norm. He sounds so much like the prophet, Habakkuk, who after seeing and being affected by violence and destruction, was nevertheless able to write these words of great faith and trust in God:

"I heard and my heart pounded,
My lips quivered at the sound;
Decay crept into my bones,
And my legs trembled.
Yet, I will wait patiently for the day
Of calamity
To come on the nation invading us.
Though the fig tree does not bud
And there are no grapes on the vine,
Though the olive crop fails
And the fields produce no food,
Though there are no sheep in the pen
And no cattle in the stalls,
Yet, I will rejoice in the Lord,
I will be joyful in God my Savior"
(Habakkuk 3:16-18 NIV).

Thanks, Dallas, for your sharing, your clear thinking and your unswerving faith that God is indeed in control and that God's Love does prevail.

Edalyn Everett

[At the start of this portion of this chapter, I am saddened to write that Edalyn Everett succumbed as the result of a stroke and heart failure. All who knew her miss her ever-ready smile, her compassionate love, and creative intelligence. Indeed, we live in the hope that we shall meet again.]

World War II played a part in our lives in so many ways that any attempt to count them would be futile. This is one example. As a young teenage high school graduate, Edalyn Everett was as patriotic as they come. In her shared experience she tells how God helped her make one of the greatest and most important decisions of her young life.

Miss Everett is now a retired elementary school principal. She is a dear friend of many, including my wife and me. Indeed, to know her is to love her. She is an active and involved member of the church where I served as pastor in Castile, New York. Edalyn served on the Board of Elders, which has the primary responsibility for worship and the spiritual concerns of the church. She was also actively involved in our overall Christian education program.

In October of 1963, when I began my ministry in Castile, Edalyn was our elementary school principal. I quickly found her to be knowledgeable and keenly sensitive to the needs of students, teachers and staff. I promptly agreed with the community perception of her, as being an intelligent and compassionate person. She was loved by all. One of the first substantive discussions I had with her was about our Sunday school program. We agreed that our United Church of Christ Sunday School material was very good. We also concurred that our teachers needed to have some training in lesson planning and presentation, if they were to teach it effectively.

Like she has done ever since, Edalyn offered to help in this endeavor. She gave a fabulous seminar on the subject to our compete staff. I had had a course or two on that topic while in college; but let me tell you, her presentation was superior to those classes in every way! I still remember her offering on that most crucial aspect of teaching. Anyone who takes teaching seriously would agree that lesson planning and presentation are priceless tools. In her usual, humble way, Miss Everett did a bang-up job in assisting our Sunday School staff. She made a lasting impression upon me.

It was a natural for me to request her to read over my doctoral project prior to its submission to Drew University in Madison, New Jersey. Her command of the English language and her eye for typos proved to be a real help in my effort. With that background you can understand why I invited her to submit something for this book. I knew her as an educator and I never would have thought that she started out to be a nurse. She shares with us now, beginning with these words:

> As teenagers my brother, sister and I were baptized and subsequently joined the Membership of the Methodist Church in Castile. It was there, with a young minister and his wife, that we became involved with the youth ministry of the church. After a few short years, due to inadequate financial support to maintain the beautiful old church building, its doors were closed and our church membership transferred to a neighboring Community's Methodist Church.

In 1940 as my high school years ended I knew that my goal was to become a nurse to help people. I wanted to become an outstanding nurse like my Aunt whom I loved dearly and admired greatly. In 1942 I had earned enough money through various local jobs to enable me to enroll in the Fall Class of the Nursing School program at Wyoming County Community Hospital in Warsaw, New York.

Our country was involved in World War II and the members of our high school graduation class were eager to help. Many of the boys entered military services and we girls did whatever we could to be helpful. I entered nurse's training along with fifteen others. We were anxious to support our nation's effort to the fullest. I thanked God again and again, for the opportunities offered that permitted me to enjoy the training and success during our probationary period.

Edalyn Everett's words triggered a thought in my mind. Probationary periods are or can be rough and tough. Her words brought to mind the concern I had over a probationary period given all of us who were seeking a further degree at Drew University. The class was told that anyone who did not maintain a "B" average or above would be excused from the program. That was a concern of mine because I knew that anyone could "bomb" a test and be "out the window" before they knew what was happening! At the same time, when I read Edalyn's words I had to smile. I am sure she had a whole lot less concern over her probationary period than I did. At any rate, she now continues.

Because the nursing staff was so limited in numbers and, due to the war needs, availability of trained personnel was so lacking, the student nurses were assigned tasks and medical procedures for which they did not feel adequately prepared. Bit by bit, I realized that although I was very successful in meeting classroom expectation, I was always uneasy whenever I had to assist the professionals in caring for a very sick patient or when I frequently had to initiate medical procedures without their specific guidance. I became very apprehensive about my ability to serve.

Consequently I was continually asking for God's intervention. In my prayers I requested the Lord to somehow show me the direction I should follow. I was seriously considering how to terminate my training in the spring at the end of my first year. I approached the director of the nursing program to discuss my insecurity and noted to her that my parents were very supportive of any decision and action I was contemplating. She encouraged me to continue.

It was a short time later that an opportunity to make a definite decision presented itself. **There was no doubt in my mind that my prayers were being answered.** I had just begun an assignment in surgery with a general orientation to a sterile environment. The supervisor for this specialty was very stern and, as required, very exact and critical.

She was an excellent professional for supervising the surgical division. With only a day or so in the Surgical

Unit, the hospital staff was seriously short-handed due to absences. Only one doctor and one student nurse were on duty. I was that student nurse. On that particular day a severe emergency occurred and surgery was necessary.

A man who had suffered a farm accident with a buzz saw, which mangled his hand, had been rushed to the hospital. I was terrified when I realized that I had to assist in his repair. It still remains a very vivid memory in my mind. God gave me strength to do my best throughout the situation as the doctor and I worked together.

Edalyn told me that it was hard to put in words but she truly felt God was present in that operating room. She knew that it was God who gave her the wherewithal to assist the doctor in helping that patient. She thought things went pretty good, considering the whole situation. Consequently, she was not expecting what happened after the surgery was over!

At the end of the ordeal I was reprimanded harshly by the doctor! It was then that I knew my final decision to terminate my goal of nursing as a career was made. Although that experience was an extremely sad one for me, I was thankful for God's answer to my prayer. God gave me the opportunity to proceed to a revised goal for serving.

In the fall of 1943, I entered college at Geneseo, New York. In the fall of 1946, I was privileged to begin a wonderful rewarding career in the profession of teaching. With all this, I now know that God gives us so many special moments as we journey through life. And **ever since that operation room experience, I have not doubted the power or importance of prayer. I know God does answer our prayers.**

I am exceedingly confident that Edalyn Everett would have been a very outstanding nurse. She is so caring and gentle and full of compassion. But as I read her story and thought about her life's work—it appears to me that God helped her to do what she was "called" to do. She had retired from her amazing career. And until her very recent death, she continued to be a real part of our church and community. Thanks Edalyn, may God's Love and Life continue to be with your soul.

War, like anger, has its own price tag. It is an age-long problem with those of the human race. In this chapter we have read how war has altered lives and caused pain in a variety of people. The message here, is how God is always with us. Those who shared with us, have demonstrated how companionship with God, gave them strength to carry on; direction for their lives and a peace greater than can be gained through war, regardless of how many bombs, missiles, or rifles are involved.

This is a truth that we should hold onto as we journey down the roads of life. God is above all the power of the world; beyond all strife and pain. God always desires an improved relationship with you and me and all people.

We give thanks to all who shared with their stories, telling us not only the horror and futility of war, but the reality of God's presence with them on land, in the air and on the sea. Yes, Praise the Lord, God is with everyone no matter where one may be—in the time of Peace and Joy, and in the time of war; despite the consequences of which side of the battle you favor! God loves all people.

Chapter Three

With Both Thumbs Down—God Amazed Them

I remember it well. It was midway through my first semester at Bangor Theological Seminary in Bangor, Maine. When a class in Hebrew ended, I remained in my chair. I was as confused as anyone studying theology could be. Classes in New Testament Studies, Old Testament Studies, Theology and Hebrew had been so stimulating, but such a jar to my prior beliefs, that I did not know which end was up!

One of the most influential men in my life looked at me with inquisitive eyes. Dr. Szikzai, who was both my Hebrew and Old Testament professor, slowly walked over beside me and sat down. In his delightful accented voice he said, "Mr. Embling, What is wrong?" He was a big man, probably six feet tall and he had large bones. We students had been told that he spoke six languages, emigrated here from Hungary or Austria, and had been in one of the infamous German concentration camps during World War II. I knew him as both an intellectual man, and a compassionate man, with a deep faith.

I did not expect him to understand or appreciate my theological turmoil. Without looking at him I said, "I am so confused that I don't know what I believe anymore!" I was shocked at his quick and startling response. He said, "That's good!" I looked at him and said, "What did you say?" The good professor continued, "Now you can begin working on building a strong faith in God." I was stunned. He continued on with words of encouragement that went something like, "Now you can read and study the Bible without preconceived ideas. You will find justification and authenticity for your experiences with God and His Son, Jesus Christ. Now Mr. Embling, you will build a faith that will be built on a rock; on a solid foundation that will not crumble."

With a couple tears of thankful relief dripping down my cheek, I thanked that man of God. HIS WISDOM, proved so right and so helpful as I was pondering why I was, where I was. I guess I would say that prior to that personal talk, my life was in a ***"both thumbs down"*** position because I was so much in need of help; help that seemed far beyond my reach. As I think of that experience, I am sure that The Reverend Dr. Szikzai was indeed an "angel" sent by God for me that day. I was so beat up, so confused and depressed that that experience changed my life.

In this chapter, I will be sharing many experiences of people who have found themselves in what I think of as a "both ***thumbs down***" position much like I was, in the discussion above. It is inspiring to hear and/or read their stories and to "see" that God's presence is not only everywhere but also beyond all understanding and expectation. As you read of their experiences, remember that these are all just ordinary people like you and me. They are people who have had their downward thumbs turned upward; their desperation replaced with the joy and the wonder of God's Love and God's Presence.

Harry and Phyllis Leathersich

I have known Harry and Phyllis for a long time. Harry was in the class behind me in school—that means all twelve grades in public school. Harry also went to Rochester Business Institute as I did, and at one time we both worked in the shoe department at McCurdy's, a downtown Rochester, New York, department store. I do not know where or how he met Phyllis, but she was a beautiful girl and so very pleasant to be around.

My wife, Audrey, and I were absolutely thrilled when Harry and Phyllis were united in marriage and came to visit us on their honeymoon. We lived in Norfolk, Virginia, at that time. Seeing such good friends and recalling our many experiences together was good for us. We were in Norfolk while I was in the Army and we had altogether too few visitors at that time.

We continue to see each other; getting together occasionally for a meal in our homes. That is how I first heard the story of what happened to them when it looked to me as if they must have had **"both thumbs down."**

> In February 2000, we were vacationing in Florida when Harry ended up quite unexpectedly in the hospital at Fort Myers. We were both shocked to find out that he had to have bypass surgery. The operation went well, for which we thanked God and also the medical team for their medical expertise. Although he had five weeks of

recuperation time before we left for home, he was neither ready nor able to drive that long distance. As you might assume, I became the designated driver!

As we headed for our home in Spencerport, New York, we ran into a torrential rain storm in Gainesville, Florida. The visibility was very poor and the roads were getting slick, so we decided to pull off to the side of the road for a while until it calmed down. After it quieted down we took off again only to run into the same torrential rainstorm a few miles down the highway. Again, we decided we'd better pull off the highway and wait.

As I started to pull over to the side of the road, Harry told me that I was driving too fast and would likely hit the car that was already parked there. As I put my foot on the brake to slow down, the car started to slide. Unpredictably and without warning, we careened down an embankment! Our car was not on skis, but it felt like it as we slithered to a stop. Harry looked at me and said, "Well, now what are we going to do?" My response was, "Call 911."

What a predicament they found themselves in. In a flash as quick as lightning, they found themselves down an embankment in the mud. With the wind and rain beating on their motionless car, they both knew there was no way they could get out and back on the highway without assistance. Now remember, Harry was basically helpless. He was in no way supposed to push or lift or even be outside in weather such as they were experiencing. (Being a heart patient myself, I can easily identify with the seriousness of their dilemma.)

I had no sooner said, "Call 911" when a young man driving a flatbed truck pulled up and asked, "Do you need some help?" Without any hesitation, my reply was, "Yes, we do, thank you." He then very reassuringly and with no doubt in his mind said, "You just sit right there and I'll have you out of there in a jiffy." With that said, he backed his truck to the back of our car and hooked us up to his and out we came, back up on the highway again. The young man came to my window. He was by now shirtless and soaking wet from head to toe. He asked if we were okay, and I quickly put a tip in his hand and said, "Yes, we are fine, thank you."

With that, the young man, who was truly our guardian angel that day, was off and on his way, and so were we. We still marvel at what happened. **It is as if God put that all together, even before we had time to become anxious or stressed over our situation**. That is, of course, exactly what Harry needed in the shape he was in.

God's presence and help truly amazed Harry and Phyllis. They, like all who have had their "thumbs turned upward," continue to thank God for their experience and help. Yes, when we have our eyes open to the presence of God amidst our daily lives, we are comforted again and again. God is always present, and our knowing that and seeing that, opens our lives to so much more peace and joy. The Psalmist of old knew that truth. He writes in Psalm 121:

"I lift up my eyes to the hills—
Where does my help come from?
My help comes from the Lord,
The Maker of heaven and earth.
He will not let your foot slip—
He who watches over you will not
Slumber;
Indeed, he who watches over Israel
Will neither slumber nor sleep.
The Lord watches over you—
The Lord is your shade at your
Right hand;
The sun will not harm you by day
Nor the moon by night.
He will watch over your life;
The Lord will keep you
From all harm—
The Lord will watch over your
Coming and going
Both now and forevermore."

Harry and Phyllis also want to share another experience they had. In discussing it with them they said that they call this next experience, "A Miracle." It is not as if the car experience was not a miracle, but this next event is of a different nature. Surely, it was a situation when they and all whom they loved had both thumbs down and God's guidance and presence turned them back up .

In 1992, our grandson, Colin, was five and, like many little five-year-olds, he started kindergarten. He enjoyed school and everything appeared to be going along just fine. However, Colin seemed overly tired every day when he came home from his half-day at school. His mom thought that was not quite normal.

After watching him closely for several days, she decided to take him to the doctor and have his blood checked. I must tell you here that his mother has a little ESP and she sensed something was very wrong. Accordingly, she took Colin into the doctor's office for the blood test. The doctor tried to assure her by saying, "I am sure it's nothing, Janelle, but we will do the blood test you request."

Well, that evening around 9:30, Colin's dad, Scott, received that dreaded phone call. Someone from the doctor's office called and told him to take Colin right into the hospital. His blood count was so low it was evident that something was not right. The next morning he was diagnosed with leukemia.

Our whole family was in shock; we had never had anything like this happen before. He went on chemo treatment and in thirty days he was in remission. We were delighted. He went through the usual protocol of two years in treatment and then back to a more normal life. He recovered very nicely, although he went though some terribly painful times that just tore our hearts out when we saw him. He lost his hair and he experienced all the other nasty things that chemo does to one's body. But Colin came out of it all just fine. He went on to play soccer and roller blade and he did all the things that ten-year-old boys love to do. We were all very thankful for his recovery.

Then in May of 1998, his mom again suspected that something was wrong. She did not like his color. Although he seemed to be acting okay, she asked to have his blood checked again. The doctors, knowing of Janelle's ESP, did not argue with her at all, they just did it. Sure enough, Colin had a relapse. Our hearts were broken. We all asked the same question, "How could this happen again?"

Once again, Colin was taken to the hospital for what we all thought would be another two years of those horrible chemo treatments. But this time, the medical staff was considering a bone marrow transplant. To help move in that direction necessitated finding someone who matched Colin's bone marrow. They first decided to check Elyse, his only sibling, to see if her bone marrow would be a match for Colin.

We were very concerned about Elyse being a match because we were well aware of another boy down the hall in that same hospital who had seven or eight siblings, and none of them matched! Our prayers were faithfully frequent and urgently spoken.

And this is where our miracle happened. Not only was the bone marrow a perfect match, but also her blood was the same type as Colin's. What more could we ask for? Our prayers had been answered and we felt so deeply thankful and blessed once again by our Creator, Sustainer and Friend. **Yes, it was truly a miracle**.

We consider Elyse and Colin to be two very lucky young people. She was able to help her brother whom she loved, and he was able to receive her lifesaving gift. Colin had that transplant in August of 1998 and today he is a healthy young sixteen-year-old boy just like other sixteen-year-old boys. We are truly grateful to God for this miracle in ours lives.

Elyse Leathersich

We do not often hear from one who has donated bone marrow to help another. But Elyse Leathersich wrote a paper entitled "Giving Life," in which she shared how she felt about being a donor. She was a student in Irondequoit High School, in the Senior Class of 2002, when the follow words were written.

> Colin, my brother, and I have always been close. We would fight and have our sibling battles about silly things as much as other siblings do, however, this would all be put aside as of the spring of 1998. In the spring of 1998, Colin had gone five years without a reoccurrence of his leukemia and we all wanted to believe that it was behind us. The doctors assured us that Colin had done so well that we could finally consider his disease cured. Except for thin hair, there were only small reminders of the two years of chemotherapy, the cranial radiation and the time spent in the Pediatric Intensive Care Unit. My family and I had moved on with our lives and were enjoying some normalcy.

While Colin and I played Frisbee in the front yard, my mom called for the blood test results from the local hospital that had previously treated my brother. "It doesn't look good," was how Colin's nurse broke the news to my mom. She mentioned that there was an outside chance that it was a virus, but both of them knew what the bone marrow aspiration would confirm the following day—Colin's cancer had returned.

While I have had many experiences in my life, none has affected me more greatly than the event that I experienced in the summer of 1998, the return of my brother's cancer. During this time, I was given the opportunity to give life without giving birth. My younger brother relapsed with leukemia when he was a vibrant, active and energetic eleven-year-old. During this time, I felt as if everything I had, had been lost or taken away from me. It became a true test of my faith and where I stood.

As a young girl on the verge of entering high school, I did not know what to expect out of life anymore. I felt as if any childhood I had was gone. While it was scary to watch my only sibling lay lifeless on a hospital bed, I grew in many ways from this experience. The hospital shows on television are meant for entertainment; the occurrences I witnessed became a frightening reality. The silent death of the child next door, or the paging of a doctor to the emergency room was nothing like it is on television.

Walking through the automatic opening doors of Strong Memorial Hospital was never my favorite thing to do. During the summer of 1998, I longed to be outside with my friends, playing soccer or chatting on the phone. When I pushed open the heavy wooden door of the isolation unit to enter my brother's room, those thoughts vanished as I looked at my brother in so much pain and discomfort. Questions of faith ran through my head. "Why would God do this to me and to my family?" "How could God let this happen to such an innocent boy?"

I was torn as to what I was to make of God and His involvement in my life. At fourteen, what I thought of as faith was quickly altered. Though I never lost my faith in God's capability to see me through this incredibly difficult time, I wondered constantly what His plan was.

In June, after much research, the doctors decided to test my blood to see if my brother and I matched so that a bone marrow transplant could be considered. They had already done chemotherapy as well as radiation and felt that a bone marrow donation from me would be his best chance. When the results came back, I matched my brother perfectly. Both Colin and I were quiet when we received the news, though Colin had a big smile on his face.

I was overwhelmed and unsure. I said that I needed some time to myself so my parents put Colin in a wheelchair, dragged his IV pole and walked around the floor of the hospital. As per my request, my mom and dad gave me some time to adjust to this new information. As my family walked around, my mom heard Colin whisper, "Tell her she doesn't have to do it." My mom informed me that Colin was adamant that it was my choice and that he would go through chemotherapy again if donating bone marrow was too much for me. When they returned to the room, Colin immediately let me know that he understood how difficult this was and that I did not have to go through with the transplant if I did not want to. I immediately said, "Of course I'll do it. I would do anything to help you regain your health."

My family and I spent the next hour outside, away from doctors, away from the phone, trying hard to sort out all that had happened and what it all meant. On August twenty-fifth, at six-thirty in the morning, I entered the Ambulatory Center to donate bone marrow for my brother. I was unsure of what to expect and was reassured that my mom would be beside me the whole way.

In a little room, the nurse prepared me for the harvest, which is what the removal of bone marrow is called. The sedation began to take effect and I was less nervous. The last thing I remember was the oncologist telling me to take three deep breaths and it would be all over. An hour later I awoke as my mother walked into the room. After the supervising doctor of the "recovery floor" was satisfied that I was feeling okay, I was allowed to leave. I could walk, however, I was very sore. I have never liked attention being on me; therefore I refused to be pushed in a wheelchair. I walked out of the recovery room in pain, in spite of being medicated.

The elevator took us to the bone marrow transplant floor, where my brother had already started receiving my bone marrow and was waiting for my arrival. As I entered his room, tears began to fill my eyes at the sight of my brother, who with a towel draped over the transfusion bag, was sitting there waiting for me. I slowly dragged my feet in and a quiet, soft voice said, "Thank you." It was a turning point in my relationship with my brother, with my family, and most importantly with myself. Never before have I looked into my brother's eyes and seen the sincerity, appreciation, and gratitude I saw in them that day. I was not the hero, I was not the miracle child, I was not the one who cured him, I just contributed to his health; I helped save my best friend.

I now look at disabilities, differences, illnesses and unique characteristics in a different light. It has made me more grateful for the people in my life. I have an appreciation for the everyday life that God gives us and the plan God has for us. I do not take the tiny matters in life so seriously, because compared to what I have been through they are irrelevant. I am, who I am today, because of my brother and the journey we have taken together.

Elyse grew in faith as she took that journey along with her brother, their family and their God. I am sure that she now has a deeper appreciation for the words of Peter in his first letter: "Cast all your worries and anxieties on God, because he cares for you" (I Peter 5:7).

Elyse and Colin and their loved ones, along with countless others who have had journeys like that, surely have a deepened faith and a more positive connection with the words of Jesus when he said,

"Therefore I tell you, do not worry about your life, what you will eat or drink; or about your body, what you will wear. Is not life more important than food, and the body more important than clothes? Look at the birds of the air, they do not sow or reap or store away in barns, and yet your heavenly Father feeds them. Are you not much more valuable than they? Who of you by worrying can add a single hour to your life? …So do not worry…but seek first God's kingdom and God's righteousness, and all these things will be given to you as well" (Matthew 6:25-27, 33-34).

Indeed, we thank Elyse for sharing with us and for her willingness to give Glory to God, as her thumbs—if you will—were turned up. I have had opportunity to visit with both Elyse and her brother, Colin, since she wrote these inspiring words. They are both doing very well and they are both solid in the faith. Like we all should do, they continue to give praise to the Lord for each new day God gives them.

Robert and Leone Bater

I have known Robert Bater most of my life and I vividly remember Leone when they first began dating each other. I knew Bob as a vocal soloist in our high school and as an industrious and determined adult. He, like Leone, is solicitously helpful to others. Bob continues to be known as a person who can fix anything that is broken. Leone is meticulously neat as is her husband. Throughout their house everything is in its place and in Bob's shop things are just as orderly. He puts my shop and most shops I've seen to shame! When I say they are neat friends, it carries both the common and the literal meaning!

Bob has always been a very good golfer and continues to this day to be a challenge to anyone who plays with him. As I remember it, they moved from their home in Churchville, New York to Fort Pierce, Florida, so that they could be near Leone's parents who had just retired. However, we used to joke with Bob, telling him that we thought he moved to Florida, so that he could play golf year round!

Leone particularly enjoys working with children. She also does some nifty sewing with her machine and she is a natural at doing many creative craft projects. She is as unassuming a person as I have ever been privileged to know. Along with that attribute, Leone is a person with grace and compassion for all.

And I must say she is a wonderful cook and baker whose table looks like it belongs in *Home Beautiful* magazine. Both Bob and Leone are very much involved in the United Church of Christ in Fort Pierce, Florida.

Here in their own words is the Baters' story. It cannot help but warm the cockles of your heart. I am confident that you will quickly learn why I say that with both thumbs down, they found that God did amazing things to comfort and assure them of His Presence with them.

> This is the most memorable experience of my life in regard to having faith in God. I retired in February 1997. That same year, my high school class had our 50th class reunion. Leone and I decided that we would attend the reunion and incorporate it into an extended trip. Camping has always been our preferred mode of travel. For us it has always been a good way to relax and see the beauty of nature that is so often missed in our everyday

lives. Now being retired, we planned to visit some places we had not had the time to see before.

In May of that year we attended my 50th class reunion that was held in Churchville, New York where I grew up and where Leone and I had purchased our first home. After visiting family and friends in the area, we left in June with our recreational vehicle. We visited a niece in Ohio, and then went onto Indiana, Michigan (Upper Peninsula), Wisconsin, Illinois and Missouri.

During this trip we camped in about every type of camping area you could find. Some with RV's almost touching each other and some where your nearest neighbor was not in sight. One particular day we were camping in a very remote area. While taking a walk, Leone and I discussed what we would do if either of us had a heart attack. Looking back on that conversation seems almost uncanny. Our concern was that we were at least a mile plus from civilization, with no cell phone or any other way of summoning help if needed. I know we both prayed that we would be protected from any such event.

Later, on July 29, 1997, a date that we will always remember, I decided to play a round of golf. We were in Springfield, Missouri. While getting ready to play, I collapsed, falling into the golf cart. Leone told me later that she did not know what else to do but pray. In fact, she had just said, "O God be with us," when I regained consciousness. Once I realized what had happened, I was sure I was experiencing food poisoning from a meal we had had the previous evening.

Leone had already called 911 but I cancelled the ambulance, after assuring her that I would be okay. A short time later she drove me back to our recreational vehicle. Then she went out to check on where we could find a doctor. About twenty minutes later she returned and I advised her that there was definitely something wrong. For a second time, she called 911.

Two ambulances responded. They put me on a body board, put me in the ambulance and headed for the hospital. Less than a half hour later, I remember seeing the most tranquil white vision. My heart had stopped, the attendant got it restarted and I heard him on the radio with the emergency room of the hospital. The staff was all ready for me when I arrived. They performed necessary tests, which determined that bypass surgery was needed. My heart stopped once again and it was restarted this time with "paddles" and I was then rushed into surgery.

A day or so later, I am not sure just how long it had been, my doctor came in to see me and informed me that when I went into surgery, **I had only a five percent chance of surviving the surgery. What a blessing I had been given**. I had made it so far!

It was only a few hours later when a nurse, our daughters, Diane and Susan, came into my room, along with doctor. **They gently informed me that my wife, Leone, had collapsed and was now in the same hospital in a room on another floor**. I was horrified and I felt so very helpless, still being in the Intensive Care

Unit myself. **I prayed to God for help. I asked for God's divine Presence to heal us.**

"I was kept abreast of her condition, which was helpful to me. And I was so thankful when they told me that her medical problem turned out to be stress related. Eventually, I was taken to her bedside for a visit, which proved to be most comforting for both of us.

In due time we were released from the hospital, feeling certain that without God's help our lives would have ended in that Missouri hospital. We are so blessed. Our faith had been strong and our Lord was our strength and peace, our healer in the time of great need!

Today, we continue to thank God for his divine presence with us. As we go one day after another, we live full and happy lives, and we thank God that we have been granted more time here on the planet earth. Praise be to God.

Bob and Leone will never forget their trip of 1997. They continue to be well aware of God's presence being with them. And they still remember the help of so many people in their time of crisis and need. The word of Paul in his Second Letter to the church at Corinth says so much, not only to the early Church but also for all of us still today.

"We have troubles all around us, but we are not defeated. We do not know what to do, but we do not give up the hope of living. We are persecuted, but God does not leave us. We are hurt sometimes, but we are not destroyed" (2 Corinthians 4:8-9).

The Baters' continue to be thankful for God's act of healing which was a gift only God could give. They both continue to be active members of their church and they continue to enjoy God's never-ending blessing upon them. No doubt about it. When they had both thumbs down, God turned them back up to where God wants them to be for Bob and Leone, and for the rest of us, too!

Helen Fletcher

I remember when my sister, Helen, and her husband, Charles, took my sister, Marjorie, and me to New York City. I was in my early teens and I have never forgotten that wonderful trip. I vividly remember the first sighting of the Empire State Building. We could see the bottom portion of it and then there was a portion of it covered with a mist or cloud. The top of the building stood above the clouds, that particular morning and made me cognizant of the height of that structure.

I also remember hearing my sister, Helen, making beautiful music with her trombone and the piano. She preferred classical music and played like a concert pianist. I still prefer classical music and I suspect her playing had a lot to do with it.

Helen was employed by Monroe County, where she was responsible for printing the paychecks for all the county employees. When their children were born, she gave up that position to be a "stay-at-home mom." That was long before those words became a common definition of mothers who cared for their own children.

Helen has always been a great sister; more willing to help her siblings than to allow those brothers and sisters to help her. That has been true to her being for as long as I can remember. This dear sister of mine has had some very tough things to deal with of late. She shares a faith experience with us that she dates Saturday, August 1, 1998.

> I was driving home after having spent several hours at Strong Memorial Hospital. My husband, Charles was in critical condition in their Intensive Care Unit. My route home took me past the very road where my beloved mother now lived in a nursing home.
>
> The night before I was in such a distressed condition and crying so hard that I thought it best not to stop in to see her, even though it was what I normally did. The next day, however, I did stop in to see her for a few minutes on my way to the hospital.
>
> When I was on my way home from the hospital**, I had the most compelling feeling that I should stop in to see my mother again, even though I had been to see her that morning.** I was very tired and distressed over my husband's condition, but something kept making me feel like I had to make that stop. As I turned onto the road that leads to her nursing home, I prayed, asking the Lord to be with me so that my emotional state wouldn't upset mother.
>
> It was about 8:30 p.m. when I arrived at her room. She was already in bed and appeared to be sleeping. I gently touched her hand and said, "Hello." She said that she was so very tired. At this point she had not yet opened her

eyes. She said that she was thirsty. I got her cup and held it for her and she took a sip of water. Still having her eyes closed, I said, "Do you know who I am?" She thought for a moment and said, "Yes—Helen."

I was pleased to know she was able to recognize my voice. Mother then opened her eyes a little and looked at me. I told her that I loved her and she said that she loved me. She then asked me how Charles was doing. I simply told her that he was not doing very well. We shared a short prayer together and then I told her I had to go home because visiting hours were over. She smiled slightly as she said, "Goodbye."

The next morning at 7:15 my phone rang. It was a call from the nursing home to tell me that Mother had passed away at 7:10 a.m. To this day I thank God for leading me to her the night before. Although I was stressed to the limit and exhausted beyond expression, God led me and gave me the strength and wherewithal to make that visit. **Yes, I still thank God for those last blessed moments with Mother, a time that was sacred for me then, and still remains the same today, as it will for evermore.**

I am so thankful that my mother was such a beautiful Christian woman. She loved my husband and he loved her and thought of her as his own mother. (His mother had died when he was fourteen years old.) When we were expecting our third child I told him we should think of some names. Back then we had no way of knowing whether a baby was a boy or girl. Charles said, "If it is a girl, it should be Marion, after your mother." I was so impressed and pleased that he loved my mother that much. Our youngest child is a girl named Marion.

Helen did not mention it, but as she described visiting her husband who was in Intensive care and our mother who was in a nursing Home—she was also at the same time caring for her daughter, Marion, who has been ill for a number of years. Marion has multifarious problems believed to have resulted from her working in a place where many patients expired with what is commonly called "Legionnaires Disease." Marion continues to be on oxygen full-time and resides at home with her mother.

Helen continues to share some holy experiences when she realized that God was with her in very real ways.

> My husband, Charles, had not been well since January of 1995. He had a heart attack at that time and along with that came other health problems, each making him very weak and fatigued. It was so unlike him to be sitting or lying around the house. He had built our house and was always busy keeping it in tip-top shape. If he was not doing that, he was forever helping others with any variety of projects. He was a skilled carpenter and others often called upon him for suggestions and/or help. His heart attack changed all that.
>
> Charles was in the hospital due to a second heart attack, when my mother passed away. It was hard for him not to be able to attend her funeral. I went to see him following the funeral. He was so very weak. The cardiologist told me that they did not think he could live six months. When I left his side that evening, I was so painfully sad. Somehow the Good Lord brought him through it. He was able to come home and he lived for nearly two years.

It was February 16, 2000, that I found myself going from one room to another in Strong Memorial Hospital. Charles was a heart patient in the Intensive Care Unit and our daughter, Marion, was in Intensive Care Unit for lung patients. It was again a painfully sad day for me. I spent the entire day going from my husband's room to my daughter's room. Although I was unaware of it then, **I know now with all my heart, that God kept me composed, strong, and able to function that day. It was as if God was leading, and guiding me with His hand in mine**. Yes, God was strengthening and supporting me every moment as I endeavored to be uplifting and faithfully supporting them in love.

Charles had been in a deep coma for two weeks before he died. I was at his bedside when he left this world. I had been praying the Lord's Prayer and repeating the 23rd Psalm. I lovingly told him it was okay to go; we would miss him dearly but we would be okay. **A Hospital Chaplain and a nurse were in the room with me when a most holy and unforgettable moment took place. Just prior to my husband taking his last breath, he opened his eyes, they had a beautiful twinkle in them, and he smiled at me. He then with one finger moved it a little and tried to squeeze my fingers. I KNEW GOD WAS PRESENT WITH US. God had not only been present, but God enabled Charles to respond, to "peek" out of his coma and share with me. I shall never forget the love he showed me in that precious moment, nor the immense peace that God had blessed him with, in that hallowed time together.**

I will never forget that Holy Experience as long as I live. I was so blessed in my deepest sorrow. I was engulfed in a peace that defies description. I was assured beyond doubt that God is Love and that that Love is Eternal.

Along with all that, I now believe Charles lived those extra years so that I could better cope with grieving over my mother's passing. We, Charles and I, had fifty-two plus years of happy married life together. God gave us three beautiful girls whom we both love dearly. And in the strongest of faith, I look forward to meeting him again in the great beyond where God's Son, Jesus, has gone to prepare a place for us."

What an absolutely wonderful and sacred experience. Thanks, Helen. God is so good. Your sharing, like other sharing in this book, is not only an inspiration and encouragement to me, but so it will be also for countless others.

Among other pertinent scriptures these words of the Apostle Paul come to my mind. He writes to the church in Ephesus:

"For this reason I kneel before the Father, from whom His whole family in heaven and on earth derives its name. I pray that out of his glorious riches he may strengthen you with power through his Spirit in your inner being, so that Christ may dwell in your hearts through faith. And I pray that you, being rooted and established in love, may have power, together with all the saints, to grasp how wide and long and high and deep is the love of Christ, and to know this love that surpasses knowledge—that you may be filled to the measure of all the fullness of God" (Ephesians 3:14-19).

Robert Fidler

Bob Fidler is a gem of a guy. I first met him and his lovely wife, Lillian, when I became Student Pastor at the Federated Church of New Sharon, Maine. It was a combined United Methodist and United Church of Christ church. Bob had served that church prior to my arrival; I am not sure how many years before. Both Bob and Lil (her preferred-shortened name) were actively involved in the church. They sang in the choir, headed up an adult fellowship group and taught Sunday school. Lil was Superintendent of the Sunday school and the Vacation Bible School as well. They were then and still are "super people, great family." After some forty years we still keep in touch and we love them dearly.

I was at the same time a Student Pastor of the United Methodist Church in Mercer—about six miles down the road. After a few months, the United Methodist appointed someone else to that church which meant that my family budget lost about thirty dollars a week. Wrong! Each week I received that amount in the mail from an anonymous donor. Just before I left that church to accept a call to a full time pastorate, a neighbor of mine told me that our benefactors were The Fidlers. I doubt that they have any idea how much their kind and generous gift meant to us. With it, we were able to remain in New Sharon until I completed my formal education.

Bob shares with us an experience in which he sensed God's concern for the direction and goals of life.

I was struggling to get through college and, at that time, taking time out to serve a student pastorate in Vermont. I had spent three years at two different colleges. I took a year off in between the two to work, and was only deeper in debt. Neither college had been satisfactory. The first had been a Christian college with strict rules and some policies I did not see as ethical. The second was a secular university whose philosophy and student conduct were out of character for my goals and outlook on life. Making my own choices on the basis of cost, availability, and my own wisdom had left me confused and discouraged. It seemed to me very apparent that a different approach was in order

"When all else fails—follow the directions." I decided to try to find out what God would have me do, and to attend the school he would direct me to. I began praying and sending for college catalogs. Just how I came upon the name of Houghton College I can't remember. In any case, as I read the catalog and thought about it, this college became especially appealing to me. A Wesleyan Methodist school with high academic standards, it seemed to fit my needs. There was neither "a voice out of the blue" nor any miraculous sign, but the place seemed right. I applied and was accepted.

The next problem was financial. Already in debt, and my family unable to help, I had no resources to borrow more. I prayed, but nothing seemed to move. Returning home for the summer, I consulted with the pastor of my home church. We prayed together. Then, as I was about to leave his office, he said to me, "Bob, the only way I can see for you to make it is to get a job as a night clerk at a hotel so you can study on the job, or to work as a night watchman in a factory where you will have time to study between rounds." No greater insights came during a summer of hard, hot work as a railroad trackman.

Summer ended and I started out for Houghton, well ahead of school opening day to look for work. Houghton is a small town, about the size of New Sharon. It is located on the Genesee River in a waning rural area about sixty-five miles southeast of Buffalo, New York. It had two small general stores, one of which housed the post office, three gas stations, a church, and a motel. The college operated the one small diner. That was it; the college on the hill above the village, and the struggling farms around the valley. It looked like this was the end of the road for my hope for a college education.

The day was well into the afternoon when I arrived at Houghton, so I drove up the hill and around the campus. Older brick buildings mixed with newer stone structures and a dormitory under construction greeted me. Little or no activity was evident. I was very disheartened. I drove back down to the town where I got a small meal at the diner, and took a room for the night at a tourist home on the main street instead of sleeping in my car as I had while traveling.

Evening dragged on slowly as I read my Bible and tried to pray. Desperation gripped me. I was over three hundred miles from home with only a little money left in my pocket and no visible prospect of a job. What could I do? Had God just dropped me? Was God around at all?

As I paced the floor I came to a decision. "Lord, God," I prayed almost defiantly, "I have just enough money left to buy gasoline home. I'm going up on that campus tomorrow to see what I can find out. If nothing turns up to help me, I'm going to get in that car and drive home!" I then flopped into bed and slept until morning.

Early the next morning, I put my suitcase in the car. After a meager breakfast, I drove up onto campus. I pulled the car onto a semi-circular drive in front of a set of some older brick buildings, one of which had a bell tower. It was early morning in the very beginning of fall. The dew was still on the grass and nothing was stirring — not even a bird! There was the deadness that only a school can have when there are no students around. I was almost ready to start the car and drive away when I suddenly decided to get out. As I put my hand on the car door a man walked around the corner of the building ahead of me. As I opened my car door, he turned and came toward the sidewalk. I proceeded around the front of the car and up onto the sidewalk. The man turned in my direction and we met face to face.

Professor Smith, as I came to know him, was a tall pleasant man with thinning gray hair. Holding out his hand, he greeted me saying, "Hello, may I help you?" "I hope so," I replied, and I poured out my situation and my desperation to him. **After listening quietly for me to finish he said, "I think God has answered both of our prayers**. I'm the Superintendent of Building and Grounds here and I am looking for a night watchman. We need an older student who can be responsible. (I was twenty-five at the time.) It will be a staff position, so you will get tuition at half price; ten percent off your purchases at the bookstore and off your meals at the dining hall. You will work seven hours a night and get paid for eight. Rounds will be each hour starting at 8:00 in the evening with about 30 to 40 minutes between each round for you to study." **I hardly knew how to respond. Within fifteen minutes of getting out of my car my dilemma was solved, and my major needs met.**

My new employer held out his hand, "I will have to look over your recommendations, but I trust they will be fine. Now, while I go back to my office and look over your records, you go over to the Registrar's Office. Tell her I sent you, and get a schedule arranged that will have all your classes in the morning so you can sleep in the afternoon. Then come over to my office. I suggest that you sell that car. You won't be able to keep up the payments and go to college. I can give you the name of a dealer in a nearby town who can help you out." All these things I did, and I started work that night.

Houghton College helped to set the course for my life. Here I met my wife, Lil, and came to know Dr. Marvin Nelson, who was my counselor and an instrument of God's healing. Here I changed my major to psychology, which eventually led to a career in school counseling. It was also here that I found my first real circle of close Christian friends. God had come through at a crucial point in my life.

What a message for us all. Indeed, God does have concerns over the direction and goals of our lives. As Bob put his trust in God, Bob found that what looked impossible was easily accomplished with God's help. God does things like that when we put ourselves devotedly into His hands. Think of how things worked out for Bob Fidler. Bob' thumbs were both down, but the good Lord did not allow them to stay that way. The pieces fell together so neatly, that it is obvious that it took some Divine intervention. Yes, God's planning and God's involvement is what helps us when we ask and allow it to take place.

Our Lord said, "Ask and it will be given to you, seek and you will find; knock and the door will be opened to you. For everyone who asks, receives; he who seeks finds; and to him who knocks, the door will be opened" (Luke 11:9-10 NIV).

Thanks Bob for sharing this experience. We will hear of more holy experiences from Bob and Lil in the pages ahead.

Robert and Dawn Gruendike

I remember playing cowboys and Indians with Bob Gruendike. We are cousins, and as children, we spent considerable time together. I thoroughly enjoyed spending the day at his place; his mom was a dear aunt who made the best fried potatoes I ever tasted! She also taught me how to tie my shoes.

As we advanced in age, we enjoyed playing baseball and soccer along with other sports. At one time, Bob and I both worked for the County of Monroe in the Photostat Department where we photographed all sorts of legal documents. At the tip-end of the Korean War I was drafted into the Army. That time away and my subsequent time in college and seminary separated us but it did not end our caring about each other. When I became pastor of the Castile United Church of Christ, Bob and Dawn asked me to baptize their daughter.

While I did not know his wife, Dawn, prior to their marriage, I have found her to be a very lovely person. She is compassionate, kind and talented. She is an Ombudsman, licensed by New York State to be an advocate for persons in nursing homes. Dawn writes about the experience they had when she was visiting her husband, Bob, when he was a patient in the Strong Memorial Hospital in Rochester, New York. Yes, they had both thumbs down, but they were quickly reversed.

> Bob was recuperating from major surgery on an unseasonably warm day in late January. He was Post-Op and still very uncomfortable. I was visiting him and we were pondering together some of life's imponderables. Feeling a bit overwhelmed and still in pain Bob was feeling "down" and I was feeling very sad for him.
>
> His room in the hospital was on the fifth floor facing north, overlooking Mt. Hope Cemetery. Both of us were concerned over what the future had in store for us. **In this forlorn and painfully confused state, we looked out the window and we saw a very big, very complete and intensely vibrant-colored rainbow. It was breathtaking and we looked at each other and we both had a peacefully calm smile on our faces.**
>
> We were both uplifted and transformed at the sight of such beauty. We realized how insignificant our troubles

seem to be in the face of that beautiful rainbow. We remembered together how the Bible tells about the rainbow. We smiled as we remembered that it was sent by God, as a promise, many thousands of years ago, and how it was still so real and vivid today.

In my joy and thanksgiving, I quickly went out to the nurses' station and pointing back north, I called attention to the huge and beautiful rainbow. Several nurses ran in Bob's room to view and exclaim over it. Its hues remained vivid for several minutes and as each person left his room we heard a soft, "Thank you for sharing your rainbow with us."

We felt so much better. The signs of nature made us feel so blessed. Bob continued to grow stronger and seemed to become ever more healthy. **The rainbow signified to us that everything would turn out right!**

And it has. Bob and Dawn continue to enjoy married life together and they continue to count their blessings. Upon reading their response to God's presence with them, the words of the old and familiar hymn came to mind:

"Open my eyes, that I may see
Glimpses of truth Thou hast for me;
Place in my hand the wonderful key,
That shall un-clasp and set me free.
(Refrain) Silently now I wait for Thee,
Ready, my God, Thy will to see;
Open my eyes, illumine me,
Spirit divine."

The words of that hymn are important for you and for me to take seriously. So many times, so many of us do not see what is before us. Dawn and Bob could have looked out that same window, at that same moment, they could have seen that same rainbow and simply thought or expressed words like, "Isn't that pretty."

Thankfully, they had their eyes opened and they were able to see "glimpses of truth" God had for them at that very moment. It was such a gift; it gave them renewed focus, a deepened assurance that God was in control. Accordingly, they knew "Everything would turn out right."

If we would keep that message in our minds and hearts, the times when we find our thumbs in a downward position would be greatly diminished. The scripture that Dawn and Bob referred to comes from the Old Testament book of Genesis.

"And God said to Noah, 'This is the sign of the covenant I am making between me and you and every living creature with you, a covenant for all generations to come. I have set my rainbow in the clouds, and it will be the sign of the covenant between me and the earth'" (Genesis 9:12-13).

Because Dawn and Bob were aware and familiar with that story of Noah and the rainbow, they found in "their" rainbow a divine message of God's love sent to them in a very timely and consequential way. Our thanks to Dawn and Bob for this sharing, and may the joy, the pleasure, and the message of God's rainbows continue to be a blessing to them and to all.

Larry LaCroix

I first met Larry when I visited him and his wife, Ellen, in their home in Castile, New York. They lived in the area of the church I served. Upon visiting them I quickly realized that these two were beautiful people. They were then and continue to be forthrightly honest, consistently supportive and sincerely compassionate people.

Larry later became a member of our church (as did Ellen), and he quickly became involved in the life of our church family. He served on the Board of Trustees and helped us to instigate numerous energy saving projects that helped conserve heating expenses, as well as general costs of electricity. Larry has been interested in old cars, belonging to an Old Car Association and owning some neat vehicles himself. He has traveled all over the world and enjoys people and the places where they live. Larry shares with us a time when he, in essence, had "two thumbs down" and was prayerfully guided by God to overcome that defeated feeling.

> We lost my dad in early October of the year 2000. When he passed over, he was in the hospice unit in a small nursing home in Spencerport, New York. It was a sad, yet comforting ending to a long life after ninety-one years. His short stay there of six months met all of his and our needs. The dedicated staff was caring and loving to Dad. And that particular nursing home turned out to be God's answer to my prayer.

This answer followed a series of painful and depressing circumstances that began during a wonderful trip that Ellen, my wife, and I took. We, along with two other couples, flew to Singapore then boarded a cruise ship that journeyed for thirty fantastically superb days to exotic ports in Southeast Asia and the Middle East, including Israel. The fare for the trip was deeply discounted and we felt we had made an excellent choice for traveling.

Because Dad was elderly and lived alone, my brother, Dick, his wife, Jackie, and I made sure that at no time would both of us be away in case he had an emergency. The trip we took happened to span the time that Dick and Jackie had planned a trip to Atlanta where their son and grandkids live.

Tragically, Dad fell and was taken to the hospital the day after we left for Singapore. The extent of his injuries was difficult to assess. This forced Dick and Jackie to cancel their trip. Unlike being retired as I was, Dick had a business to run, which meant he could not reschedule. Their trip was planned before ours and we took a chance that nothing would happen when we were both away. We were wrong in going. We should have been there.

Understandably, Dick's anger toward me grew. In fact, his anger exploded at me when I called him upon our return. This deeply affected me because I had no defense for my actions. Prior to this, we had never had an angry exchange. I was devastated.

I carried a heavy emotional load in the weeks that followed that painful phone call. After awhile, Dick and

I reconciled our differences, but I knew there were hard feelings and I continued to feel guilt and depression that resulted in sleepless nights. I needed help.

Before too long, I began waking up at night with terrifying panic attacks and a strange sensation in my head that would last for an hour or more. It was then that I began praying for help. I had prayed before, certainly, but never for myself. After such intensive communing with our Lord, I soon began to feel that everything was going to be all right.

What follows here is a description of a series of events that I believe was the work of our living God. It begins with a phone call from my Uncle Ray. He said that Dad had taken another fall and had badly cut his hand. Ellen drove to Rochester to help. I wasn't able to go with her. She took Dad to the hospital emergency room, where he was admitted. They suspected some additional heart problems, even though he had had bypass surgery earlier, which had improved his condition considerably.

Dad was okay, but his physician advised us to begin a search for a nursing home, as Dad was unable to be alone in his own home anymore.

Prior to this event, our friend and pastor, the Reverend Doctor Clyde Embling and his wife, Audrey, had advised us to consider a small nursing home in Spencerport, New York. It just happened to be in the same village where my brother, Dick and his wife, Jackie lived. Our hastily arranged visit to this nursing home confirmed that this home was caring, friendly, and well staffed. **Even more**

miraculous was that the very night prior to our visit, the only private room had become available!

Dad was able to fast-track from the hospital directly to the home with the help of an understanding social worker. While all of this was happening Dick and Jackie had been on a short trip. There was some anxious apprehension on my part over making the decision without them.

Upon their return, they were truly pleased with what had transpired. Dad would be safe and cared for in our absences. I felt immediate relief and exoneration. Added to that comforting feeling was the fact that Dad very quickly adjusted to his new residence. The staff took an immediate liking to him, as did the resident cat.

Dick and I came full circle…back to the positive feeling that brothers should feel for each other. In truth, my prayers had been answered. I'm not surprised that God's instrument was the advice given by Reverend Embling, whom we love. After reading his book, *When God Walked With Me*, it struck me that my experience had too many coincidences, to be random luck.

My misery led to prayer which led to sharing with my pastor which resulted in Dad's timely placement into a private room that had just recently become vacant, and all this took place while my brother was away. And, with all that, the nursing home was located in my brother's hometown. But, even more importantly, it healed my relationship with my brother whom I love dearly. It is no longer uncomfortable for us to be together; it is instead, a refreshing, joyful and affirming experience.

> I believe in the power of prayer. You may not yet have seen that prayer can change events for you, as I believe it did for me. But prayer will calm your taut nerves. It will quiet your irrational fears and heal your tired body, even during your darkest of hours. I have experienced the healing touch of prayer and I am confident that it will continue to be there for the taking.

Larry LaCroix's sharing, highlights within me the words of a Christian hymn that has long been so very meaningful to me.

"Sweet Hour of Prayer"

…That calls me from a world of care,
And bids me at my Father's throne
Make all my wants and wishes known
In seasons of distress and grief
My soul has often found relief;
And oft escaped the tempter's snare,
By thy return, sweet hour of prayer!

The other two verses of that hymn complement the first as they go on to affirm the continued wonder of prayer. Those words are so very true to life's experience. Larry just demonstrated that truth very notably. Nevertheless, it is such a shortcoming for so very many people. Like the child, who was visiting his neighbor. When they sat down at the table for lunch, as was there custom, they said Grace. After that prayer, the host asked the child, "Do you say a prayer at home, before you eat?" "No," said the child, "We don't have to, my mom is a good cook!" Prayer has to be more than that. As Larry wrote about prayer, he spoke of it as a tremendous gift, free for all to make use of, as we will.

Scripture has these words, which also seems to be appropriate as we ponder the whole of Larry's sharing: "God is not a God of confusion but a God of peace" (I Corinthians 14:33a). Thanks, Larry, for this sharing and reminding us all of the importance of prayer. Talking with God, is without doubt one of the most splendiferous gifts afforded us by our Creator, Sustainer and Friend.

Julia and Gordon Brodie

As a way of letting you know a little about Julia and Gordon, let me first say that I have referred to them elsewhere in this book, as I endeavored to "set the stage" for the experiences that people shared in relationship to World War II. In addition to that let me share a few quick remembrances of these two beautiful people.

When I started school in the first grade, I was greatly comforted knowing that my sister, Julia, was in the school office as a secretary to the principal. She had been a student there for twelve years before graduating. From there she attended the School of Commerce in Rochester, and upon graduating was hired by her alma mater.

It was comforting to me having her in the school office because I was basically a shy child. That first year of school, I boarded the school bus in fear, trembling. It was also comforting to me because in my eyes, Julia was so special. She was the eldest child of eight, and me being mother's sixth child, meant that Julia assumed an almost parental role at times. as did my sister, Helen, who was next in line! When Mom and Dad were away, it was Julia (or Helen) who was in charge! It was she who gathered all of us together when strong thunder and lightning storms would hit in the middle of the night.

That is how I first learned the hymn, "Sing the Clouds Away." It included words like if you sing and sing and sing, you'll drive the clouds away; and if you pray and pray and pray you'll pray the clouds away. She was so reassuring and calm; that was especially true when the thunder rumbled and the lightning struck. Her almost casual manner, while some of her younger siblings were scared stiff and usually crying in fear, had a very positive effect on us.

Following WWII, Gordon became a physical education teacher. He had graduated from high school in Churchville, as did Julia. He went for further education, graduating from Springfield College. His first position was in Rushford, New York. There he was a high school physical education teacher.

At one time, Julia and Gordon ran a small grocery store at Rushford Lake. It was a convenient place for lake visitors and those who had summer cottages on the lake. I was so thrilled one summer when they asked me to run the store for a week or so while they were to be away. As a teenager, it felt good to be trusted, and it also proved to be a lot of fun.

Another time when I was visiting them in Rushford, they asked me to take their brand new Mercury to have it serviced. I drove it some ten or fifteen miles each way and truly felt like I was "King of the Road." I did not realize it then, but I now know that it was a very good self-esteem building experience for me. When I got my own car, I appreciated the trust they had put in me as a new teenage driver.

Gordon moved from Rushford Central to the Rochester School system. He remained a physical education teacher until he retired. Accordingly, Judy and Gordon moved back to Churchville, just a few miles from Rochester. It was then that Churchville-Chili Central School hired Judy again.

After being away for a number of years and having had two of their three children, she was hired as Secretary to the Business Manager. Later, her devotion, skill, and hard work found her being promoted to Treasurer of the Central School System, where she quickly became known as a caring and compassionate financial whiz.

After their retirement they purchased a Condominium in Florida, where they spent winters. Summers they spent on Rushford Lake, near where they had previously lived. Both places were delightful and beautifully decorated as only they could do it. The following experience that they share with us, all but overwhelmed them with the awareness of God's divine participation in their lives. When they decided they no longer could make those long journeys to Florida, God's help became a treasured gift.

> One of our most recent blessings from our Lord is almost impossible to believe. That is the speed and smoothness of our relocating from Florida to Virginia. When we made the decision we were at our summer place in Rushford, New York. We had thought about it for quite some time and discussed it with our three children, Larry, Linda, and Harold. They all considered it with us and they concurred that our thinking was the right thing

to do. Once we finally made our decision in late August the rush was on.

Time was of essence because our place on Rushford Lake was not winterized and we did not have much time before we would have to vacate it. We decided on a realtor in Florida to sell our condominium in St. Petersburg and we signed on with her. She helped us find a reliable mover and got that all arranged for us. Our daughter, Linda, and Gordon got airline tickets and flew to St. Petersburg to pack up a full condominium of furnishings and personal effects. What a job it must have been. We had left the place ready for our expected return in early fall.

We planned to move near our son in Lynchburg, Virginia. He and his wife had been looking for a desirable place for us in that area. We were delighted when he called to tell us that they had found a nice place for sale not far from them. It was ideal. We could actually see their place across the small lake, which bordered both of our properties. Larry also made arrangements for us to rent a storage place for our belongings until we had purchased something.

I'm trying to limit the length of my explanation but needless to say, everything was happening so fast and yet so smoothly that it was almost overwhelming. We obtained a mortgage and quickly closed on the new condo. Not only that, our Florida condominium sold without needing to have an open house. Our neighbor who lived above us gave us our asking price IN CASH.

Now then, look at what happened during this short span of time. We found and purchased a condominium in Lynchburg, Virginia. The location was as perfect as anything could be. We moved into our new place in early October, just a little over two months from the time we made our decision to relocate. In addition we sold our condominium in Florida and received the money; all that we were asking, no less.

We unmistakably feel the direction of God's hand on our lives daily. But, during those two months, we felt it even more acutely, for we never could have done all that we accomplished, so smoothly, and so quickly, without God's help.

I actually believe and feel that I talk endlessly with God. He is my most treasured friend and guide. When I try to share how I "see" the Holy Spirit, I say that it is like waves in the air; like radio waves; or waves over which we are able to use our cell phones. We cannot see those waves—only what they do—like electricity for example. God's Spirit is always with us. To know this truth, all we have to do is to focus on God and/or call out to God. Yes, if we plug ourselves in to God, the light of God's Son, Jesus will shine on us.

We must take time to pray and mediate if we are to know this great blessing. To know this is to have a peace that passes all understanding, and the assurance of a life that is never ending.

"My brain does not tell me this—my soul tells me."

Upon reading and typing Julia and Gordon's experience, I was reminded of the words of a beautiful hymn. Perhaps this particular hymn came to mind because as Julia penned her words and later discussed them with me, she knew she was near death. At one point in our sharing she asked how soon my book would be published. When I said, "Not for several months," she responded by saying, "Clyde, that's too late for me, you will have to read me what I have shared." I did, and the expression on her face, upon Gordon's face and their son, Larry's face was one of peaceful serenity and praise to the God of Love and Life. That was a Holy moment that I shall not forget. Read carefully these beautiful words from the hymn: "It Is Well With My Soul:"

When peace like a river attendeth my way,
When sorrows like sea billows roll;
Whatever my lot, Thou hast taught me to say,
'It is well, it is well with my soul.'
Though Satan should buffet, tho' trials should come,
Let this blest assurance control;
That Christ has regarded my helpless estate,
And hath shed His own blood for my soul.
My sin— O, the bliss of this glorious thought,
My sin—not in part but in whole,
Is nailed to the cross and I bear it no more,
Praise the Lord, praise the Lord, O my soul!
And, Lord, haste the day when the faith shall be sight,
The clouds be rolled back as a scroll,
The trump shall resound and the Lord shall descend,
Even so—it is well with my soul.

Along with those words of that hymn, God's Holy Word also pushed it's way into my thinking. Our Lord spoke these words:

"Do not let your hearts be troubled. Believe in God believe also in me. In my Father's house there are many dwelling places. If it were not so, would I have told you that I go to prepare a place for you? And if I go and prepare a place for you, I will come again and will take you to myself, so that where I am, there you may be also" (John 14:1-3).

We miss them so. Shortly after I shared with them their shared experience, as I had it prepared for this book, Julia, as she expected, left this planet Earth and joined with those who have advanced to the Eternal Kingdom of God. Not many months thereafter, Gordon followed his dear wife into the Eternal Kingdom. They were both a blessing to all who knew them well. They were kind, loving, generous people whom will be missed but never forgotten by yours truly, nor by their family and many others.

The Reverend Larry Brodie

You were "introduced" to Larry Brodie in the first chapter. Julia and Gordon are his parents. The Easter following his mother's death, he shared these words of faith with his congregation:

> Easter and hope are synonymous. Easter Sunday morning never arrives without its refreshing reminder that there is life beyond this one. True life. Eternal life.
>
> "Like many other families, in our family, we are dealing with the dreaded disease cancer this Easter. The battle

makes your emotions rise and fall. For even the strongest of Christians have moments when you feel like you live on what Charles Swindoll has called "The outskirts of hope." That feeling can become so very real when one hears the news: "There is nothing more we can do." We have heard that news, and for a while the hope disappears. The setting of your house in order, the prearrangements with a funeral home, the contacting of lawyers and updating one's Will, the signing up with Hospice—it all has a tendency to keep a family on the "outskirts of hope."

"Then comes Easter morning. There is nothing like Easter to bring hope back to life. Easter has its own anthems. Easter has its own scriptures. And Easter has its own proclamation: "He is not here, for He has risen, just as He said."

Easter Sunday moves us from the "outskirts of hope" to the "center of heaven." I will stand shoulder to shoulder with those of like precious faith and sing together, ***"Christ the Lord is risen today, Alleluia!"*** And my heart will feel a transfusion of hope. My tear filled eyes will be the result of the mixture of sorrow and hope. All of a sudden there will be a power surge of hope that will flood over me. And not only me, but all those like me who find themselves on the "outskirts of hope." Fears will fade and lose their grip. Illnesses and death don't seem so final. Grief over those who have gone on ahead is diminished. Our desire to press on, in spite of the obstacles, is rejuvenated. And the grace of another week is poured out to my soul. It happens every Easter. But better than that, it happens every Sunday!

The worst I ever experience is the "outskirts of hope." And it's only temporary until next Sunday. And even throughout the week I hear the 'Whispers of Easter hope.' You continue to be used by God to be those whispers of hope in our ears. In behalf of my entire family I want to thank you, and Happy Easter.

I felt I had to use those poignantly significant words of Rev. Brodie for the testimony they give us and the challenging reminder that is ours…sharing the Gospel of Jesus with others. A word of encouragement, a gesture of understanding support, a touch of compassionate love or a word in prayer are examples of the "whispers of hope" we can offer to one another. That offering is so very simple and so easy for all of us to give. But, those "whispers" can help to move mountains of suffering, loneliness, and unspeakable pain of sorrow.

We thank you, Larry for your sharing the Gospel of our Lord, and for what you mean to us.

Dorothy Klein

Dorothy Klein is a native of Buffalo, New York. She now resides in Fort Pierce, Florida. I had met Dottie (as she is commonly known) when she was at a celebration for her aunt and uncle, the Huels, in their church in Buffalo. I was pleased to see her again in Florida at the Fort Pierce United Church of Christ. She is an actively involved member of that church.

Dottie is in food service and works at the Fort Pierce Nuclear Power Plant. She is single and truly enjoys living in Florida, where she has resided for a number of ears. Each

Sunday at that United Church of Christ where we attend regularly, they have a coffee hour following worship. On one such occasion, as Dottie and I chatted, she inquired about my book. When I explained to her what this book was about, I asked her if she had something to contribute? Without hesitation she said, "Yes, I do have something to share; it has completely changed my life and I would like others to know just how wonderful God really is to us."

We then found a seat in the church garden area where she poured out her heart-felt story amidst thankful tears and joyful laughter. My notes share the words and experience of a dear lady, who indeed had both thumbs down, when the miracle of God's love turned them upward.

It was after that horrific hurricane in 2004 that I anxiously and wonderingly returned to my home to see what damage was done. One look and I knew my home had been totally destroyed.

At first I tried to pick up pieces as if I could somehow put the thing back together. All four walls of my primary living space were on the ground and all the contents that once graced my home had been tossed and scattered by the fierce and violent wind. The copious shredded pieces appeared like so many feathers, abandoned after an old-fashioned pillow fight. What was left of my house was no longer livable, although I did manage to stay there in a portion of the banged up trailer for a few days. It was no picnic! The hurricane had done massive damage to this part of my house as well. Water had destroyed the ceiling and walls; the carpets were like a wet sponge left too long in a tub.

I think you should know that I am about sixty years old. I am a single person and virtually all of my earthly belongings were, to a great extent, in that broken residence that included a nice trailer home with a large living area attached. I took a long walk through that park; seeing place after place in tangled disarray. Some seemed not to be in very bad shape at all, but they did all have some damage. I prayed as I walked around that "war zone" trailer park.

In a stupor of confusion and disbelief I prayed asking God for guidance as to what I should do. I asked God to help me with questions like, "How am I going to manage my living," realizing that I was living alone in a time when it usually took two incomes per household to get along. No doubt about it, I felt as devastated as my home appeared. I also felt and continue to feel so incredibly blessed, knowing that I can converse with God whenever or wherever I find myself.

Then one evening a man knocked on my door. When I opened the door he said, "Young lady, I think you need to come over to the next street with me. I will take you in my car." He looked okay, he appeared kind and he was very polite, but I had never seen him before this evening. So, as I hesitated, he said, "I want you to come and look at my home."

I finally cleared my head enough to say, "Alright, but I'll follow you with my car." He drove ahead of me. We circled around the park filled with debris. Soon we were at his home that looked very nice and seemed by its appearance to have had very little hurricane damage.

That, in fact, proved to be the case. We went inside and he introduced me to his lovely wife who was waiting at the door.

They showed me around their home that was very impressive, to say the least. It had a large Florida room that reminded me of what mine used to be. After a thorough, all-inclusive tour of their house, I was invited to have a seat in their strikingly attractive living room. Almost immediately upon sitting the gentlemen said, "Young lady, we are moving to St. Augustine. If you can give us our moving expenses and one month's rent, this place is yours."

"I could not believe what I was hearing. "What?" I said. In response his petite wife repeated his words and added that she thought it would be considerably less than one thousand dollars. In joyful exhilaration I said that I could come up with that amount of money!

In a day or so I got the money together. I gave them one thousand dollars for which I had an absolutely beautiful trailer home in which I now reside. **I did not know why that man knocked on my door that evening. I knew neither the man nor his wife.** I have wondered if they saw me walking around the park? How was it that they chose me among so many others?

With all the wondering and with all the questioning of why me, the amazing thing is that there is no other answer, other than that GOD WATCHED OVER ME; INDEED, GOD ANSWERS PRAYER!

Before that benevolent man knocked on my door and before he and his compassionate caring wife were so kind and generous to me, I was in a shattered residence, receiving food from the Salvation Army, living in one hundred five degree heat with no water to bathe, no electricity and feeling DESPERATE! My world had caved in around me and I was befuddled as to how I was ever going to make it.

I thank God for such a wonderful and timely gift. With the exception of God's gift of life and the gift of God's Son, no greater gift have I received. Just think of it. Two strangers gave me a house of which I have now made a home; a gift beyond my wildest dreams, a gift given because of God's love and compassion. Yes, my Creator, Sustainer, and Friend used two strangers, people unknown to me, to share God's love with me.

I am thankful to be able to share this awesome experience. My greatest desire now is to share the Love of God and God's Son, Jesus with as many people as possible. I want everyone to know God's Love for them and the promise that that love never ends.

We thank Dottie for sharing her remarkable experience with us. She was in a real position of despair. She certainly had both thumbs down, prior to that knock upon her door. She was down but not out. She knew God's presence and through it all she maintained a close relationship with God.

Surely, her experience ought to remind us to work at having that kind of close communion with God. And not only for those moments when our thumbs are down, so to speak, but equally for the heightened peace and joy that becomes so real, when our relationship with God and God's Son is intact.

The prophet, Ezekiel had a vision of a valley filled with many dried bones. In that vision, God asked the prophet if those bones could live. Ezekiel was aware enough of God's power to say to God that only God knew that answer. God then directed him to prophesy to those bones and God would put breath and life into them.

Ezekiel did as God directed and as he did the bones came together (as expressed so joyfully in the song, "Dry Bones") and God gave them new life. Dottie can relate to that. So can endless numbers of others, because God is forever granting renewal of life within and around us (Ezekiel 37:1-14).

Donna Sanford

I was Donna's pastor for most of her life. I still see her at worship in the church that I served for many years. She grew up in Castile, attended the local school and was involved in our church family. I had the sacred privilege of officiating at her wedding, and later baptizing her three children.

We shared many joys and some sorrows as well. Her beautiful daughter, Julia, is a very dear person. But she sure had both thumbs turned down during her high school years. Upon having some medical tests she was found to have cancer. The news was devastating to her family, to all of us in her church family, and to all those who knew her at school.

Donna shares with us her experiences as she and her daughter, Julia, dealt with that malignant disease.

"The experiences I want to share pertain to Julia's diagnosis and treatment. I was so concerned for my daughter and I was frightened with the possible outcome. Shortly after we discovered that Julia had cancer (Ewing Sarcoma), I was having a particularly difficult day. Not that any day was very easy after hearing the news of her illness, but as it goes, this day in question was predominantly an agonizing and nerve-racking day for me.

I was in our master bathroom and I suspect that I was there getting ready to take Julia for another appointment with a doctor. We sure had them often enough to warrant that speculation. Thankfully, our doctors and medical personnel were always very caring and professional.

It may seem out of the ordinary, but I do a lot of praying in our bathroom, it seems to be a quiet place where I can calm down and draw myself into closer communion with God. It is probably in part because it becomes a place where I can be away from the many distractions that meet our everyday lives.

Yes, it was a day when I felt deeply stressed over my child who was undergoing treatment for cancer, when a most uplifting thing happened. In the quietness of that place, as I was sharing my innermost concerns with God, **I distinctly heard a voice! I will never forget it. The voice was awesome, gentle and compassionate. The short sentence verbalized before me changed my entire life. From on high came the words: "I'M NOT GOING TO TAKE YOUR DAUGHTER."**

I'm sure you can appreciate why I said, "I will never forget it." It was a holy moment for me; an indescribable experience with the Presence of God. I did not share that incident with very many people because I was afraid that people might think I was losing it.

Nevertheless, I always held those beautiful words close to my heart. I always carried those words in the back of my mind—especially when we were having one of those bad or stressful days. They were frequent, but as I remembered those words, it was like a huge weight being taken off from my shoulders. I continue to thank God for that time together and for those words that were a blessing to me then and still today.

Another time it seems to me that a doctor became a messenger from God to give me help and assurance. I was walking the halls of that great and well-known cancer hospital, Roswell Park. As I strolled the floors, while my daughter was having a treatment, I saw so many children who were coming back to the clinic or to the hospital due to having a relapse. I felt so sad for them; I wanted to help each one but realized all that could be done physically and medically was being done. But I prayed for them as I walked the halls. The burden I felt on that walk was all but overwhelming.

I found myself getting more and more stressed, depressed and simply worn out, physically, emotionally and spiritually. Then all of a sudden, when I felt as though I would drop from the burdens I carried, **I felt a tug on my shoulders. In my mind I still think they were**

angels, and I heard the words, "Keep going, you can do it!"

About that time, Julia's doctor appeared on the same floor where I happened to be. I approached her, and asked, "Doctor, is this what happens—I mean the relapses? Do we really have any hope?" Julia's doctor was so filled with compassion and professional insight that I clung on to the words that came from her mouth. She said, "You see only the few coming back for additional help. But what you do not see is all the healthy kids that are cured." Wow, that was what I needed to hear at that moment of complete fatigue, both physical and emotional.

Donna was really down when our Lord sent angels to encourage her. The experience of being tapped on her shoulder must have been a bit surprising at first. Feeling a tap on the shoulder and not seeing anyone or anything around would be baffling. But then she heard the voice of an angel speaking to her. That experience is not all that different from the time when Moses saw the burning bush that did not burn.

In Donna's journey she continued to be close by the side of her daughter. She writes now of another experience that was a beautiful message given by God for her comfort and reassurance.

Another time that God spoke to me was an absolutely stunning experience. Julia was in the hospital again for another treatment. I was a bit weary. It was the end of another busy and arduous day. Just after I had tucked her into bed, she fell into a much-needed sleep. As she fell asleep there appeared a glow over her and on her face that made her look so precious and so watched over by God and His Son, Jesus. There was a light that was on over her bed, but this was a totally different light. It gave me great comfort and a reassurance of God's divine presence with her and also with me.

As I have thought about that experience over and over again, I find that it is still so very difficult to describe. But somehow it made me realize there was a Presence in that room with her and me that was more than we humans can wholly understand. For this reminder of God's never ending love, I continue to give praise to God.

Those shared experiences are so valuable for us to read and/ or hear about. They are experiences not unlike what God has used to help many down through the ages. Donna's sharing brings to my mind the experience that Paul had while he was in prison. He was there because he would not stop proclaiming the Gospel. Acts of the Apostles, chapter seventeen records that when Paul and Silas were in prison, in chains and their feet in stocks, as they were praying and singing hymns to the glory of God, an earthquake hit the prison. It caused a shaking of its foundation and making the chains and stocks to open and the doors of the cells and of the prison itself to swing freely. (Now, Paul and Silas did not flee the prison but stayed and thus saved the prison guard's life from certain doom.)

I bring up this experience of Paul in prison because it is an experience that is hard to explain. Have you ever heard of an earthquake being so violent that it would loosen chained stocks on one's feet and chain clamps on their hands—and still leave the building standing? I do not think so. The violent action was to free Paul and Silas and they in turn used the opportunity to proclaim the Gospel. Thanks, Donna for sharing how the Gospel of Jesus Christ has shone brightly in your life and in the life of your dear daughter, Julia.

People are forever finding themselves in situations that we may refer to as having both thumbs down. It happens to all of us. We have seen in this chapter how God is ever enabling us to have that reversed. What a blessing it is to have that understanding of God's enduring love. Jesus came to share that truth, to live that love and to assure us that that eternal love of God is not only present in this world but is itself never ending.

Rosalyn Dressel

I have known Rosalyn and her husband, Paul, for a couple of years now. They reside in Florida during the winter months, and we happen to live in the same park. Here at the Road Runner Travel Resort in Fort Pierce, your are apt to see Rosalyn and Paul playing tennis at any time of the day. Likewise, you catch a glimpse of them taking off with their canoe on top of their ever-shining vehicle.

Rosalyn sings in the choir here and also in their home church, where she has been involved with education and worship committees. She not only taught in public school but also continued her influence on children and adults by teaching Sunday School. It is not surprising to learn that she is involved in the Red Cross, Habitat for Humanity and active in the Ohio University Women's Club.

Before he retired, Paul was a Superintendent in the Public School system, after which he concluded his career in education at the University of Ohio. Both Paul and Rosalyn are cheerful people and it is always a delight to be in their presence.

Both Rosalyn and Paul are people who would endeavor to help anyone turn their downed thumbs upward. She writes about something that is so important to her and to all people. She puts a title on her sharing:

Smile—Be Happy.

This is the day which the Lord has made; Rejoice and be glad in it" (Psalms 118:24). Rejoice means to be full of joy, to be cheerful, to be happy.

Years ago I read an item about an old man who was a guest on a popular television show. He was very alert, appeared to be incredibly intelligent, and full of unending humor. The television host for the program was impressed with this elderly guest. Just before the program came to a close the flamboyant host said, "You are terrific!" He then asked, "Tell me, why are you so happy at your age?" The man replied, "When you wake up in the morning, you have two choices. You can choose to happy or unhappy. It is that easy, I always choose to be happy."

Those words sort of stood out for Rosalyn as she heard them. It was as if they came "from on high." She remembers the words and the occasion upon which she heard them.

Without doubt, those words have a great deal to do with our dealing with life, whether our thumbs may be down or up. Indeed, we can help ourselves so much by making the right decision. A Christian hymn that supports this, speaks of an action we can take that will help us to make that right choice; the decision to make an effort to be happy. It is:

"COUNT YOUR BLESSINGS"

When upon life's billows you are tempest tossed,
When you are discouraged, thinking all is lost
Count your many blessings; name them one by one,
And it will surprise you what the Lord has done.

Are you ever burdened with a load of care?
Does the cross seem heavy you are called to bear?
Count your many blessings, every doubt will fly,
And you will be singing as the days go by.

So, amid the conflict, whether great or small,
Do not be discouraged, God is over all;
Count your many blessings, angels will attend,
Help and comfort give you to your journey's end.

As we go through each new day there are many little and/or modest things we can do to help facilitate other people to be happy. It may be a simple effortless smile. It could be a pleasant or kind word. In fact, we can touch others in so many ways that would help them to be significantly happier. A happy or cheerful thought given to a friend can do wonders, be it by sending a card or talking over the phone or a pleasant note can always be a charge for the batteries of their faith, resulting in increased happiness and joy.

It is never too soon to do a kindness because one never knows how soon it may be too late.

God not only helps us to turn our thumbs up, but as Rosalyn implied, God also calls us to assist in helping others do the same. It is a beautiful fact, that as we endeavor to help others, we help ourselves even more. As you go from day to day and year to year, try intently to count your blessings, it straightforwardly will help you keep your thumbs up.

Thanks for sharing that message with us. Indeed, to be happy try to cheer others up. It is yet another of the treasured truths in Jesus' words: "Give and it shall be given to you" (Luke 6:38).

CHAPTER FOUR

In the Wilderness of Life God Does Astounding Feats

Remember how Moses led the people of Israel out of Egypt? It was a tough time. In the wilderness, they were repeatedly up against situations and predicaments beyond their comprehension. Trapped by the sea and afraid to cross it, God directed Moses what to do and the waters parted, allowing them to cross to safety to the other shore. That was an amazing experience; an astounding fete.

Hungry and without water, God again instructed Moses how to carry out God's Will. They were miraculously fed each day and had water to quench their thirst. Over and over again, the people found that God traveled closely with them in their wildernesses. God rescued them, time and again, from the doom that covered their paths.

This chapter shares the happenings and events of individuals who found themselves in the wilderness of this life and felt desperately in need of help. These experiences are shared, because of the depth of meaning they have for those involved and with the hope, that they will become very meaningful and inspirational to all who read them. Indeed,

God does astounding fetes all around us, in us, and for us, as we journey along the many diverse paths of life.

Jacquelyn Tepas

I have known Jackie Tepas for only a short time, perhaps three or four years. Prior to that I only knew of her through the kind words and supporting comments of her husband, Bill. He has been one of our financial advisors for many years. He's the kind of guy who is always "up" regardless of conditions that surround him. At those times when our investments were in a slump, when he came to see us, he was always very positive. His upbeat presence would leave us feeling good about transactions he recommended. And yes, his advice has been very good to us.

But totally unknown to me, his wife Jackie was for a number of those years living in a wilderness filled with more questions than answers. Today, we see her working side-by-side with her husband and their two sons at yearly gatherings for his clients. Her friendliness and pleasant smile makes everyone feel welcome and special. She is indeed a sweetheart.

Jackie is a neat, trim, fit forty-some-year-old who lives in Williamsville, New York (near Buffalo). As I previously indicated, she is happily married to her husband, Bill.

They have two delightful sons, whom anyone would be proud to claim. Both are now college age young men with a politeness, a sense of compassion for others, and an interest in people, all of which puts them above the norm for today's populace.

You should also know that Jackie is a licensed physical therapist, a private practitioner with a Holistic Emphasis. True to her professional emphasis, she loves to ski in the winter and roller blade in the summer! She and her husband are both actively involved in their church and in their professions.

Her cheerfulness and demeanor would never find you guessing that she ever had a pain or problem in her life. She informs me that she is thankful, and truly blessed to have such a wonderfully supportive family and circle of friends in her life. If you were to meet her today, her presence would never portray the pain and agony that she once endured.

Here is her story; an experience that ultimately gave strength to her faith and finds her praising God for that Presence with her, in those dark times and difficult years.

> I was humbled and remain in a state of awe! Ten years has passed but it feels like a lifetime ago. Once I was an energetic, physically fit mother, wife, homemaker and health professional, whose life seemed to be rather typical until I was brought to my knees!
>
> What happened in the spring of 1996, I never thought would happen to me, or anyone else for that matter! You see, if I had been injured in an automobile or skiing accident, that could be explained or justified. But quite to the contrary, I experienced a slow decline in my energy, a weight loss with a myriad of unexplained alarming symptoms. Because I had no known reason, my condition was something altogether different from normal. I was bewildered.
>
> So there I was, the supposed role model for my patients and family, determined to find an answer. **I could no longer devote my energy towards working,**

so I was forced to take a leave of absence from my professional work. My stamina was declining rapidly. And being the wife and mom I expected of myself, was becoming more challenging every day.

What was initially considered a minor inconvenience, had become a major preoccupation! A significant amount of time was necessary to visit physicians and specialists. I had blood tests, scans, ultrasounds and who knows what else. And waiting for the results, you could say that I was a model patient.

However, soon my patience turned into frustration. As the days turned into weeks there were still no answers. My condition regressed, as symptoms increased. I was nutritionally depleted, sleep deprived, and experiencing a plethora of symptoms from headaches, shortness of breath to tingling in my extremities.

Twice I required visits to the emergency room only to find myself back home with memories of a perplexed physician, reassuring me that I was not having a heart attack or a stroke. As his patient, I recall reiterating to him that I felt better outdoors, and adding that I was sleeping every night in a chair with my head propped up close to an open window.

More and more I began playing "home physician," pulling out every medical book I owned, trying to make some sense of this! (This is one of the burdens of having some medical knowledge…self-diagnosis. I started thinking I had every disease from beriberi to myasthenia Gratis!)

Gradually fear took over; I thought I was going to die. By the sixth week, a diagnosis still was not determined. Since there were no conclusive findings on any of the tests, my physician felt that I required the intervention of a professional psychologist. He prescribed Xanex to assist me during this stressful time in my life. It should not surprise you that that was the last time I recall seeing that particular physician.

Shook by the finality of it all, I decided that I needed to take a more radical approach. It was obvious that I had to find a health care provider who looked beyond the limits of conventional medicine. My husband, who helped me forge through those two months, lovingly and compassionately persevered and cautiously provided support. Yes, he tenderly held me as I cried in his arms more than once!

Feeling lonely and discouraged, I surrendered and knew more than ever that it was in God's hands now. I was not giving up. I was following where the Spirit led me. **The continuous prayers and words of encouragement from family, friends, clergy and fellow parishioners were more powerful than I had ever imagined**. Soon, I realized that I was not alone; a new world was being seeded and growing.

An old friend from grammar school paid me a visit. We had not seen each other in months and she planted the first seed. This seed was in the form of a book. Its contents contained details of individuals coping with Environmental Illness (EI), Chemical Sensitivity (CS), and Associated Food Allergies.

Once I started reading that book, I WAS RIVETED. It was as if the author knew me personally! The similarities in patients' testimonials were uncanny. The book was about our world, sadly, our toxic world. What we are eating, drinking, touching and smelling is negatively taxing our immune system. It all began to make sense to me.

Suddenly, I thought about what was happening in our home when I first noticed my symptoms. It was by now several weeks ago. We were doing extensive remodeling of our master bathroom plus painting and wallpapering. There were strong fumes from the sealants and adhesives permeating throughout our home, even with the windows open!

The children were at school and my husband was at work. And guess where I was; there were problems with the job, so I remained on the premises. And to make matters worse, the workmen's estimated day of completion was weeks longer than quoted when hired.

The author of this informative book, a physician, had no contact information available. **I prayed and asked of the Lord again, "Where can I find this kind of help?"** There was a cabinet in our family room where I store brochures, note cards, etc. One day I decided to write thank you notes. When I looked in the cabinet to get some note cards, right there next to the cards was an envelope. In that envelope was found information on alternative therapies. A former patient had given me this long-forgotten envelope years ago.

I started to shake inside when I saw it and a voice from within me instructed me to "OPEN it!" On one particular page, there was a letterhead with the complete address and phone number of a Physician specializing in

EI. The very next morning I called that physician, and guess what? She had had a cancellation for that afternoon. I BOWED MY HEAD, LOOKED UP AND GAVE THANKS TO THE LORD.

And who said prayer has no power! Jackie's prayer and the results of God's response are astonishing to say the least. This reminds me so much of the journey in the wilderness when Moses led the Hebrews to the Promised Land. Step by step, God was their strength and help. Upon crossing the sea and seeing the pursuing Egyptian Army with their horses and chariots stuck in the mud, they responded in humble praise and thanksgiving. Exodus 15th chapter begins:

> Then Moses and the Israelites sang this
> song: 'I will sing to the Lord, for He is highly
> exalted. The horse and its rider He has
> hurled into the sea. The Lord is my strength
> and my song; He has become my salvation.

Jackie gave thanks to the Lord for her astounding find, the name of a doctor who deals with EI (Environmental Illness), and then securing an appointment the very day she called.

Think about that for a moment. A patient of hers had given Jackie that informative pamphlet a number of years prior to it becoming a real part of God's answer to her humble prayer! Miraculous? Astounding? I'd say so.

The doctor was from India, went to medical school in the United States. She was a "cutting edge" practitioner and very knowledgeable in Environmental Medicine. It was an intense four-hour session of history taking, evaluation, and answering questions. The doctor simply explained that exposure to toxins over a long period of time, hide and build up in your system. If the load is high enough, when an individual becomes exposed to an even more toxic environment, their immune system reaches its limit and then malfunctions. After this, there is a point of chaos where even some natural scents can be troublesome, and seasonal allergies develop.

Toxins can be emitted from a natural source such as mold found in damp basements or synthetics, from pesticides, petrochemicals, etc. (which are all around us). Those were quantitatively measured. A toxic blood panel confirmed that I had all the latter with the highest ranges being that of benzene.

The treatment started with avoidance, avoidance of any object, food or scent that triggered adverse reactions. This required altering our home environment so that I would have a safe haven to heal. Some necessities were air and water purifiers, ozonators, elimination of carpets, toxic household cleaners and like kinds of things, plus an organic rotation diet. I myself had physical work to do. This consisted of cleanses, nutritional replenishing and rebuilding.

After a few months I had improved physically. My husband was relieved to see any improvement and we both were grateful that we could financially afford this program. Bill also expressed that he felt some satisfaction in seeing positive improvements in my health resulting from the external changes he had orchestrated in creating my place of refuge. He had felt so helpless for a long time, as I did myself.

Now looking back, I think of the burden he must have carried. The worrying and watching of someone he loved, slowly deteriorate in health. It must have been horrible for him. The many home projects that we had to do kept him focused on the present. God was watching him and surely knew that he was an ambitious and loving person. God also helped him endure by providing him with undertakings which would assist in my restoration and give him a real part in that effort. Also in the long term, we now know, all that work benefitted the entire family. We are so thankful that the Lord knew exactly what he was doing.

Improvements in my health also meant short outings from home. The first was going to church for Sunday Mass. Being unable to attend mass for a few months left a void in my life. The physical environment in the church was tough on me. Fighting the scents in the air from perfumes, flowers and the paraffin candles was a struggle. But it was important for me to express to the Lord my gratitude for all he had done for my family and me. I also asked Him for his forgiveness during all those times I displayed anger and self-pity. Most importantly, I wanted to thank the Lord for His endless love, even though I continue to ask petitions for myself. At that time, I made a promise to Him that my self-centeredness would be replaced with more selflessness and service to others.

I soon realized that forging ahead and attempting to resume daily activities was not an easy level to achieve. Leaving the confines of our home left me vulnerable and usually ill, for the remainder of that day. I always felt unprotected, like a glass doll, almost breakable. Again, I asked the Lord for some help. "I do not want to live like this Lord. What am I doing wrong?" Soon thereafter, another health practitioner approached me and offered her experiences. She told me she had been helped by traditional Chinese medicine (TCM). Quickly I realized that this is where I was being led and where I should walk. THE LORD PROVIDED ME WITH ANOTHER SEED TO PLANT AND CULTIVATE.

GC was that health practitioner. He was warmhearted, non-judgmental, insightful, disciplined; a healer trained by Shaolin Monks. He lived their traditions and stood by their philosophies. He briefly explained, our CHI (QI) flow. The energy within us (and surrounding us) needs to flow freely and be strong in order for us to remain in a state of balance and good health. The methods used to purify, cultivate and circulate our QI are through QIGONG (working energy). This is active work consisting of repetitive movement with breathing. Also QI can be strengthened by absorbing nature's QI, whether it is through ingestion of food or by walking in the forest.

As I worked and progressed through different levels with QIGONG I was feeling changes in strength and stamina. Cautiously, from a distance, exploring this world of Eastern Buddhist culture, I realized being here was not just-simply for a remedy. It was also to draw from the wisdom of this individual in order to validate my own truths and beliefs in Christianity.

This was a "spiritual test" for which I required a cleansing and replenishment. I thought about QI, and my intentions. In my eyes, it was always (and remains) the Spirit, particularly the Holy Spirit that flows within me. Nature, God's Creation, has it's own vibrations of energy (spirit) and that was why I am drawn to nature. I'm reaping the benefits, feeling stronger internally because of these natural wonders from God. The symbolic and practical use of incense, candles and essential oils had intrigued me. My desire to learn more about them provided for me a new appreciation of their use in church and in our home.

The burning of the pure incense had bothered me initially. But eventually I found myself welcoming the scent. Frankincense in particular not only has the power to cleanse but it was well known back in Christ's time on earth for its healing powers. The oil was used to anoint for thousands of years. I understand more clearly now why this was one of the gifts presented to Jesus at His birth. To this present time, I apply incensial oil on my family, my patients and myself. These oils are the extracted life from plants and carry powerful healing spiritual energy. To me, oils are gifts from our Creator. Why should I not share them with others? They are for everyone but particularly for the sick.

Today, I look forward to my daily walks. I found trails in my town that many did not know existed. The natural terrain and scents of the leaves and grasses invigorate me. Looking back, I used to find walking very boring, I needed headsets and I listened to Bruce Springstein. I gained a deeper respect for our earth and continue to do all I can to protect the environment we live in.

My children were in their early and preteen age years during the acute phase of my illness. But they observed and learned a whole lot. They were concerned about their mom but confused and sometimes rebellious. They too developed a healthier lifestyle, such as making healthier food choices and using unscented natural hair products. Even some of their friends stopped wearing their colognes. I am blessed with two wonderful boys who are now young men. I hope they know how much I appreciate their prayers, encouraging words, non-judgmental characters and their unconditional love. I thank God every day for protecting them and keeping them in good health.

I often meditate outdoors. There are many forms of meditation; visualization was very effective for whatever purpose I required it. Through visualization I reduce external stressors, induced relaxation but also prepared myself for prayer. I would use imagery and talk with the Lord. I later started to use these techniques with the teens at our church preparing for confirmation, assisting them with another way to pray. Since then I have used meditation techniques and imagery during our church youth retreats. I have been told that the response from the youth has been very positive. Thanks be to the Lord.

There were many times during this journey when I did not like where I was going. But actually, that did not matter. Why? Because eventually I began realizing that God had His own plans for me. I had deep-rooted anger to deal with. It was directed towards both others and myself. Forgiveness and spiritual healing really began when I recognized that most of my anger was based on fear.

Speaking for myself, I now realize that it was fear of the unknown, fear of being considered vulnerable or being judged by others. I suspect that this was the basis for some people I considered "my friends" to cease communicating with me at a time when I thought I needed them most.

I let this go and permitted myself to focus on the numerous individuals who provided support, aided me and offered to me their seeds of hope. I let my eyes and heart open up to all of these extraordinary people and the Lord who rewarded me with a fruitful harvest.

Not only the gift of restored health, but also a better capacity to look at others (and myself) with a deeper appreciation for who they are inside. Your physical body is only a manifestation of your inner spirit. Your God-like spirit is a precious gift, protect, nourish and love it. In the light of this miraculous journey, I suspect that you can appreciate why 2 Corinthians 1-5 is so very meaningful to me; it reads: "Now we know that if this earthly tent we live in is destroyed, we have a building from God, an eternal house in heaven, not built by human hands. Meanwhile we groan, longing to be clothed with our heavenly dwelling, because when we are clothed, we will not be found naked. For while we are in this tent, we groan and are burdened, because we do not wish to be unclothed but to be clothed with our heavenly dwelling, so that what is mortal may be swallowed up by life. Now it is God who has made us for this very purpose and has given us the Spirit as a deposit, guaranteeing what is to come."

In her wilderness, Jackie indeed found that the Lord was with her. God directed her and gave her the wherewithal to proceed in spite of all the unanswered questions that her physical condition produced. Ever so slowly, but also ever so consistently, God led her to the living waters that brought new life to her body, her faith, and her relationship with God and with God's children. Praise be to God.

In her journey, in the wilderness of life on this planet earth, Jackie walked where no one would seek to travel. In her travels she found a truth that should be endeared to all of us. In addition to having her health restored, she found that God was always with her. And added to that, she attained an enhanced capacity to perceive others and herself, as God would have us see.

Thanks, Jacquelyn, for your shared experience. Your steady determination, and your trust and faith in God is an inspiration for all of us in our own journeys.

Roger and Irene Schwedt

I have known Roger and Irene for just a few years. We became friends by way of friends! Once we became acquainted, we soon included them in our "list" of dear friends.

I suspect that one reason we continue to enjoy their company is that they are truly "down to earth" people. Their honesty, trustworthiness, kindness, friendship and love make them a joy to be around. Roger is now a retired farmer (if farmers ever retire) and Irene is a retired schoolteacher. She has also authored a children's book that is delightful.

Most of my good friends have read my first book, either because they were "shamed" into it or otherwise! When these two read it and heard that I was writing another, they agreed to submit some of their experiences for me to consider using. Now just to set the record straight, NO, I did not include their experiences because I felt compelled to because of our friendship! Roger and Irene are members of the First United Methodist Church in Warsaw, New York and their love of the Lord is too real for me to do anything but include their inspiring and astounding experiences.

Here now are their words, penned by Irene.

> I have given lots of thought to the incidents in my life that testify to my "walk with God," to use your words, Clyde. It was hard to choose just one, so I have written about a few. They all seem to tie in with my first profound experience that made me fully aware that God's Presence was involved in directing my life.
>
> In some ways my "walk with God" began when I was born to immigrant parents in 1932. It was in the depths of the Great Depression and we were living in Buffalo, New York. There were no possibilities of employment in that large city. For that reason, my parents moved with my brother and me to a small dairy farm in central New York,

near Utica. In that rural area we had no electricity. This meant that all household tasks and farm work had to be done by hand. Mother scrubbed clothes on a washboard. Cows were milked by hand. It was a hard life, but with God's help we survived on that farm for eight years.

My little sister was born in 1938. She became very ill with pneumonia while she was still an infant. My mother and dad had previously lost two babies due to pneumonia. It was not surprising that my mother cried bitterly with fear when this dear child also became ill with the same disease. This was prior to the antibiotics of today. To care for my sister, Dr. MacNaughton came every day for a week to change the mustard plasters he put on the baby's chest.

I did not realize it then, but I know now that God's hand was working through our doctor. Yes, my sister survived; my mother's tears of fear changed to tears of joy!

In 1941 our family moved back to Buffalo, just as our country became involved in World War II. After working in defense plants for two years, we moved again to a farm near Warsaw, New York. Those war years required many sacrifices, but again we survived, sharing a special bond with others who were a part of that courageous generation.

I was fifteen years old when I had a life-changing experience. It was on Easter morning when I was at our Roman Catholic Church service of worship. As I sat in a pew near a beautiful stained glass window, I began to feel the warmth of the sun's rays streaming onto my left shoulder, neck and head. I noticed that the sun's ray continued on to dance and glow on the statue of Mary holding baby Jesus.

As the warmth continued to penetrate my body, and as I beheld the beautiful vision, I became aware of a special Presence among us. It was the Spirit of God calling to me. I felt as if my soul was reborn. I was incredibly calm and so happy to have been claimed by God. IT WAS A LIFE-CHANGING EXPERIENCE FOR ME.

Since that Easter morning experience I have diligently tried to be sure that all of my decisions pass a test. The test is this: "Whatever I do must comply with God's teaching first, and then let the chips fall where they may." I know I have failed at times, but that still is my philosophy and goal—God first—Me second.

In my lifetime I have had many serious decisions to make. Like most people, some of these decisions were made, realizing that they would make an immense difference in my life. Not the least of these was the challenging decision to convert from the Roman Catholic Church to the Protestant side of the Church.

It probably never would have come up, had it not been that my husband had no desire to become a Roman Catholic. For me, unity in the family is very important and the expression of our faith should draw us together, not pull us apart. It was only after much soul-searching, and as I seriously tried to "put God first," that I came to the conclusion that I did. I know God loves us all, regardless of what denomination we may be involved in, and I also knew I could never lose God.

I have never regretted making that decision. I am sure I have been happy with that important decision in my life, because of **my effort to be true to my decision when I had my soul's rebirth experience. As I sincerely sought to put God first,** God was able to guide me in the way God knew would be the better for all involved."

Irene's decision to convert from Roman Catholicism to Protestantism proved to be so very interesting to me. I too, think ecumenically, as she expressed about herself. But what is so intriguing to me, is that for the same reasons, I encouraged my dear sister to convert from Protestantism to Roman Catholicism! Irene is right. When we honestly seek to put God first, there is no other answer that is any better.

Irene's decision after sensing God calling her is indeed that which all of us should purposely strive to do. Putting God's Will ahead of our own is NEVER a wrong choice.

One of the most painful events in my life was losing my mother to a massive heart attack. She was only fifty-four, and I was expecting our son at that time.

The death of a loved one is very hard for those left behind. When that death is totally unexpected it is doubly difficult. When my mother's life on earth ended, I was terribly shaken and had all the negative feelings of sadness, anger, numbness, disbelief and more. My dear husband eased my pain with understanding, comforting love, and patience. I realize that it was once again, God working through someone else to speak to me, guide and help me when I needed that help so intensely. Thanks to God, we all survived, baby and all.

Even as I had prayed for my mother's life, I still had to say, "God may Thy Will be done." Yes, at times it is very painful and extremely difficult to remember and accept the fact that God's Will is always the way to travel in this world.

Roger has himself had untold number of experiences wherein he has been keenly aware of God's Presence with him. In fact, on many occasions my husband has "dodged the bullet" as he went about his daily tasks. I say that, trusting you agree with me, that no one can "dodge a bullet" by his own doing!

One day he was sawing large limbs from a felled tree. It was a typical day and he was doing what he had done on numerous occasions before. All was going along so well, even the chain saw was running at its best, when totally unexpected and without any forewarning a huge limb broke. Somehow it gave aim and hit Roger's leg and shattered it.

Roger was alone in the woods, far from the house. He was in shock and his one leg was pathetically helpless. Yet, he somehow managed to get free from the outsized limb and maneuver himself over to the tractor. The tractor he had with him was a very large John Deere that is difficult enough to get into with two good legs.

Once he got himself onboard that tough strapping piece of machinery, he figured out a way to drive it home to get help. Roger is a physically strong man who is also a quiet kind of person. Of this horrific experience he simply says, "Somebody up there was looking out for me!"

Having taken time to think about all these experiences, with the obvious presence of God with us, reminds me of the poem, "Footsteps" where God is ever present to carry us when we need to be lifted above the terrain upon which we find ourselves needing to walk.

These are just a few experiences or incidents that have happened in our lives. May God continue to bless us all everyday, with God's care and love. Amen.

When I read over Irene and Roger's sharing I remembered the words of an old hymn. It seems especially significant as I pondered the impact that Irene's rebirth experience has had upon her decision-making and life.

"I have decided to follow Jesus, {repeated 3 times]
(refrain after each verse) No turning back, no turning back.
The world behind me, the cross before me, [3 times]
Though none go with me, I still will follow [3 times]
Will you decide now, to follow Jesus? [3 times]

Thanks, Irene and Roger, for your sharing and may you continue to have blessings to share, as you journey down the roads of life.

Nancy Gebauer

I have known Nancy for many years. It may be forty years, but regardless she has always been the same pleasant, kind, helpful, ambitious and compassionate person. She is a member of the church where I was pastor and continue to belong. Nancy served on our Board of Elders and has been our Financial Secretary among other positions in the church.

She is retired from her work with the U.S. Postal Service and keeps busy with five children in their combined family. When Audrey and I had our house built, Nancy was vice-president of the corporation that did the construction. Her husband, Paul, was our builder and we are still pleased with his work after some 30 years!

Nancy began her shared experience with a quote from the Gospel of Luke 12:6 "What is the price of five sparrows? A couple of pennies? Not much more than that. Yet, God does not forget a single one of them." She put a title on her sharing experience: "Molly's Miracle." Nancy's experience is really a cause for us to pause and contemplate the expansive inclusiveness and wonder of God's love and involvement in all of life. It can be mind-boggling; it is astounding. Here is Nancy's sharing of an experience when it became very clear to her that God was somehow involved.

JUNE 8, 2000, will forever be etched in my memory. It was the night our Quaker Parrot, Molly, spent the night in the nearby cemetery all by herself.

We live in a very friendly neighborhood where we often vacation together, spend New Year's Eve together and are always there for each other. Molly is one year old.

She is so much a part of our family that if we go to sit with the neighbors on their porch, Molly goes along with us. She not only loves the change of scenery, but she relishes all the attention she predictably receives.

It was on a Thursday about 7:30 that our neighbors, Mary Jane and Pete, returned home from an evening out. It was not unusual that Mary Jane then came to get us to sit on their porch. It was a nice summer evening. But we had just taken a few steps toward their residence when a gust of wind burst upon us, taking Molly with it! She made a quick landing on the street and then she was immediately engulfed in the swirling wind that took her high in the air above the cemetery that is across the street.

The cemetery is a beautiful old cemetery about the size of a village block. Within and around it there are many big old trees that give their embrace to the burial ground. The streets that border the cemetery are interestingly named "Lovers' Lane" (on the south) and "East Park Road" on the east. That whole area is a great place to walk with children, not only because of nature's beauty, but also the lack of traffic.

As Molly flew out of sight I followed after her yelling with all the strength and capacity within me, "Oh Molly, Oh Molly!" Neighbors came running from all directions, knowing that something was wrong. One boy on his bike said he thought that he had seen Molly flying over Park Road East. I kept calling and soon Pete and Mary Jane saw her fly from one tree to a big maple that was very high up and at the edge of a sheer-drop bank that ended on Lovers' Lane some twenty feet below.

By this time a crowd had gathered. I was concerned that such a group of people might scare Molly even more, so gently suggested that some of them go back home. Molly loves peanut butter cookies, so I sent the boy on his bike to our house to get some cookies. At that same time, Paul, my husband and Molly's "Dad," arrived on the scene. Paul spotted Molly in a tree, which was a phenomenal fete because she was the same color as the leaves and blended in extraordinarily well.

Molly was eager to talk to us but she wasn't about to venture out from her safe perch in that sturdy well anchored tree. I sent Mary Jane down on Lover's Lane in case Molly happened to fly across the road instead of going back into the trees in the cemetery. I did that so we would at least have that information, if she indeed took that course.

All this time, it was getting darker and darker. In an act of desperation I called Linda, Molly's breeder, to see if she had any ideas on how we might capture her. Mostly all I succeeded in doing was upsetting Linda. She said she would come and bring another Quaker Parrot to call to Molly, but by the time she could get here it would be too dark. Linda also offered to have her husband get a bucket truck from where he works, but we decided that Molly was up higher in the tree than the bucket truck would extend. Her final suggestion was to take Molly's cage over to the cemetery where the bird could see it. We did that. We also waved peanut butter cookies in the air. Nothing worked.

Darkness arrived and Molly apparently decided to bed down for the night. At least we assumed that because she was quiet and we could not see her anymore. Many prayers in addition to our own were offered for Molly that night.

Needless to say there was little sleep for us that night. Wanting to be there at daybreak, Paul and I went over to the cemetery at 4:45 the next morning. We took our chairs, binoculars, Molly's favorite bell and her food. To my pleasant surprise, at 5 o'clock, Mary Jane, who is not an early riser by choice, arrived to help us. She is a neat friend!

As the sun rose on that otherwise pleasant morning, we called and called to Molly but heard no answer. The wind was blowing and we could no longer see her, nor the very place where she was the night before. We continued to call and ring her bell, but if heard she did not know for whom the bell tolled!

At 5:30 that morning I called my daughter Marge and asked for her help. Marge "baby-sits" Molly when we're away and is very familiar with her. The wind continued and we were starting to feel this situation was not going to have a happy ending. In an effort to beat the odds, Mary Jane and I decided to walk in a big circle around the fields, calling to Molly and watching for any movement. This walk took about thirty minutes and ended up on the other side of Lover's Lane. Feeling rather gloomy and dismal we began walking down that street toward home. All dismay evaporated from us as Marge came driving towards us yelling, "We got her! We got her!"

After Mary Jane and I had left to tour the fields, Paul started looking in other trees. Marge stayed right where we had left Molly the night before. Although she had no idea where Molly was, Marge started talking to her as though she was right beside her. Immediately Molly answered.

At that, Marge yelled to Paul but that must have frightened the already bewildered bird because she took off, flying to another tree. Paul decided to go stand among the gravestones in a spot where there weren't any trees in order to have a better view. At the same time Molly took off higher than ever, heading towards Park Road East.

Paul yelled, "Molly, Molly" over and over again until all of a sudden Molly turned and did a gigantic circle of the cemetery. She then landed about fifteen feet from Paul. By 6:30 a.m. Molly was safe at home, in her cage, under her self made blanket where she stayed most of the day.

Now, if you are wondering why we would take a bird outside and risk her flying away, you have every right to do so. We had clipped her wings thinking she could not fly, but obviously we did not do it correctly. A trip to Linda corrected that.

An interesting side story to this is that Linda still owned Molly's mother and the night all this happened, Molly's mother passed away.

Wow. I have been wondering if somehow Molly's mother was aware of her child's fearful experience—or whether somehow Molly knew of her mother's condition. I suspect the former since the sudden-burst of wind initially caused

Molly's initial flight that must have been a frightful experience for her.

Do we dare consider God's role in all of this? I go along with the quote from Luke that Nancy used at the beginning of her sharing with us. "What is the price of five sparrows? A couple of pennies? Not much more than that. Yet, God does not forget a single one of them."

In like thought, Jesus used the example of how all-inclusive God's love was for the birds of the air and why we therefore should not worry. "Look at the birds of the air, they neither sow nor reap, nor gather into barns, and yet your heavenly Father feeds them. Are you not of more value than they?" (Matthew 6:26) All that is to say that God does care for all Creatures in Creation. Just how God goes about expressing that care and love is open to speculation!

I have had the pleasure of being around Molly on a number of occasions. It is interesting to me how she made that big circle and then landed close to Paul. When Audrey and I were at Nancy and Paul's home for dinner one evening, as we sat around the table, Molly was quiet and content. That is until Paul would move out of her range of sight! When he did that Molly would begin putting up a fuss and calling for him. She obviously felt comforted by his mere presence and she (at least in her mind, regardless of what Paul may verbalize) felt a close kinship with him. That close relationship carried itself over into the hour of Molly's frightful experience and ultimate return.

That too, is a lesson to be remembered in all this. The neighbor's demonstration of concern and love was precious.

Yes, the concern and love of Molly's previous owner was also precious. And the love of God seen in all this is precious. Yet, more precious than what may or may not have been envisioned in Molly's astounding story is God's Love for you and for all people, including the likes of me. Yes, God's Love is more precious than envisioned anywhere—-save in the life, death and resurrection of God's Son, our Lord, Jesus the Christ. Praise God, be thankful and be happy, for God's Love is real and it is endless.

Thanks, Nancy, for sharing this most unusual experience. It indeed makes us think, discuss, and wonder about the omnipresent, omnipotent, and loving Creator of all there is, or ever shall be.

David Reding

I first became acquainted with David when he was a student at Letchworth Central School. It is the public school system that includes the area around where I have lived for some forty-three years. David was a star athlete, good student and he was a well-liked young man by his peers and all who knew him. His family and relatives loved him.

Nevertheless, one evening something unbelievable happened to David. In a state of utter confusion, in a time when what was reality slipped from his consciousness, in a moment that changed his life forever, he shot and killed a friend. His world collapsed around him. His family, like his fellow students, teachers, and staff, were devastated. The community at large, who knew and loved him and his whole family, were stalemated in disbelief.

David is currently an inmate at the Wyoming Correctional Facility in Attica, New York. He is very much involved in the chaplains' program; he is active in their sports program where teams are made up and play against each other (similar to the outside world). David is also working on his education and last but perhaps not least, he is learning to repair antique clocks. It is difficult to move very fast in that effort because I cannot take tools nor old clocks in to use for demonstration nor upon which he could work.

When David read my first book we were able to discuss it together. When I told him I was going to write another book using the experiences of people who had read my book and then shared their experiences with me, he began writing. Dave is such a sharp young man; such a caring and openly honest person. I am pleased that he wanted to share the astounding miracle he experienced. David put a title on his shared experience, "God Heals and is Real!" Here now are his words, sharing an experience when he knew God was with him.

> "On October 25, 1992, I woke up at eight o'clock in the morning feeling short of breath. My heart was racing and I could not seem to breathe. A few hours later I felt cold, and damp and a mixture of unsettling feelings. I could not eat anything. I remember praying, "God, I know I have not been doing my best as a Christian, but please heal me."
>
> Being in prison, I had to go see the nurse on an emergency. Saturday I visited the nurse twice, however the nurse could not find anything wrong. On Sunday my

condition was worse. I visited the nurse two more times.

Finally, on my third visit that day, they rushed me to the Albany Medical Center. Twenty-four hours later, with no diagnosis to my problem, I was placed in the Intensive Care Unit. I clearly remember my last words prior to my slipping into a coma, I said, "God, I need you."

What I am sharing next is bits and pieces of what my family told me several days later after I came out of the coma. They told me that the doctors knew that I had some kind of rare pneumonia. The scary thing was hearing them say that they did not know how to treat it!

They went on to say something even more horrifying to my family. They alleged that they had only seen this kind of disease once before. In that instance, the individual did not survive. "But," my mother said, "I know a way, God and Prayer!" That was in fact the only option left.

My mother told me that the chaplain from the prison came to visit me about some twenty-four hours after I went into the coma. She shared with me that the chaplain prayed over me. I do remember the incident. I remember opening my eyes and seeing the chaplain laying his hands over me. That is all I can recall and it is not at all surprising because I was told that I fell right back into the coma. A few days later I remembered that scene very vividly.

Although it was several days after the Chaplain's visit when I came out of the coma, I still believe it was at that moment that God intervened (Psalm 40:1-5, 12-14). **Yes, at that precise moment when I briefly came out of the coma and saw the chaplain laying his hands over me, God told all sickness to depart. In essence, God was saying, "He is my child."**

As I look back, I was dead to the doctors. All that my family and friends had was hope. In that experience I "see" that a loving and healing God pulled me up and God worked in my life. Why for me? The answer to that question is at least in part answered in Psalm 91. God healed me because God was not done with me. This has been a great help to me as I ponder my future. God loves me, and I love God.

At that point, God not only healed me, but God opened my eyes to His call on my life. I am called to truly work for God's glory by being God's servant as I live day by day.

There is no question in my mind. I can honestly say that prayer works. I can honestly say, if it were not for God, I would not be writing these words today. God is real! And when God has a call for you to do, whether now or ten years from now remember this: There is no power, or principality, nor depth, nor height that can stop you. God will go the distance for you.

I NOW MUST GO THE DISTANCE FOR GOD.

God is so wonderful. God does astounding things to help us know his love and compassion for us. Dave knows himself as a recipient of God's embrace. He is resolved in his heart and mind to respond as he has been called.

I hope you who are reading this will take time to read the entire scripture that Dave has found so meaningful for him. Psalm 40 begins:

I waited patiently for the Lord,
He inclined to me and heard my cry.
He drew me up from the desolate pit'
Out of the miry bog,
And set my feet upon a rock,
Making my steps secure.
He put a new song in my mouth,
A song of praise to our God….

Those words do indeed speak volumes to us all; I am sure they are packed with intense meaning for my friend, Dave. He also refers to Psalm 91 and it begins: "You who live in the shelter of the Most High…."

The Psalm concludes with these beautiful words:

Those who love me, I will deliver;
I will protect those who know my name.
When they call upon me, I will answer them;
I will be with them in trouble,
I will rescue them and honor them,
With long life I will satisfy them,
And show them my salvation.

Thanks for sharing your experience with us, David. God is without question a God of Love. God sent Jesus, His Son, to let us know just how real that truth actually is and what it means to us and to all humankind.

Rocco Bellucci

I first heard about Rocco from a neighbor who told me that anytime they had a clock problem they would just call the "Clock Man" from Silver Springs. After hearing him referred to that way a few times, I began asking who he was and where did he live? I was told that "everyone" knows Rocky; he's a barber and he repairs antique clocks.

Eventually, not being able to withstand knowing this person myself, I went over to get a haircut. You would not believe the clocks he had in his barbershop; all four walls have shelves and every shelf has clocks; beautiful clocks. Some are antiques one might expect to find in a high-class Antique Shop and others are beautiful novelty clocks that are hard to find. Still others are rare antique clocks that are not very easy to find.

It was not apparent to me on that first visit, but I soon found out that Rocco also builds clocks. Some of the very best looking and best-built wall clocks and grandfather clocks that I have ever seen, are housed in his shop and/or home. He built many of those clocks himself.

In Rocco's shop he used to have homemade candy for sale and if my memory serves me right, he also sold some homemade cookies. His wife, Pauline, whom he lovingly called "Polly," is now deceased. She made those delicious baked goods and the mouth-watering candy.

From the first time I met his wife, Pauline, I loved her. The same was true when my wife first met her. Pauline was one of those people whom you quickly feel like you have known for a long time. When polio was so prevalent and so difficult to treat, Pauline had that disease. Remember hearing about "the iron lung" in which people were put in order to help them deal with polio? Well, Pauline experienced all that and she ended up cured but unable to walk.

Rocco totally redid the kitchen, making it wheel chair friendly. Together they raised their two beautiful children, Carol and Larry. Both children have told me that she was an excellent mother and their father was such a great dad. All who knew Rocco and Pauline also knew of their special relationship. Their marriage and their lives were an active demonstration of a solid partnership of love. People also marveled at how magnificently and gracefully they dealt with her physical handicap. If you did not see the wheel chair, you would never know she needed one.

If you have not guessed it, Audrey and I quickly became close friends with these two remarkable and superbly interesting people. When people heard that these two were celebrating their 50th Wedding Anniversary, the only surprise was that they were old enough!

Following Pauline's death, Rocco missed her companionship so very much. They loved and cared for each other without reservation. We can appreciate his feelings of loss. For whoever we may be, when a loved one goes on to the Eternal Kingdom of God, we sorely miss them.

In addition to the above, in order to more deeply appreciate Rocco's shared experience, I want to say that Audrey and I and their loved ones and friends were deeply saddened when Rock and Pauline's son, Larry, left this world after a short but brave effort to defeat cancer. It was after his mother's death that Larry was diagnosed with the malignant disease. In a short few months he left this world. Rocco and his daughter, Carol, had to deal with the pain and loss of both.

But, with all that being said, Rocco is sharing with us because he knows that God is so good. God never leaves us alone in times of joy or sorrow. In times of death, God endeavors to remind us of a life that has no end; of a relationship in love that is eternal. Rocco experienced some of these outright astounding happenings. He quickly understood that God was seeking to help him deal with his pain and anguish over the death of one dear to his heart.

Rocco Belucci shared and discussed the following events with me. He and Pauline had both read my first book and he was so very accepting of my request to include these experiences of his, which are truly astounding. He verbalized these experiences with me and I shall try to use his words as much as possible. However, let me now share his experiences using a collection of our words.

Rocco told me that following his wife, Pauline's death he was awe-struck when he later looked at her watch. Both Pauline and he had a lifelong interest in timepieces. God used that same avenue, to speak to him with an almost unbelievable fete.

Rocky said that when he looked at his wife's watch, the very watch she regularly wore, and wore the day she died, had **the date of the month, the 17th, and it had the precise hour and minute that she expired! When she died, her watch "died" also.** What an absolutely astounding fete.

Why did this happen? Rocky believes, and I concur with him, that it was just one way that God used to make God's presence known to him! It is as if God was saying, "Tell me how it happened that that dependable watch stopped precisely and accurately the very moment your dear wife left the world? You repair clocks; you build clocks, you collect clocks and watches—Tell me, How could that happen?"

As I mentioned, prior to sharing Rocco's experience, it was only a few months after his wife died that their son, Larry, also died. That was a horrific blow and it was very hard to accept. Larry had just retired and now, instead of seeing him more often, he would not see him at all.

Rocco and I shared all this along with our faith. We are both Christian men and our sharing surely helped me as I hope it did him. But what really helped Rocco, was the way God once again did an astounding, seemingly impossible fete.

It was eight months after Larry had died. Rock was doing extremely well, although he still missed (and always will miss) Pauline and Larry. One day he called me to say I would never guess what happened. He was right! He went on to say that he had been "hit over the head" once again! At first I thought a clock fell or tipped over and clobbered him.

He went on to share what happened. It proved to be more consequential than any mere bump on the head could be. **He reminded me that it was just eight months after Larry's death, when he was given a reminder of God's Love and Presence**. He has a calendar clock in his barbershop that he kept running regularly. Well, it stopped running! However, it did not just stop, it stopped at exactly 2:23 on the 10th day of the month.

I was wondering what was so astounding about a clock stopping as that one had. That is, I wondered until he went on to tell the rest of the story. He told me that Larry took his last breath eight months ago. It was on the 10th day and the time was exactly 2:23.

I have seen the clock a number of times before and since that event. It is still on the 10th day at 2:23. Rocco tells me he has never started the clock since, and doesn't think he ever will. It hangs there in the barbershop, a constant reminder of how God seeks to give us strength and courage to carry on. And it is also a reminder of the reality of God's never ending Love and Promise of life Eternal.

Rocco's experiences have been so helpful and meaningful. But guess what? If he was not "tuned in" to God's Presence he very well could have missed it all! **God is still speaking, our universal problem is that too often we are not listening nor seeking to see.**

Thanks, Rocco for sharing these awesome happenings and what they really mean to you and now to us. Thinking about these experiences and the immense power they have for us, this hymn came to mind:

Open my eyes that I may see,
Glimpses of truth Thou hast for me;
Place in my hands the wonderful key,
That shall unclasp and set me free.
"Open my ears, that I may hear
Voices of truth, Thou sendest clear
And while the wave-notes fall on my ear,

Everything false will disappear.
(The refrain after each verse:)
Silently now I wait for Thee,
Ready my God, Thy will to see;
Open my eyes [ears] illumine me,
Spirit, Divine!

Lorraine Hendrickson

Lorraine is my baby sister! I don't think of her in that way, but reality is what it is. She is the youngest of my seven siblings. She married a high school friend and before long they moved all the way from upstate New York to Texas—of all places. I thought they would move back soon, missing the cold winters and shoveling snow. But they seem very content to stay right there.

They live in Colleyville, which is close to the Dallas-Fort Worth International Airport. The proximity to the airport has been important, being that her husband, Jack was a commercial airline pilot.

Jack is no "fly by night," even though he did at one time fly cargo during nighttime hours. He is a great guy, raised in a strict Roman Catholic family and he is a member of the Roman Catholic Church. I am not sure of my actual influence in the matter, but I did encourage my sister to join with Jack so that they could worship together as a family.

My sister's shared experience is new to me. As I read it over, I thought to myself, "My what younger sisters don't get themselves into? Here are the words of my dearly loved sister, Lorraine.

God walks with us, and there are times when I seem not to take full advantage of that knowledge. There was an experience that I had when I was a young girl dating the young man who is now my husband.

He had returned home from college over the Thanksgiving holiday. His parents owned an airplane. They lived near to Rochester, New York. One afternoon it was decided that the four of us would fly to New York City for a cup of coffee. You have to understand that in order to become a commercial airline pilot, you have to have many hours of flying time. This was a dream and goal for that young college boy who became my husband.

So off we went on our trip, having every intention of being back home by sundown. Well, things did not turn out as such! Jack and I were in the back seat; his college friend and Jack's father were up front. After flying for quite some time, it did not seem to me that the engine was sounding the same as it had been!

I often had flown with Jack on dates. We would fly to nearby airports where we would stop for a hamburger and coke. The engine sounded different to me now. It was getting late and I heard conversations taking place and my mind was running wild! We landed at LaGuardia and they had a mechanic look at the plane and fix it. I recall falling asleep on the wooden benches inside the terminal while waiting and waiting.

It was hours later when I was told the plane was all fixed and we were cleared to take off. We were, at last, on our way back to his home that was in the Rochester area.

It was nighttime and I went back to sleep. Shortly thereafter the guys talking awakened me. When I opened my blurry eyes, I saw the guys upfront using a flashlight to look at the instrument panel. I then heard the unbelievable. One of them said, "We are almost out of fuel." And then I came to the realization that on top of that, they did not even know where we were!

There were mountains on each side of us, so that made it easy to decide which direction to keep flying. Eventually, they spotted dim lights ahead, and after what seemed like an extremely long time, they saw a cow pasture and without circling it for safety, made a landing.

A kind farmer came out to see us and opened up his home to us, fed us and invited us to spend the night in their home. The next day, Jack's mother had to drive to Pennsylvania to pick us up. That was due to weight restriction that made it impossible for us to take off from that small field with all four of us on board.

Do you think I continued to like flying after that trip to the Big Apple to get a cup of coffee? You are correct if you think I did not. After that experience**, I had an intense fear of flying that would last for years**. I would agonize over any trip in which I had to fly.

It was several years later, when my mother, who also happens to be this author's mother, helped me overcome this nightmarish horror that had been a heavy burden for me. She was my inspiration, her faith example and the sharing conversations I had with her became the instrument God used to help me. I have now overcome this fear of flying that had haunted me so miserably and for so many years.

Prior to this fear eradicating experience, I had so many opportunities to travel with my airline pilot husband. And in every case, as we planned a trip I was relentlessly tormented. Now, as I think of that flying weekend when we flew to New York City for a cup of coffee—**I marvel how the Almighty kept our sputtering engine going until we reached LaGuardia Airport. And then, who would not take comfort in God's guidance that same night. When we were running out of gas, not knowing where we were in the darkness that night, we were somehow assisted to that small but sufficient cow pasture, where we were able to land without a hitch.**

When my mother so nonchalantly and perhaps unknowingly helped me, she was at that time an elderly widow. She would fly to Texas on commercial airlines by herself, in order to spend some time with us during the cold winter in New York. **On one of those stays with us she casually commented that she just places herself in the Lord's hands, and let's His Will Be Done.**

WOW——-What a change that has made in my life. I prayed that I could go forth with such peace and serenity; to realize that God was always with me; to appreciate that my flying opportunities are truly a gift from God, a blessing. Today I am comfortable flying and I truly enjoy the travel and the words as Mother said them to me, **"Thy Will Be Done."**

Mother is now deceased, but I think that she would be astounded to hear that her casual words had such an impact and lasting effect on Lorraine. I have seen this transition in Lorraine's life. Although I had never heard how it happened or why, I knew that her thoughts about flying surely had a most impressive change. She now flies all over the place! Let's think about it for a moment. The words we use in everyday conversations are indubitably important. Without ever realizing it, our expressed thoughts can become "messages from on high," or they can be very much the opposite.

Lorraine's sharing is a beautiful example of the influence a word or two spoken can have on others. May this sharing serve to reinforce our understanding of our call to the discipleship of Jesus Christ our Lord. It is, undeniably, all encompassing, including our words, our examples and our lives as we live them each day.

Thanks, Lorraine, for sharing this experience. Your light continues to shine for the glory of God. And I am confident that to all who read your words, you are an inspiration. These treasured words of Jesus come to my mind as I ponder Mother's words to you and her life in the faith:

Jesus said, "All authority in heaven and on earth has been given to me. Go therefore and make disciples of all nations, baptizing them in the name of the Father and of the Son and of the Holy Spirit, and teaching them to obey everything that I have commanded you. **AND REMEMBER, I AM WITH YOU ALWAYS, [on land, in the air or on the sea ALWAYS] TO THE END OF THE AGE."**

Doris Daycock

In an attempt to introduce Doris to you, I must say that I have known more "of" her than I have known her. She is a delightful person who happens to be the wife of an almost life-long friend. I guess it is because we are now retired that we have been able to spend some time with those with whom we grew up. This has enabled me to get to know Charles' wife, Doris, much better. She is strong of faith, a solidly compassionate person, who cares about and loves her family without reservation.

Doris has written about an absolutely astounding feat. As we contemplate her sharing it becomes abundantly clear that our Creator, Sustainer and Friend is very much involved in our everyday lives. She shares her experience with us.

Hoopins

Born in Korea, Kimmy, our granddaughter, came into our family on April 7, 1989, at the age of six months. She bonded with our son and daughter-in-law right away. Happily for us, she also bonded with her new grandparents, who lived next door on the family farm.

She was a healthy and happy little girl who was always smiling. Then one day when she was only 22 months old she became very ill. At the time, we were on a family vacation with the whole family. Kimmy's parents took her to a nearby emergency room. The medical staff ran some tests on her without finding anything wrong. Accordingly, they said she probably had a virus.

When we got back home, her parents took her to their own pediatrician. He knew something was not quite right. He also did a few tests and concluded that she needed one additional test. He sent her to have an ultrasound on August 6, 1990.

After the ultrasound test we took the x-rays to her doctor's office. He took us right in and told us Kimmy had a softball size tumor on her right kidney. He then sent us right over to a surgeon's office. From there, we were sent directly to the hospital to have the cancerous kidney removed.

We always felt that God had placed this dear child in our family for a reason. We now realized that if she had remained in Korea, she probably would have died. Many prayers went out for her and we put our faith in the Lord, as we started a long battle with Kimmy's cancer.

The first chemotherapy treatment that they gave her actually blew out a vein around her ankle. The second chemo treatment blew out a vein on her wrist! The medical staff was concerned that she not lose any more veins. They concurred that they needed a different approach. Due to this dilemma, a second operation was scheduled to put two ports into her chest through which blood and chemo could be given.

It was at this time in Kimmy's life that "Hoopins" became an active partner for her. Right after the operation she started talking and playing with her new friend, "Hoopins." This new friend of hers was a mystery, if not a concern. Eventually, I looked at

my son and daughter-in-law and said, "Hoopins is Kimmy's guardian angel!"

In the following months there were many trips in and out of the hospital for Kimmy. And always "Hoopins" came right along with her. Then one day when my daughter-in-law and I were sitting in our living room, we watched as Kimmy was playing in there with "Hoopins."

The time seemed right so I nonchalantly asked Kimmy, "Is Hoopins a girl or a boy?"

"Gramma," she said, "She's girl!"

I then asked her how old she was and what she looked like.

"Gramma,' she said, "She is a little bit taller than me and she looks just like me."

I then asked how 'Hoopins' came to be with her. She looked at me as if I should know, and she said, "A tall man brought her to me and then he grew real tall and went up into the sky."

As we sat there my daughter-in-law and I looked at each other with tears in our eyes; we knew who had brought "Hoopins" to Kimmy!

As years went by, now and then we would hear Kimmy talking to "Hoopin'" as she played and walked around the house. When she was older I asked Kimmy if "Hoopins" was still with her. She looked so peacefully at me and said with a big smile on her face, **"No Gramma, but she told me if I ever needed her, she will be here with me."**

Kimmy is going to be seventeen years old on October 1 and she is doing very well. She still has to visit the hospital once a year for tests. This check up is to see if there were any side effects to the chemo they used to keep her alive. They keep close check on her heart, because the medications did have an adverse effect on her heart muscle.

"We found out later that our dear Kimmy was not expected to live-out the first year, after her malignant tumor was removed. That just makes all the more astounding what God has done. **We know in our hearts that the Lord gave us a miracle and sent "Hoopins" to Kimmy to comfort and give her assurance and companionship as she went through the difficult time of Chemotherapy, pain and healing.**

The astounding feats of God are indeed astounding! Doris has shared with us an on-going journey in which the miraculous presence of God was so evident. God travels the roads of life to help us on our journey here. In an effort to surmise the reason for "Hoopins" to be so real for that dear little child, it occurred to me that she needed something visible to "hang on to." We have the same "Hoopins"—if you will—in the presence of the Holy Spirit.

Remember after his resurrection. Jesus said to Thomas who had doubted the astounding truth of the resurrection, "Have you believed because you have seen me? Blessed are those who have not seen and yet have come to believe" (John 20:29). Little Kimmy was not like doubting Thomas; she had no knowledge or experience to grasp or hang on to. God gave her an astounding gift, to assure her that she was not alone nor without a friend who loved her dearly.

I hope this chapter will serve to remind all who read it or share it with others, that God's astounding feats are celebrated by people every day. Maintaining a close-personal relationship with God, and keeping our eyes open for God's presence with us, will bring into focus the many astounding things that God has planned for you and for others. As our sharing-contributors realize, it is indeed incredible what we see when we keep our eyes of Faith wide open.

CHAPTER FIVE

Wondrous Miracles Experienced

This chapter will share some specific experiences of people who have been blessed by miracles. Miracles are happening all around us, all the time. For me, many miracles are a way of God's presence being assured; somewhat like a "tap on the shoulder" by our Creator. Such wondrous miracles give us self-confidence in our understanding of God's presence and love. And at the same time, miracles are very often a stimulant to our discipleship.

Our most common reason for not being more aware of God's incredible miracles in our midst is that while we have eyes to view them, we do not attentively look. In juxtaposition, while we have ears to hear, we do not wisely, nor carefully, listen. In Matthew's Gospel account Jesus was at one point speaking to his disciples, telling them how blessed they were because they could understand what he was saying to them. As he spoke with them he said, "But blessed are your eyes because they see, and your ears because they hear"(Matthew 13:16f).

That blessing remains for all who experience; who see and/ or hear any of the wondrous miracles given by God. We will start our sharing in this chapter by one whom I love dearly. It is a life-embracing experience that was so powerful, it's effect on she who is sharing it has never diminished.

Cynthia E. Hadley, M.D.

I shall never forget the day Cynthia was born. She was our first child and the miracle of birth and life was full-bloom within me. Just a few minutes after her arrival, I sat in a small room with the doctor who had delivered her. It was long before we knew smoking was so damaging to one's health. It was quite normal at that time to have a doctor pull out cigarettes, and it was not unusual that he/she offered me one.

Sitting there in that cozy room, we lit the tobacco-filled cylinders. I took a couple good puffs and immediately began to cough. I coughed some more. At that, Dr. Trombetta said, "What's wrong? Between gasps for air, I was barely able to reply, "I don't smoke!"

Yeah, I guess the birth of that dear child sent me into some kind of unusual "orbit." I say that because an hour or so later when I went to work, I told my office friends that my daughter weighed twenty pounds and was seven inches long! I had her weight and length all mixed up, which is this father's way of saying, "When our first child was born, I was conspicuously excited."

Cindy grew and it soon became obvious that she had a love for horses. She began riding at about eight or nine years old. She rode in the county fair and in the state fair, doing very well and collecting many ostentatious ribbons.

She was always an excellent student and she had a keen interest in music, which found her taking piano lessons. She did well enough that subsequently at the age of twelve she played our church's pipe organ for a wedding on Christmas Eve. In high school she accompanied choruses and played for area churches when they needed a substitute organist. During Cindy's college years she earned considerable spending money by playing the organ for two different churches each Sunday.

For most of her "growing up" years we lived next door to Dr. and Mrs. J. Stanley Baker. They were great neighbors and became the dearest of friends to Audrey and me. They were both very active in our church and lived their faith "on their coat sleeves."

Dr. Baker was a general family practitioner and he had his office in his home. Cindy's bedroom windows looked out at the Bakers' home. She tells of being awakened in the dark of the night when their outside lights would come on. She would then see patients of all ages hurrying in for some emergency care. She could see into the waiting room (not the medical care rooms) and she continually marveled at how the doctor helped so many people, both night and day. I suspect that played an important part in her decision to become a doctor of family medicine.

Cindy is married to Stephen Hadley, who is a high school teacher in nearby Letchworth Central School. Here, he offers some classes with college credit, along with the regular-school classes. They have two girls: Allison recently graduated from the New York State College at Fredonia and writes for a small newspaper, and Kristen is in the ninth grade at the Geneseo Central High School. Now you know something about Dr. Cindy, who is doing this sharing. The following experience is of an affirming wondrous miracle.

Gifts

On July 1, 1985, I started the most intense and grueling "adventure" of my life. As a first-year resident in family practice, I was both excited and terrified that, for the first time, my orders as a physician would be accepted and followed—and have life or death consequences.

As luck would have it, my first monthly rotation was in cardiology. And my first night on call was in the Cardiology Intensive Care Unit. I felt fairly confident in the presence of my attending physician and senior resident during the daylight hours. We discussed cases, saw patients in the emergency room and reviewed standard orders and protocols. But then, suddenly, it was evening and everyone else felt very comfortable leaving me "in charge."

My superiors were only a phone call away, but I found myself praying desperately that I would have an uneventful night. As I found my way to the cafeteria, medical library, and call room, I kept calmly reminding myself that the Intensive Care Unit patients were all stable and any new cardiology emergencies would be first assessed by the emergency room physicians who would guide me through their care.

The call came abruptly at 2:00 a.m. I wasn't yet accustomed to these shocking wake-up calls, but I shot to attention when the ICU nurse beckoned me to come quickly—Mrs. S. had gone into cardiac arrest. (If adrenaline were sold in cans, caffeine would be out of business!) I remember running the short distance to the bedside of the patient and wondering what my heart rate was!

The next hour of my life was a fast-motion blur, yet I remember every detail to this hour. The nurses and respiratory therapist were efficient and my orders and directions were amazingly clear and accurate. Was that really me running that code? This was the moment when all that bookwork finally held some meaning. Mrs. S. was successfully resuscitated. I finished my charting and retreated once again to the call room. I must admit that the event finally hit me when I sat down alone—***whew!*** Three deep breaths—stop shaking—three more years….

I was lucky to get some sleep before 7:00 a.m. Of course, by this hour my attending and senior resident were well aware of the night's activities. We all went in together to see Mrs. S. Much to my surprise, she was awake and alert and able to tell us she was feeling quite well. I stayed to check her monitor readings after our exam. I had never actually met this woman face-to-face before. In fact, I had not seen her before the "code" earlier that morning, and she was completely unconscious the entire time I spent in her room.

But **something amazing happened that morning of my second day in training.** This dear woman whose life I had saved during the night looked at me with an expression of deep appreciation on her face. "Thank you," she said unfalteringly, "for what you did for me last night."

I'm sure my jaw must have hit the floor and bounced back up into place. No one had told her I was even present in her room. **As I gazed into her eyes, she accurately recounted my every move as we had brought her back to life a few hours earlier. She knew things that would have been impossible to know, if she had not been watching, as she explained, from above the scene.**

Well if I ever had needed a confirmation that this was my calling, this was it. The peaceful reassurance and inner conviction I obtained that day has been enough to sustain me through not only three years of residency, but in the many years of being actively involved in the medical profession.

Before reaching this point in my career, I had developed an interest and done intensive reading about near-death experiences. After this day, with it's wondrous miracle harmoniously embedded in my very being, I am no longer hesitant to ask appropriate patients about their experiences. This has helped me to come to terms with my own understanding of life and death—the miracles of healing I have witnessed, as well as the inexplicable suffering that my patients have sometimes endured. ***I know that God is always there—and though I may not always understand why, I accept that God knows all and is always with us and there to sustain us, even in the toughest situations.***

I feel blessed because I have been able to help others through God's guidance. Many other times in my life,

God has "whispered in my ear."* [* A quote from my wonderful nurse, Sue Gillett.]

Thank you, Dr. Hadley, for sharing with us. The wondrous miracle that took place in that patient's room, speaks to us ever so strongly. Without doubt, these kinds of experiences occur to give us support and a clearer understanding of life here and life eternal that is to come. They are indeed meant to give us inspiration and the assurance of God's Presence and never-ending Love.

When Dr. Hadley graduated from high school she won a number of awards, among them was a scholarship for writing about her goals for her life. Cindy included these words in the writing she did for this award. The words "fit her" very well as she goes about extending herself to help others. We should all try hard to pursue that sort of goal for our own lives.

I shall pass through this world but once,
Any good therefore that I can do
Or any kindness that I can show to any human being,
Let me do it now, let me not defer or neglect it,
For I shall not pass this way again."

(Written by Etienne de Grellet, also know as Stephen Grelier.)

God's Wondrous Miracles happen. As we see them, participate in them and/or hear about them—the God of Love, the Father of our Lord, Jesus Christ surely must intend for them to be instrumental in the building and strengthening of our faith.

Alvah Hart

I have known Alvah Hart for over forty years. She and her husband, Harold, owned and operated the local grocery store. They were active members of the church I served in Castile, New York.

Alvah served on the Board of Elders—the board that had primary responsibility for the spiritual and worship aspects of the church.

On a vacation trip, we visited the Harts who now live in Cookesville, Tennessee. Having read my first book and hearing about my intentions to write this one, Alvah verbalized this holy miraculous experience. As she spoke, my wife penned her words that we now use for her sharing.

> I went to see my doctor for a checkup and upon being examined he told me that I was in the process of having a heart attack! Talk about being shocked; I could not believe my ears, although, I had been feeling weaker than usual of late.
>
> My doctor asked me to be admitted to the hospital. Being in a state of shock, I readily agreed with her request. I was put in the Intensive Care Unit of the hospital. The heart surgeon, Dr. Fleet, wanted an angiogram. This, of course, meant that I had to sign all those papers that heart patients usually must do. I also had to sign papers to allow for heart surgery, just in case an emergency occurred and that operation was needed.
>
> I was on the stretcher in the downstairs hallway, just outside the operating room door. As I rested, waiting my turn in the operating room, **something breath-taking**

happened. As I intermittingly prayed for God's presence and contemplated my soon to take place surgery, a cloud appeared over me.

I felt my body lift up and float backwards. I rubbed my eyes, and as I did, the cloud went backwards. As that happened I felt a tingling throughout my whole body. At that point, an angel came out of the cloud that was over me. The angel was gold colored and had glittering wings. It also had a pair of smaller wings on the inside that came out like unfolding wings. I felt very much at peace and unafraid all through this experience. I asked the angel if she was healing me, and the angel just smiled peacefully and joyfully.

I was thereafter wheeled into the operating room where Dr. Fleet performed the angiogram. I was not at all surprised to hear him tell me that everything was fine. The camera they inserted showed no heart problems whatsoever.

Later, my husband, Harold, and our pastor told me that the doctor came out to see them. He explained what he did, and said that everything was fine. "I can not explain it," he said, "but she has no heart problems."

My pastor, doctor, nor husband had no awareness of what had happened to me in that hallway. I knew I had been healed. It was not until I shared the experience with them that they began to fully appreciate what had actually happened to me.

God is so great; in a time of immense need, God heard my voice and performed a Wondrous Miracle within me, which I shall never forget. Praise be to God!

What a joy it was to have Alvah share her experience with us. After many months, her emotions were yet so tender. It was very obvious that that experience will be forever a most holy moment in her life. We thank her for sharing her wondrous miracle with us. A hymn that she appreciates more than ever, although it has been a much-loved hymn for years is: "My Jesus, I Love Thee"

My Jesus, I love Thee, I know Thou art mine—
For Thee all the follies of sin I resign;
My gracious Redeemer, my Savior art Thou;
If ever I loved Thee, my Jesus 'tis now.
I love Thee because Thou hast first loved me
And purchased my pardon on Calvary's tree;
I love Thee for wearing the thorns on Thy brow;
If ever I loved Thee, my Jesus 'tis now.
I'll love Thee in life, I will love Thee in death,
And praise Thee as long as Thou lendest me breath;
And say with the death-dew lies cold on my brow;
If ever I loved Thee, my Jesus 'tis now.
In mansions of glory and endless delight,
I'll ever adore Thee, in heaven so bright;
I'll sing with the glittering crown on my brow,
If ever I loved Thee, my Jesus 'tis now.

Robert and Lillian Fidler

You will remember that in the Chapter Three I introduced Bob Fidler and his wife, Lillian (whom we know as "Lil"). They are a delightful couple with a dear family all of whom we love.

As if setting the stage for this shared experience, Bob wrote: "I am trying hard to seek the face of God and to see God in the hurly-burly of my life and in the way things are going in our church. I have been praying lately that God would reveal himself to me and increase my faith…."

Well, dear reader, you are about to read how God did just that very thing in a puzzling-miraculous way. This is indeed what happens when we endeavor to walk more closely with God, and speak sincerely with God in prayer after prayer.

> In just the lasts two weeks I had this experience. Lil and I had gone to Farmington to do some errands, and do our stint at the University of Maine at Farmington Fitness Center. On the way, I stopped at the Savings Bank to make a payment. There was money left over from the check, so I went to our other bank to deposit it in my checking account. I made the deposit and handed the receipt to Lil to put in the front of my checkbook.
>
> We then drove to the fitness center. I dropped Lil off at the door before parking the car. After our exercise, we drove to church where Lil was going to work on the Sunday bulletin, while I went to Wal-Mart. When I started to get out of the car, I noticed that my checkbook was not on the seat.
>
> In a panic I searched under and between the seats, but no checkbook! Back to the church I scurried to see if it had been accidentally scraped out onto the ground when Lil got out. No checkbook; back to the banks I hustled to see if I had somehow left it there. No checkbook. Back to the fitness center I dashed, to search the ground where I

had parked the car and to inquire at the receptionist's desk if a checkbook had been found. Absolutely no checkbook!

Upon returning home, Lil and I both thoroughly searched under and between the car seats. I searched the car at least three times, carefully feeling between the seats and using a flashlight to peer into every nook and cranny. I eventually gave up, concluding that it was thoroughly lost.

The next business day I went to the bank and put a "stop payment" on all the checks left in the lost checkbook. I then went to the fitness center to post a notice of the lost checkbook, asking any finder to return it. I also noted that the checks were unusable. I went home convinced that I would never see that checkbook again.

In our morning prayer together, Lil prayed that we would find our lost checkbook. I went about daily affairs convinced that it was a hopeless loss. That next Wednesday evening as I returned from Prayer Meeting **I had a sudden unexplainable thought come to my mind. The thought was "Look under the car seat."** Now that is foolish, I thought, that car has been methodically and meticulously searched many times.

Still, the thought was frustratingly insistent. By now, the thought was more specific, "Look under the car front passenger seat." Oh, all right, I consented, as I drove slowly in the driveway of our stately red brick home. I am going to feel foolish, I confessed, but I will do it. Exiting my van, I inaudibly and reluctantly walked over to the car, hoping no one would see me. I obediently opened the rear door behind the passenger seat. Reaching in I felt and looked under the driver's seat. Nothing.

Then as I turned my head, I saw something under the passenger seat. YES, there it was right where Lil and I had looked several times before. It was squarely in the center of the space as if being carefully placed! The envelope and the bank receipt were neatly tucked in the front of the checkbook just as I expected Lil would have placed them.

Something wondrously miraculous happened. That checkbook was not there, and then suddenly it was there. As startling and surprising, as it was to find it, **it was more amazing to me to experience the insistent thought assailing my mind even when I was convinced that such a search would be useless.**

Perhaps that is because several days before this, I had been praying for God, to do something to increase my faith. I left the options up to God just asking that He let me know that He was around, caring for me. Coincidence? I don't think so. This whole event in my life is too consistent with the way God has dealt with me in the past.

Yes, wondrous miracles happen. We know they are legitimate because we are involved in so many of them. How do they happen, only God knows the answer to that frequently asked question. Again, thanks for sharing with us, Bob and Lil.

George and Ellen Off

I am so grateful that one of those taking cardiac rehabilitation when I did was George Off. Both of us were there due to our heart problems and we both were seeking to make ourselves physically stronger. Unbeknown to me at the time was what he had been through and just how real and meaningful was his faith. We had competent, efficient and professional nurses and others who were in charge of the rehab center. They guided us through one period of exercise and on to another, and another, and another. Yet, these beautiful people knew our predicaments of health. In a very helpful way, they enabled us a minute here and there to chat with each other, and they would give us things to laugh about, all of which was good therapy.

Outside the Rehab Center there was a waiting room where one would often find spouses of those in therapy. Unbeknown to me, was that my wife, Audrey, was visiting with George's wife, Ellen. When we were at home, Audrey would occasionally speak of a wife whom she had been talking to during my rehab session. In turn, I had shared with her things about one of the guys going through the course with me.

I do not remember just how it happened, but somehow we finally realized "her wife" and "my guy" were husband and wife. We have been friends ever since. I didn't have to pay them to do it, but somehow I got them to read my book! When we discussed the book, I also shared with them about my writing this book. After telling them that I was using all sorts and conditions of people who shared their personal experiences with me, they quickly consented to be a part of this effort.

They begin their sharing with these words that they both confess to be very real in their lives. Then both George and Ellen will share an experience of their own.

God walks with us each and every day,
but some days we need him to be closer.

In 1984 I developed pain over the Maxillary Sinus area. The discomfort was additionally present with radiation down into my neck. The persistence of this pain and soreness found me seeking medical attention.

An alert doctor sent me for a stress test. Upon receiving the results, I was sent to have an angiogram. With a feeling of surprise and disbelief, two days later I had my first emergency bypass operation. What is rather routine surgery today proved in my case to be quite something else. Unfortunately, the surgeon did not graft far enough on one end of the bypass vessel, which then resulted in giving me angina.

With all this problem I was given blood. It too, is a rather routine procedure, but in my particular case the blood was contaminated. Accordingly, in addition to angina, I was infected with the type 'C' Hepatitis virus.

I began to think of Murphy's Law, "If anything can go wrong it will!" That is not really the best thought to have in one's mind when going into surgery. But I could not help from thinking about it as I was told that I had to have a second surgery in July 1996. Unbelievably, during surgery a vessel was attached to the right side of the heart, instead of the left side!

This surgical slip-up found me having yet another surgery. It was in September 1996 that the medical staff took me into surgery for a third time. It was in this surgery that the surgeon finally removed the wrongly placed graft. It was taken from the right side of the heart and put where it belonged on the left side.

During this mistake-repairing surgery, guess what? In the midst of it, the changing of the vessel caused my heart to beat irregularly.

As I have repeatedly thought about all the above experiences, I cannot help but thank God for His Presence that never leaves us alone. I know without a doubt that **without God's intervention I would not be alive in this world today!**

What a story. What a chain of events, any of which could have been lethal. His experience reminds me that no matter where we find ourselves, God is already there.

Ellen is a neat, compassionate, and exceptional registered nurse. Her knowledge was helpful as we shared physical changes due to my heart attacks. Like her husband, George, she is active in her church, which means a great deal to them (and me). Because they are Roman Catholics, it has been especially interesting discussing the likes and differences of our two Christian Churches.

Ellen now shares her experience that has a depth of meaning for her.

I was undergoing a routine physical examination when my doctor heard something that he did not like. As he was checking my aorta, he paused and checked it again and again. The doctor heard a bruit (abnormal sound) over the aorta. Due to the seriousness of the possibilities that may be causing the bruit, he recommended an ultrasound.

Upon setting up an appointment for me, he explained that he wanted to rule out an aortic aneurysm. With what medical knowledge I did have, I realized that this could be something rather serious.

I asked God and His mother, Mary, to intervene and to be at my side. When the day arrived for the ultrasound, I was concerned, but confident. The test came back, NEGATIVE! I have no doubt whatsoever that my medical doctor had heard the sound, but I also have no doubt that God heard my prayers and intervened.

I was reminded of the verses found in Psalm 27 as I read the shared examples of George and Ellen. The Psalm speaks of having a faith that remains strong in spite of the challenges that life may give us.

> "One thing I ask of the Lord, that will I seek after;
> To live in the house of the Lord all the days of my life,
> To behold the beauty of the Lord, and inquire in his temple.
> For he will hide me in his shelter in the day of trouble;
> He will conceal me under the cover of his tent;
> He will set me high on a rock. Now my head is lifted up
> Above my enemies all around me, and I will offer in his tent
> Sacrifices with shouts of joy, I will sing and make melody
> To the Lord" (Psalm 27:4-6).

It was this kind of enduring faith, grounded in the never-ending love of God that gave our dear friends the ability to trust God in spite of what did or might happen to them. It is the faith seen in God's Son, Jesus and promised to all who will be his disciple. Thanks, George and Ellen for your sharing and continued faith.

Mary Sternal

I became acquainted with Mary Sternal shortly after I arrived at the Road Runner Travel Resort in Fort Pierce, Florida. She and her husband, Bob, are friends of people who have been our friends for a long time. We were invited to group dinners as they were and our friendship became ever more real. Mary's husband is a talented handyman, who helped me repair some hurricane damage to our Florida Room, that is attached to our trailer. Bob was an Administrator in Public Service, prior to his retirement.

Mary and Bob journey here for the winter months. They otherwise reside in Saint Paul, Minnesota. They are involved in the church at both times of the year. They sing in church choirs and involve themselves in a variety of activities.

I am not sure how it came about, but Mary read my book and in sharing with her she agreed to write something for this new endeavor. She is a kind, pleasant and lovable person. Her sharing will inspire you.

> One time during my childhood when I was perhaps ten years old, I was sick in bed with pleurisy. I awoke one morning and attempted to get out of bed, only to fall back on my pillow in pain. I made a couple more efforts to move but each time the pain in my chest stopped me.

I quietly laid in bed, puzzled, frightened, and began to pray for help. Suddenly, I popped up like a jack-in-the-box. I hadn't been attempting to move but there I was, still in pain, but sitting up and able to get out of bed.

It was such a strange experience that I have not told anyone about it—until now.

It is truly amazing how something like that can effect us so very much. All these years, she has undoubtedly carried that wondrous miracle close to her heart. God is so wonderfully astounding. Gifts, like what Mary shared with us, cannot be tabulated as to their value, because they are priceless. Further, one cannot decipher how much influence they may have over an individual, because they actually affect everything—who we are, who we become, and whom we will ever be.

I say all that, because once a person has experienced the very presence of God in his/her life, the words of this hymn become extraordinarily meaningful and real:

Anywhere with Jesus I can safely go;
Anywhere He leads me in this world below;
Anywhere without Him dearest joy would fade;
Anywhere with Jesus I am not afraid.
"Anywhere with Jesus I am not alone;
Other friends may fail me, He is still my own;
Though his hand may lead me over dreary ways,
Anywhere with Jesus is a house of praise."
(Words by Jessie Pounds; 3rd vs. by Helen C. Dixon not included)

Thanks, Mary for sharing with us that wondrous Miracle that has meant much to you, and now to us!

The Reverend Larry Brodie

I first introduced you to the Reverend Larry Brodie in Chapter One, where he shared his call to the Christian Ministry. He also shared a message he gave to his congregation. Larry is now going to share an experience that he had included in his personal diary on Saturday, September 6, 2003. It is like the others in this chapter, unexplainable. His diary notes began with a full day of ministerial activities that would not be foreign to any of us in the Christian Ministry.

Rev. Brodie speaks of returning home, and a wondrous miracle that took place as he responded to the input of God's Spirit directing him.

> While driving home there were many thoughts running through my head. I finished listening to a leadership tape and was thinking about Tim's ordination. As I'm driving, my thought patterns went to Gene Blair and how he would have loved to be at Tim's ordination.
>
> Well, then I got this thought to stop at Gene's grave. That thought seemed so strange that I dismissed it. But the thought kept coming back into my mind. So, I decided to stop and see his grave. I was not even sure exactly where it was. I parked the car and began looking for it. Don't ask me why—what was I planning on doing, if I found it?

Well, it was weird, but I followed my feelings and guess where it led me? There was a man sitting on the ground who was wearing a sleeveless T-shirt, a pair of shorts and boots. His knees were up, his head down sort of like on his knees. He was close to where I thought Gene's body was buried.

I did not recognize the man until he looked up. It was Mike Kelley. I couldn't believe my eyes and I'm sure he couldn't believe his. He said, "Hi Larry, I didn't expect to see you here." I responded, "Hi Mike, I didn't expect to see you either." He got up as I walked over and we greeted each other with a handshake and hug.

Mike was visiting his son's grave. Jonathan took his own life one year ago, on September 1. Mike had been on a camping trip, up in the peaks by himself to be alone with God, and to pray. He was on his way back and stopped here to talk with the Lord at the graveside.

We had some "God Appointed" fellowship together. I listened, I read him a scripture passage, I tried to encourage him. We knelt there in the grass, near Jonathan's grave. I prayed for him and he prayed for me. We then embraced and parted. Believe me, I tingled all the way home, believing God, for His purposes arranged that meeting in the cemetery.

Can you explain that wondrous miracle? I can't, except to say that God is in control. And God can do, what God wants to do. We, ourselves, are richly blessed when we realize that God is wherever we find ourselves, be it traveling the highways of life or wandering around in a cemetery.

My dear nephew, Reverend Larry, has a strong faith and a strong desire to serve God in the discipleship of Jesus the Christ. His shared experience reminds me of a favorite hymn of mine.

He leadeth me! O blessed thought!
O words with heavenly comfort fraught!
What-e'er I do, where'er I be,
Still 'tis God's hand that leadeth me.
Lord, I would clasp Thy hand in mine,
Nor ever murmur nor repine,
Content, what ever lot I see,
Since 'tis Thy hand that leadeth me!

Refrain: He leadeth me, He leadeth me,
By His own hand He leadeth me;
His faithful follower I would be,
For by His hand He leadeth me.

Thanks Larry for sharing this wondrous miracle with us. Like all miracles, while we may not be able to explain them, we can and we should accept them as a treasured gift from God.

Charles Daycock

I have known Charlie Daycock for about as long as I can remember. I introduced his wife, Doris, in Chapter Four and there also made reference to Charles. We attended the same high school, and later on he and his wife owned a farm separated from our family farm by Black Creek. I never remember swimming over there, but Charlie has long been a friend. We sang in our church choir together, all during our high school days, and perhaps some thereafter.

Charlie has a positive outlook on life; he has a strong faith in God, and continues to be actively involved in the Church wherever he goes. He shares with us a wondrous miracle that will be an inspiration to all who read about it.

In February of 1968, my mother's brother, Wally, had severe abdominal pains. I took him to the Emergency Room at St. Mary's Hospital late at night. Doctors thought he had appendicitis and performed an appendectomy. During the emergency procedure they found that he had liver and pancreatic cancer. The medical staff estimated that my Uncle Wally had three to six months to live. It was devastating news.

Some time later, having said our goodbyes to my parents and Uncle Wally, my wife and I and our four children left for the Gulf Coast for a much needed vacation. Mom was caring for her brother at home while he was having cancer treatments. He seldom showed his pain, and none of us remotely considered that we might not see him again. Uncle Wally had walked us to the door and he seemed to be doing very well as we exchanged hugs and kisses. We had rented a new pop-up tent trailer in Rochester and on April fourth we picked it up. The six of us then headed southwest to Warren, Ohio. There we made our first stop. We stayed at the home of some good friends. It was at that time in early April, while we were traveling down I-90 near Erie, Pennsylvania, that we heard the news on our radio that Dr. Martin Luther King, Jr. had been slain that evening.

It was helpful that night that we were visiting a close friend. After a good night;s rest, we headed for Lexington, Kentucky to see Uncle Carl's new foal which was only a few days old. We took many pictures to have when we got back home. That night we spent our first night in a campground in our camper. We were all pleased at how good it worked for the six of us.

The campground was near Mammoth Cave, Kentucky. The tour of this huge cave was awesome. From there we went on to Huntsville, Alabama, where we finally met the sister of Doris' mom, Aunt Jewell, her son, Bob, and his wife, Eva. Wonderful people. Bob worked at Redstone Missile Arsenal and he arranged for us to have a tour. What a thrill that was for all of us.

As we traveled south to New Orleans, every main street of the cities, as well as in each small town, were lined with mostly black faces mourning the death of their great and esteemed leader. I prayed a lot during our journey for each of those mourners as well as for our own safety. It was an unsettling time, to say the least.

As we continued on our vacation we visited New Orleans, touring it from stem to stern. We even rode up the Mississippi on a paddle wheel boat. Then going east, we passed through Biloxi, and on to the beautiful Gardens, south of Mobile, Alabama. The roadway to the Gardens was lined with huge pine trees and the grass was covered with the largest pinecones we had ever seen. They were eight to ten inches long with a diameter of six inches. We gathered a few, but as our station wagon began to fill up we decided, "No more of that!"

We were having a wonderful carefree vacation until we were about midway between Tallahassee and Perry, Florida. As we were driving leisurely along, all of a sudden I heard a loud noise. I glanced in my rear view mirror, and my heart jumped! I saw the trailer bouncing up and down like crazy. I hit the brakes and quickly pulled to the side of the road and stopped.

When I first got out and looked, I could see no left side tires at all. But as I reached up into the wheel well, I could feel the bottom of the tire about a foot above the road surface. I could also see two prominent parallel lines in the hot pavement where the 'U' bolts had dug into the asphalt.

Before I did anything, I closed my eyes and prayed to my Lord that He would guide me as to what to do to get out of this mess. The whole time I felt like the Lord had his hand on my shoulder, as he had done so many times before. By now the four kids were upset and crying. I helped them relax by assuring them that all was going to be okay, even though I knew not how!

I then followed the trail made by the 'U' bolts which went back as far as fifty to seventy five yards. There at the beginning of the marked pavement, I was assured that God was guiding me. I was stunned to see three of the wheel bolts lying in the road. They were arranged in approximately a twenty-foot circle.

I thanked the Lord right then and there for His guidance. I unbelievably carried the three wheel bolts back to our car to see what was next. I took out the car jack and figured out a way to lift the trailer high enough to get the wheel out of the wheel well. And lo and behold, it dropped down as we jacked the trailer up. We aligned the lug bolts and incredibly we were able to get all three of them back in place. None of them were damaged at all. This all happened on the Saturday between Good Friday and Easter—April thirteenth.

Again, I prayed that we might find a better fix because I had no wrenches to tighten the wheel bolts. As we headed to Perry, Florida, within two or three miles we came to an old service station. I related to the mechanic what had happened and he said, "Give me a minute to see what I've got." In less than a minute, the mechanic came out with a wheel bolt and wrench in hand. The bolt fit perfectly, he tightened all the others, and he would not take any money whatsoever. I had him fill our gas tank in an effort to help him recoup something for his time and kindness to us. Another prayer was offered for the amazing guidance and astounding answer to our prayers.

That same evening we had a small campfire at the campground. Sue, Steve, Ken, Kathy, Doris and I sat around the fire, all of us thankful for the beautiful day we had shared together. And guess what? As we looked up at the dazzling sky we saw a full moon above the horizon. The shadow of the earth began to slowly cover the moon until the moon was entirely covered.

As we observed God's gorgeous creation and witnessed the full eclipse of that beautiful full moon, we again gave thanks to God for his love and guidance on that 13th day of April in 1968. We then headed for Clearwater, Florida. We shall never forget how surprised we were when we arrived at Uncle Henry's home. He is my mother's other brother. We were taken aback when Aunt Mart's sister, Irene, answered the door. She said that Uncle Hank and Aunt Mart had left before Good Friday for Churchville. They wanted to visit Wally while they could.

After camping in their driveway Easter Sunday night, we decided, we too should head back north. On Monday morning we left for home, stopping in the Great Smoky National Park. I still felt that everything was okay at home. But that morning at 3:00 o'clock, on April 16, I had a dream that would change our lives forever.

In my dream I was on the family farm in Churchville, New York. I was sitting in my Uncle Wally's chair in the kitchen, when suddenly I heard the sound of rubber boots coming across the side porch.

The sound was coming toward the kitchen. I saw the door open, my granddad's hand was on the doorknob. He looked at me and said, "Charlie, take good care of the farm for me." I sat straight up in the camper with tears streaming down my face. Doris also sat up and asked me what was wrong? I told her that I thought Uncle Wally might have died. It was the most real dream I have ever had.

Upon arriving home we found out that my Uncle Wally had died on the same night of my dream! Following the funeral service we read his will. In the reading of it we found that Uncle Wally had left us a one acre parcel to the north of the original farm house. When his brothers asked me if I was interested in the farm, I told them about my dream. I then said that I was interested in the farm. We lived there for thirty-six years

We moved into the 1877 farm house on Halloween night in 1968. We owned and operated the farm until July 2004 when we sold it to a local veterinarian who wants to continue it as a farm. **I HOPE MY GRANDDAD'S REQUEST WAS WELL KEPT**.

Wondrous miracles continue to be beyond all expectation and full understanding. Charlie's miracle experience on the highway when his trailer lost a wheel was really something. One would never expect to find those bolts. Normally they dance and skip all over the place, landing in the ditch or some other hiding place! And consider how he found such a helpful service station so close to where the wheel did its thing. Wow! Wondrous miracles continued to happen on that whole trip. What a trip that was for them. I suspect, that as they pondered all the wondrous things that took place, there was no question in their minds about how closely God was involved in their journey.

Thanks for your sharing, Charlie. Your wondrous miracles experienced have been a part of your whole life; we hope your sharing will help us all to keep our eyes and ears open to the presence of God in our midst. God's love is so real and so all-inclusive. Praise be to God.

Roxann Muller

Roxann grew up in Pike, New York, which is just, down the road from Castile. She attended the local Central School, which gave me an opportunity to become acquainted with her. The fact that she dated a young man, who was a member of our church, also helped me to get to know her. She married her high school sweetheart, but like so many marital relationships, their marriage ended in divorce. Thankfully, although they parted, they remained friends and are still kind to each other. I am sure their two boys, now young men, have been blessed by this relationship that exemplifies how divorced couples should act toward one another.

In a letter that Roxann sent with her shared experiences, she said some very nice things about my first book. Then she wrote, "Most of all, your experiences affirmed my own experiences with God. As you revealed the examples of God's hand in your life, I felt a kinship with you. I have had many such experiences, too." In those words, she expressed one of the main reasons for my writing. God is always with us; God is still speaking, we need only to open ourselves to that Presence.

> I want to share a few stories of God's love for me.... One instance was brief and simple, but made all the difference in my life at the same time. When my husband left me, I think I was in shock for a few weeks. I went about my daily routines and made some changes in my work outside the home to be better able to provide for the boys on my own. Gradually, the reality of the future I was facing began to sink in and I began to feel very frightened and alone. One night after putting the boys to bed, I began to cry. Now I had done plenty of that already, but this was not just a sad, hurt cry. This was a desperate cry.

Suddenly, I felt a presence in the room, and an embrace more warm and comforting than anything I had ever experienced. I knew immediately that it was from God. Somehow God assured me that everything would be all right. He had things under control and He would be with me. I did not know it then, but God certainly had wonderful plans for me.

Reading of her wondrous miracle that she experienced brought to mind these words from Psalm 91:14-16:

Those who love me, I will deliver;
I will protect those who know my name.
When they call to me, I will answer them;
I will be with them in trouble,
I will rescue them and honor them.
With long life I will satisfy them,
And show them my salvation.

Roxann shares another wondrous experience that again touched her very being and brought about a prayer of Thanksgiving to our Creator, Sustainer and Friend.

Another amazing example of God's wondrous work and love occurred some nine years ago. We had just started Little Lambs Preschool at our church and I was the director/teacher. Our first year was going well and we believed that this was certainly a God-inspired direction for us.

I had been having some problems with fibroid tumors, but did not think it was the best course to have a hysterectomy. We found a doctor in New York City who was willing to just remove fibroids. During the prep work for surgery, I had an ultrasound; a growth was discovered that the doctor believed was cancer.

We were very confused at this new turn of events. Wasn't the preschool the right path for me? Don and I had only been married a short time. Was our future together going to be a short one? Hadn't Don had enough hardship with the death of two of his children and a bitter wife leaving him? (You know how the mind goes on and on!)

We began praying and asked other to pray too. The night before I was to have a CAT scan to figure out exactly what needed to be done, Don said a special prayer, laying his hand over the area of the tumor. The next day, as the scan proceeded, there seemed to be a lot of confusion and bewildered discussion about what they were seeing. Other doctors were called in and more and more people were looking at the screen.

Finally, my doctor came to Don and me and explained that they could find absolutely no trace of the tumor which was so clearly visible in the ultrasound. He went on to say, "We have no explanation for this, but it simply isn't there any more."

We of course began to laugh and cry, as we said that we had a very good explanation for what had happened. God answers prayer! As we checked out of the hospital, a friend who works in the Radiology Department told me that word was spreading like wildfire through the hospital that I was the "miracle lady"! What a privilege for me to have been the vehicle for others to witness a miracle.

And the wondrous miracles of God continue to be experienced on and on. We thank you for sharing those experiences with us, Roxann. In some of her writing to me Mrs. Muller had written these beautiful words. "What an amazing thing it is that God, who is all powerful and in control of every intricate little system that holds our world together, still takes the time to listen to me and help me with such trivial things as missing keys." I treasure those words for they express a truth of God that passes all understanding; God's Love is omnipresent and eternal.

I find the words of this familiar hymn to be significant here:

Be still, my soul! the Lord is on thy side;
Bear patiently the cross of grief or pain;
Leave to thy God to order and provide;
In every change He faithful will remain,
Be still, my soul! thy best, thy heavenly Friend
Thro thorny ways leads to a joyful end.

Praise Be to God!

Mae and Larry Wheeler

It seems to me that I have known Mae and Larry all my life. However, I actually met Mae when she was a young, pretty girl, who happened to also be the younger sister of Audrey, who is now my wife. She has been very dear to Audrey and to me from those early days, and she always will be.

I first got to know Larry when we were both in high school. I have always considered him an exceptional person. His mannerism, his humility, and jovial personality make him fun to be around.

The Wheelers live in Churchville, New York, in a home they purchased shortly after they were married. It was a new house then and looks like a new house today. In general terms, Mae and Larry have had a marriage filled with love, good times, and a rich flow of blessing from on high. They have both worked very hard and have much appreciated the fruits of their labor.

Included in their joy and blessings were two children, a girl and a boy—Patricia and Thomas respectively. They are now the proud grandparents of three grandsons and two granddaughters. Their youngest granddaughter, Kristi and youngest grandson, Matthew, are very active in sports. They are gifted and fast on the soccer field or in whatever sport in which they may be engaged. They remind me of Tom, their father, when he was their age. From what I hear about their mother, Karen, I suspect they get their talent and agility from both of their parents.

Mae and Larry have one grandson, Mike, who recently graduated from college. He was also recently married. He and his wife, Lauren, just purchased a house and live in the area. Tristan is another granddaughter; she will graduate from Cornell University this year. Mae and Larry's family is one that they are proud of and should be!

Sadly, their eldest grandson, Wyatt, was killed in a tragic farm accident at the early age of twenty-one. His death was an absolute painful experience for him and for everyone who knew him. And many knew him. He was an amazing young man who was known in dairy circles for his gifted ability in grooming cattle, as well as in showmanship. As young as he was, Wyatt was at times engaged by farmers to prepare their livestock for showing in competition and/or for auctions.

As hard and painful as it has been and is for all of us, Wyatt's death was, quite naturally, much more severe on his mother and father, his siblings and his grandparents. Wyatt's mother and father were divorced, quite some time prior to his death. This may very well have made his relationship with his grandparents more intense. I have, and I am sure you have, seen this to be the case in many families.

Mae and Larry have been involved in the life of the church for years. They know the Presence of God has been with them as the have journeyed through life together. Their sharing with us has to do with Wyatt's death, their faith in God, and their faith journey since then.

To tell of their wondrous miraculous experiences they spoke with my wife and me, in addition to giving us some written notes, all of which are used to tell their story.

> Wyatt William Zuber was born on July 4, 1980, and entered into God's Eternal Home on August 29, 2001. We miss his sense of humor, his phone calls and visits. Along with that, we just miss his loving ways and his being here on this planet Earth.
>
> We have continued our faith in God's Eternal love and we have prayed that God's peace, joy, and life would be with him. Our faith enables us to have that hope, that we shall meet again. And it is indeed a wondrous miracle that keeps us smiling in the presence of our pain.

We feel that in the great mystery of the universe, God's love is exemplified in, for example, those events that "cannot happen" and yet, still happen. It is clear to us that our Grandson, Wyatt, has been able to assure us of his love and continued life in the Kingdom of God. How it is done, we do not even begin to speculate. But, we know why it is done! Be it by a miracle, by or through God's intervention or by any other label one might put on it, let us share the wondrous miracles we have experienced.

On several occasions, we feel that he has somehow made "contact" with us by sending "pennies from heaven." When Wyatt was a small child, like many children, he had a piggy bank at Grandma and Grandpa's house. It seems that he always wanted pennies to "feed" his pig. It was always a happy time when we would help and/or watch him put the pennies in his bank. Over the years, as he grew and matured, we have talked about this with him and laughed with him about how he "stretched" it out as long as he possibly could! This is probably the significance of the pennies that we have received.

One of our wondrous miracles experienced in this regard took place on his birthday in 2005. Because we knew it would be a difficult day for us all, we took Wyatt's mother and his siblings out to dinner. **When we came out of the restaurant we found a penny. Not just any penny, but a penny dated 1980, the year of his birth. That made us feel good but when we reached our car, we became ecstatic. There beside our car we found a quarter. Not just any quarter, but a quarter**

dated 2001. That was the year of his death. On his birthday, we found a penny with the year of his birth. Then, we found a quarter, with the year of his death! We thought about why we found a quarter this time and not a penny. Guess What? It was on what would have been his 25th birthday! Think about that. You can not expect to pile twenty-five pennies and not have the tower fall asunder. No, a quarter was needed in order to be sure that we got the message that was being conveyed.

These kinds of experiences have helped us to deal with the most painful experience of our lives. We hope those "pennies from heaven" will keep coming, for they help us in sensing Wyatt's presence. They put a smile on our faces, as we remember helping him "feed" his piggy bank, and recall many happy memories we have had with that dear, dear, grandchild.

God's way of giving us support comes in so many different ways. From Mae and Larry's experience and the joy, laughter and fun they had had with Wyatt as a small child, pennies (and quarters) just have to have a significant meaning. Thanks, Mae and Larry for sharing with us; your experience now has become for us all a treasured gift. As we walk the trails of life, any coins we see on the path will remind us of your holy experience.

Shared Experiences with the Holy, that we as human beings experience are so momentous to our appreciation of God's Love for us. As Jesus told his disciples, and as he would say to us over and over again, "Blessed are your eyes because they see, and your ears because they hear" (Matthew 13:16f). The seeing and the hearing that Jesus refers to here, speaks more of our hearts than any other organs of the body. Yes, the wondrous miracles of God continue to take place. As disciples of our Lord and Savior, it seems to me that we should be eager to share the meaningful, supporting, faith-building experiences we are blessed to have as a part of our life's journey. That is, of course, one big reason for my writing this book.

As this chapter comes to its conclusion, please try hard to endow others with the rich and wondrous miracles that you experience. As you share with others, the blessings you give to them, will also be a blessing for you.

CHAPTER SIX

Holy Moments of Assurance and Peace

This chapter will share some of those Holy Moments that we have when we somehow know that God is with us in a very real and significant way. I mean, those times in our lives, when God is so real that the experience becomes cemented into our very being. It is so strongly felt, that it is ever a part of who we are, and of who we are not.

These Holy Moments come to us in all sorts of places, in all kinds of situations and at any time in our lives. I deem that these experiences are given to us by God. The full impact of such Holy Moments upon us is truly beyond our grasp. But the reason we experience them, must include the fact that by them, we are given an increasing assurance of God's Presence, and a greater appreciation of God's Love. Most certainly they help us to create within us a stronger faith, resulting in a more real and unyielding peace. The sharing you are about to read comes from a wide variety of people, who vary in age, come from many different denominations in the Christian Faith, and live in a wide spectrum of these United States of America.

Audrey Baker Embling

Audrey and I have been married for fifty-three years. I can still vividly remember the first time I ever saw her. I was at a neighbor's home on a warm midweek evening. We decided to play "Kick-the-Can" which is a game similar to "Hide-N-Seek." The difference is that in an effort to keep from being caught, one could kick the can and then go hide again. All the others who had been previously caught could then also go hide again.

Well, I was "It," meaning that I had to find the others and run to the can, putting my foot on it, before someone kicked it. In the process of the game I had caught three or four of the group, which meant I was really being sure no one would kick the can and set them free. That is until out of nowhere came this new kid heading for the can at full speed. I was surprised to see her, but more significantly, I just stopped in my tracks. She went on to kick the can like a professional football player kicks a field goal!

That all happened because from my side of the "can" I was stunned by the glowing beauty of this new kicker! She was only six years old. I was two plus years beyond her. But, I never forgot about this, Audrey, who attended a one-room school. It was not until she started attending the junior high school, where I also attended, that I remember seeing her again. She was by now more beautiful than before and once I was able to get to know her, I quickly realized that her beauty was more than skin deep.

After a few years of knowing her and after a few more years of dating her, we were married. Audrey was a sharp student, National Honor Society type. Her faith has always been a real part of who she is.

When she was a child (I think it was about age nine), Audrey had rheumatic fever. At that time her doctor told her she would never be healthy and/or strong enough to have children. This was a severe concern for both of us. After some three years of married life, and after consulting with a doctor, she became pregnant for our first of two children.

We kind of pretended we had no worries about her giving birth, but we both were placidly concerned and we prayed regularly for God's help and assurance. I was not surprised, a few years later when my dear wife shared with me the experience she had. As you will see, it was a Holy Moment of Assurance and Peace, a mere moment that she will never forget.

> On the first Sunday in January in the year 1957, I experienced a Holy Moment of which I will never forget. It was at a Sunday morning Worship Service at the Union Congregational (United Church of Christ) in Churchville, New York. The Reverend Ellwyn Merriam was our pastor. As we shared in the Sacrament of Holy Communion, I prayed that we would have a very special child. It did not concern me whether it would be a boy or girl. That was before the days of ultrasounds, when every child's gender was a surprise.
>
> I asked God to give me a sign that I would truly have a healthy and special child. The answer to my prayer came before I expected it. I really wasn't ready for what happened when I tasted the 'juice' in the individual Communion Cup that was passed to me. **It was blood. It looked like blood. It tasted like blood. No one will**

ever convince me that it wasn't. It was truly blood and I had a hard time swallowing it. Like Jesus' mother Mary, I pondered it over and over. But I did not tell anyone. It was a Holy Moment for me that I shall never forget. I was given assurance and a new sense of peace settled within me.

Cindy was born sixteen days early and the doctor was concerned that she might not be quite ready for life on the outside. That fear was soon alleviated. After being delivered, the doctor laid her on a wide counter beside the large stainless steel sink. While he was very busy with me for a couple minutes, she was on her tummy. Of course, I was attentively watching her. Then all of a sudden she boosted herself up with her little arms and began to peer over the edge of the counter—looking at the hard tile floor beneath her. I anxiously summoned the doctor to "Get my baby!"

The doctor ran, as did the intern who was assisting him. They got to Cindy just before she would have fallen. Dr. George Trombetta gave a sigh and turned to the intern and said, "That is a first for me; newborns don't pull tricks like that." He then placed the baby beside me on the bed and said, "Don't leave your little rascal unattended anywhere!"

That Holy Moment while taking the Sacrament gave me the assurance that my child would be a healthy and special child. Upon her birth, she proved it within minutes. As the weeks and months went by we were often reminded of our prayer for a healthy and special child. When we would take her to the doctor for her regular checkups, he would say things like: "You do realize, don't you, that she is not supposed to be talking yet?"

Another time the doctor examined her and came out with words like: "She is only seven months old and she is calling everyone by their first names!" On another doctor's visit, the doctor looked at us and confessed, "I don't envy you trying to parent her, she is not a normal child." I simply replied, "The Good Lord will help us." And He did!

The assurance and peace that God gave me in that Holy Moment years ago, has been a tremendous support ever since. I continue to thank God for that incredible experience in the pew. It was as I worshipped God in Jesus' name some forty-nine or so years ago. **Nonetheless, it is as real each new day as it was the very day it happened**.

Audrey's "Holy Moment" has been with her ever since. It was a private experience that took place as others sat beside her, in front of her and behind her. Yet, as far as we know, no one else experienced it. Think of it. No one else in the whole worship experience was aware of the special blessing Audrey was given that day. God does things like that all the time. Her experience was truly an uplifting occurrence for her, and I am confident it will be to those who hear or read her sharing of it.

Thanks, Audrey, for sharing that Holy Moment and for being so faithful to our Lord in your sharing of it and in your living in the faith each day. Yes, God is still speaking and one is richly blessed by joining in the dialogue.

Mary Sternal

I first introduced Mary Sternal to you in the last chapter. She is a delightful lady with a strong faith in God and a very pleasant demeanor. She shares a Holy Moment that gave her a very positive sense of assurance and peace. Here is her gift to us as she shares a very personal moment, to which any parent can easily relate.

> Our home is in Minnesota most of the year, but we spend our winter months in southern Florida. During that time, we live in a park model, in the Road Runner Travel Resort in Fort Pierce. One year our son and his family, who live in northern Minnesota, made plans to drive down to see us. They also had a real desire to escape from some of the cold they had to deal with in the North Country
>
> My husband, Bob, and I were excited about their plans to visit us. This would be a nineteen hundred mile trip for them. They had three drivers and they were determined to drive straight through, with no motel stops. Naturally, I was very concerned about their safety. I worried about icy roads, a snowstorm, other careless drivers, and their being too tired to drive safely. So, I prayed that God would watch over them.
>
> **Suddenly, in my mind, I saw a clear picture of a car traveling on the highway with a giant hand cupped protectively over it.**
>
> I believed that God was telling me not to worry—so I didn't. My son and his family arrived safely and we had a wonderful week together.

Wasn't that something? When one seriously turns to God in times of joy or sorrow, in times of need or concern it is utterly amazing how God may respond. This had to be a heart-warming gift for Mary to receive.

Thanks, Mary, for your sharing of this Holy Moment in your life. I had never heard of such a pictorial response from God that was any more beautiful. It is incredible how God meets our needs and gives us an assurance and a peace not to be found elsewhere. Never forget the importance, of speaking with God.

Jack Hendrickson

I think I have known Jack for close to fifty years. I checked him out quite soon after I heard his name. He was, after all, dating my little sister. He proved to be an honest, sincere, and compassionate guy, with lots of ambition. Not only that, but he was intelligent, a gentleman, and he had high goals for himself.

Equally important, perhaps more important, he was a young man with a strong Christian faith. Some years later he married my sister, Lorraine. He did that, I might say, without any sanction from me! I am glad they married; he has turned out to be a brother-in-law par excellence.

Following his college graduation, Jack found a variety of jobs that gave him flying time. I understand that these were important work opportunities that helped him to accumulate hours in flight. Among the jobs, I remember is his working for a business that had an underground pipeline. He flew over the pipeline looking for possible leaks or problems of any sort.

Jack was steadily working toward the fulfillment of his life-long dream, becoming a commercial airline pilot.

He was in "seventh heaven" so to speak, when Texas International Airlines hired him. Some years later, he became a pilot for American Airlines where he became a Captain and flew all over the country. In his retirement from piloting commercial airlines, Jack now tests pilots in simulators, still working for American Airlines.

When I inquired about his contributing to my effort in this book, he readily agreed. His Holy Moments proved to be faith enriching and the increased assurance that God's Presence was with him.

I was on a trip to Albuquerque when I had a dream. In the dream I remember seeing a casket, brown in color, with the initials WBH on the side. I woke up in a sweat, wondering what in the world that was all about. Thankfully, it was only a dream.

It wasn't until after my dad's death that it hit me! Then I realized that the Lord was telling me, in the dream, to prepare for Dad's demise. I was at the same time shown what the color of the casket would be, plus what initials would be on the side.

I also had another Holy Moment that I would like to share. It was an entirely unrelated experience. I was driving in the car one day with my family and Aunt Marie. We happened to be near the location where one of my uncles lived. My aunt suggested we might stop by to see him. Well, our family had not seen nor been in contact with him for a number of years.

My aunt was insistent and I was beginning to get frustrated! So, in order to keep the peace, I stopped and we had a very nice visit. A month later my uncle was dead!

Now that I am in the autumn of my life and looking back, I realize that the Lord has always been with me. The problem has been me! How in the world could I have had the audacity to try to shackle the Lord in the manner He chose to guide me? I have a free will, therefore, I can hear but not listen; I can ignore or act. In every case, when I heard and chose not to act, I suffered the consequences.

Jack is a deep thinker. As he pondered the Holy Moments in his life, he knew that he, like the rest of us, often push the Lord aside for some lesser obsession. In Paul's Letter to the Romans, chapter twelve, he writes to those who were involved in the worship of God and in the service of Jesus the Christ.

> "Do not model yourselves on the behavior
> of the world around you, but let your behavior
> change, modeled on your new mind. This is
> the only way to discover the will of God and know
> what is good, what it is that God wants, what is the
> perfect thing to do" (Romans 12:2 The Jerusalem Bible).

The point I want to draw attention to here is that once we become a Christian, then we have what Paul would refer to as a "new mind." Our Holy Moments are that significant to us. They give us assurance of God's Presence and Love. They help us to know God's Will for us.

As Jack brought out, God's Word also leaves it to us whether we listen, pay attention, or close the door. Jack saw that clearly and we thank him for sharing with us. Our Holy Moments are indeed blessings to our lives as God endeavors to assure us, of God's Presence and Eternal Love.

Elaine Keif

Elaine has been a family friend for many years. Her two girls, Carla and Jodel, attended the same public school as our children. They lived in Castile and our friendship grew over the years. After she had been divorced for a number of years, I was honored to officiate at the wedding that united her with a very good friend of mine, David Keif.

Elaine and Dave owned and operated a family restaurant in nearby Perry, where I would occasionally drop in about mid-morning for a cup of coffee and a good ol' chat with my friend. In fifteen minutes we were able to solve the problems of the world, I would "unwind," he would relax, and then we would be off and running again.

I forget the particulars, but I remember that Dave bought Elaine a dozen yellow roses and had them delivered to her. The florist inadvertently brought only eleven. They later brought her two roses, delivering them to the office where she worked. The story was the butt of considerable humor among us as we kidded about not sending quite a dozen.

In addition to all that, as you might expect, roses took on a special meaning for these two dear people. It was their flower! We were saddened, though hopeful, when Dave began to have some health problems. He had numerous treatments, doctors' appointments, and days in the hospital. His sense of humor did not diminish, nor did his Christian Faith ever waver, through all those ups and downs, good days and not so good ones.

With a full awareness of his impending death, Dave expressed his love for his family and he was without a doubt aware of their love and concern for him. He left us peacefully and in the assurance that we would meet again—in a "place beyond"— where life has no end.

Following his funeral and burial, God gave a beautiful gift to Elaine (and all of us). His burial was on a Monday, the following Sunday when Elaine went to the gravesite, she saw that the scores of beautiful flowers covering the grave were all frozen. She also saw that almost all of them looked quite poorly. In the course of their cemetery visit, Elaine told her daughter that she hoped the cemetery caretakers would take all the flowers away. That was Sunday.

On Monday, which would have been their eighteenth wedding anniversary, all the flowers were completely demolished by the cold winter weather. All except for ONE PEACH ROSE that stood upright and had a bright glowing appearance as it waved in the softly blowing wind, greeting all who approached or passed by. It was called to Elaine's attention when her daughter, Jodel said, "Look Mom, Dave left you an anniversary gift!"

Yes, the Holy Moments of Assurance and Peace happen over and over again. While we are apt to simply ask, "How did that happen? How come just one flower blooming when all the others had been trashed by the frigid cold and stormy weather?"

We might ask, how come it was a "rose" that appeared alone in that ever to be sacred place? Those are the wrong questions. The eyes of faith, the eyes that behold the beauty of God's Creation and Presence—see way beyond the need to ask such questions as those.

Our Creator is always in our midst, declaring Love to one and to all. An old Christian hymn has words so poignantly significant to the experience shared by Elaine that I want to include them here. The hymn's first stanza has these words:

There is a land of pure delight
Where saints immortal reign;
Infinite day excludes the night,
And pleasures banish pain.
There everlasting spring abides,
And never withering flowers;
Death, like a narrow sea, divides
This heavenly land of ours.

Thanks for sharing that Holy Moment of which you deem never to forget. May the assurance and peace it gave you on your anniversary, be yours for infinity. It surely is a "shot" in the arm of faith to all who hear the story. The rose was indeed, a beautiful and meaningful gift. To God be the Glory.

J. Thomas Reagan

I first met Thomas when he joined the family medical practice in Perry, New York. He became a partner to Dr. Thomas Rosenthal, who at the time was our family's physician.

I became better acquainted with Dr. Reagan when he established and chaired the Ethics Committee of the Wyoming County Community Hospital. I served on the committee and every time we met, I was more impressed by his compassionate understanding, and the diversity and depth of his medical knowledge.

But, I must confess, I really got to know this delightful man when he joined our family, by marrying our daughter, Mary. He has proven to be a neat son-in-law, a devoted husband and father. And in addition to all that, he has a solo voice and continues to sing in our Church Choir, direct our Hand Bell Choir and is involved in the life of our church family.

Tom is a Quaker. His faith is solid. His appreciation of silence before God is a treasured gift that he has helped me to more fully develop, although he may not be aware of that fact.

Dr. Reagan is also my family physician, who has already saved my life at least once following a flawed diagnosis by someone else. I had a major heart attack caused by a nearly complete blockage of an artery. Once Tom came on the scene, he quickly recognized my dire condition and immediately changed the course of my medical treatment. His corrected diagnosis and his quick action proved beneficial. Without his intervention, I am quite confident that I would not be writing this book today.

Two weeks ago, I think, you asked if I would like to share with you any experience of the Divine which I may have had. There is one which was not very exciting, but still feels good.

A month or so after Mom died I had awakened much earlier than I usually do and as I was not going to go back to sleep. I set a lawn chair out on the front yard, overlooking the valley. I wrapped up in a blanket and sat down to think about Mom's death, or really life, to think about God, and perhaps to meditate. It was not to pray. The day was beautiful with the clear golden light of early morning.

As I sat there, the light became perhaps even more clear and I was filled with a certainty that God exists, and if God exists, things are basically right with the world. No claps of thunder, no revelations about the nature of God, no miracles, just a certainty or conviction.

This experience has relieved me of having to stew on the question of whether or not there is a God. I can accept that as a given. I then get to wrestle with how to live appropriately, although most of the time I do not give that nearly enough attention. Too often, I simply live comfortably, which is perhaps not the best thing to do.

One person described meeting for worship as the opportunity to become uncomfortable as we examine ourselves. I think we should live in a state of appreciation of the Holy at all times, whether on our way to church, or on our away to work or play. Unfortunately, if I am not distracted by things, I often distract myself because I fear that the message might prove uncomfortable and lead me places I do not want go. I try to be good, but sometimes it seems that we should be a little more radical than that.

Upon reading Tom's message I thought of these words from Jeremiah the prophet, "This is what the Lord says: 'Stand at the crossroads and look; ask for the ancient paths, ask where the good way is, and walk in it, and you will find rest for your souls' (Jeremiah 6:16 New International Version)."

Dr. Tom's sharing of that Holy Moment speaks to me about what can and usually does happen, when one becomes quiet before God. We are given insight, enhanced faith, and an improved appreciation of our rightful relationship with God. Unquestionably, we all need to "Be still and know that God is God." as the Psalmist proclaimed so long ago (Psalm 46:10). This sharing is so reminiscent of Elijah, who ran up into the hills in fear of his life. On the mountain (Horeb), Elijah was seeking the presence of God. I Kings 17:11-13 reads, "…The Lord was not in the wind, and after the wind an earthquake, but the Lord was not in the earthquake; and after the earthquake a fire, but the Lord was not in the fire, and after a fire the **sound of sheer silence…then there came a voice to him….**"

We do live in a noisy world. We have distractions all about us. Once we allow those distractions to detain us, we are easily "taken in." In a flash, the distractions "own" us. To take time to be still, to be quiet before God, is vital to maintaining our faith and wholeness.

Holy Moments happen and/or come to us whenever or wherever we may be. There is a beautiful hymn that speaks to all this.

"Near to the Heart of God."
There is a place of quiet rest, Near to the heart of God,
A place where sin cannot molest, Near to the heart of God.
(Refrain) O Jesus, blest Redeemer,
Sent from the heart of God,
Hold us who wait before Thee,
Near to the heart of God.

As people traveling here and there, in distance and in thought, we will do well to take time to be close "to the heart of God." One biblically sound method and one proven to be most helpful today, is to take time to be still and hear the awesome messages from God. Thanks, Tom, for your sharing of a Holy Moment, and your honest assessment of it's effect upon you.

For us to find time to be still before God will have an impressive impact upon our total being; it will do wonders for our soul, and be an additive, that is certain to give strength to our faith in the Almighty, compassionate, and loving God.

Marjorie and Robert Dix

I first introduced you to Marge and Bob in Chapter One. They are Christian missionaries serving with Wycliffe. You will remember how they were world travelers. A Holy Moment of Assurance and Peace came to them, on an airplane flight, piloted by Bob.

I have taken many flights in small aircraft with my husband as pilot. The most beautiful long trip was from

North Carolina to Cuiaba M T in Brazil. It was a beautiful trip. Our daughter, Janet, was twelve years old at the time. She and I sat in the back, and our son was up front. Every once in awhile Janet would ask if we were over W or L. I knew she meant Water or Land. If I said L, she would look out the window but if I said W, she would keep her head down.

Most of our trips were very nice and uneventful. However, I often recall the flight we were taking from Texas to Chicago. The weather was beautiful, that is, most of the way. When we were getting near Illinois the weather was very cloudy. Bob knew what the weather was forecasted to be, so he filed his flight plan and would be flying by instruments.

As we got near to Chicago and were flying above the clouds, we had beautiful weather. However, in order to land we had to come down through the thick layer of clouds. I had learned from experience that in such times when he was having any difficulties, I was to keep my mouth shut. I was to remain calm so as not to distract him. With my mouth shut, Bible open on my lap, I sure did a lot of talking to God!

Several minutes went by as we circled around the airport waiting for our turn to land. This waiting was not easy. It seemed like eternity waiting for the control tower to clear us for landing. The time finely arrived. All we could see in front of us were black clouds. Bob did all the things he was taught by using and trusting in his instruments to show the way.

I thought sure we were headed the wrong direction. As we came out from under the massively dense clouds, it was a gorgeous clear day and we were right on course at the end of the designated runway. Oh, how marvelous and electrifying that moment was for us. God is so good.

Our lives are like this experience. We all go through dark times in or lives. Each life is different. There may be days, weeks and sometimes years when someone (maybe you) goes through a very difficult time. Like it being in the dark, not knowing where or when to turn.

In dark times like that, we can not understand it, we don't like it, and we wonder "How long Lord?" It is in those difficult times that we must trust our pilot, our Creator God, our Sustainer and Friend. God is the one who gives us wisdom, strength, family, friends, medical care or whatever the need may be.

We still may not completely understand, but if we have given our hearts and lives over to God, God has promised us that magnificently wonderful place at the end of the road. That is a place so incredible, where we will live with our Lord forever and ever. How marvelous and exciting that will be.

What a Holy Moment it must have been coming out of those dark clouds to see the shining sun and the exact place where you were supposed to be! I agree with her suggested scripture that speaks to their shared moment. 2 Corinthians 1:4: "He comforts us in all our troubles so that we can comfort others." Our blessings are given so we can share them, enabling others to be strengthened in faith and life.

Be aware of God's presence; it is a reality whether you are in an airplane, on a hillside overlooking the valley, confined in prison, at home or at work or anywhere else in the universe. You are never alone. Thanks be to God. And thanks Marge and Bob for your sharing with us and for your continued sharing of the Gospel in Jesus' name.

Glenn C. Harris

I first met Glenn at a Genesee Valley Association meeting. He was a delegate to the meeting, from one of our churches. I got to know him better when I was moderator of the New York Conference. He was not only a delegate to that State meeting, but it was there that I got to know him as a candidate for the Lay Ministry Program in the United Church of Christ.

I felt honored when Glenn asked me if I would be his mentor for that program. After we considered it together, we decided that my living some fifty miles from him would be a little much for any regular meeting together for discussion and/or study.

Upon becoming more acquainted with Glenn, I shared with him my effort to write this book and invited his contribution. Glenn promptly agreed to participate and soon sent his experience to me.

More than a Simple Telephone Call

I had spent most of the week at the hospital sitting with my aunt. My uncle was in dire medical distress and not expected to live very long. I spent much of the time reading the Bible and praying that my aunt would have the strength needed to understand, or at least accept God's Will in the coming days.

My aunt looked to me as a son, and I suppose I felt a special nearness to her, because my mother had already been called home to the Lord. My mom and aunt were sisters. They were part of a family of eight girls and one boy. My aunt had four children of her own; a son who lived in California and another son who was on active duty in the United States Army. She also had two girls who lived in the area, but their relationships were strained. Their fathers soon expected death did bring them closer together.

In the morning I would go to my aunt's home, pick her up, and take her to the hospital. The three of us would then spend the day together, with a few visitors that might stop by. The decisions as to what should be done, at a time like this had already been answered. My aunt and uncle had decided that no special medical procedures were to be used, other than making them comfortable. This removed a lot of stress for the family that often becomes a part of the decisions to be made by me at times such as this.

Yet, from time to time, my aunt would start to second guess their previous decisions. Both of them had written living wills expressing their desires to be made comfortable, but there was to be nothing heroic or use of machines to keep them alive.

Many times my aunt would show strength to carry the world and support her children, then there were times when she showed anger. Anger that her husband was leaving her, and sometimes anger toward her husband because he was leaving before her. I would talk with her, trying to help her with her faith, which was so much like a lot of people's faith. When there is trouble and we need help, we turn to the Lord. When life is moving along slowly and peacefully, we forget that these times are a blessing from God. They are times when we ought to be singing praises to God. I have been like that, forgetful, myself.

Upon hearing the call of the Lord to become involved in the program of Lay Ministry, my life's actions changed a great deal. As a result of joining that program, my faith has been growing and I began to sense the Holy Spirit working in my life. I was witnessing the Good News at times when I was unaware of it. This was another step forward as I grew closer to God.

On Sunday, my uncle showed signs of improving, and he was sitting up eating his dinner. My aunt started to get excited with his apparent improvement. Her daughter and I tried to caution her, explaining that this improvement could be very temporary.

On Monday morning, I was in our kitchen preparing to spend another day at the hospital, when the phone rang. It was my aunt who said she was very upset because the hospital had just called to tell her that her husband had slipped closer to death and that she should come quickly. I assured her I would leave to get her in the next few minutes.

From that phone call in the kitchen, I walked to the room that we use as an office. It is where we have our computer. I looked, and to my surprise, my wife was on line working for "America On Line." At that time we used a dial up connection to get on the Internet. We have only one telephone line, so when she is working on line, we do not receive telephone calls.

As I went to tell her of my uncle's turn for the worse, I realized that she was on line. Upon my inquiry, she told me she had been on line working for fifteen to twenty minutes. I then told her that I had to leave and that my aunt had just called. **We both did a "double take" at the same time. We realized that a great power beyond us was at work here. I had just talked to my aunt on the telephone, and yet my wife was on the computer at the same time, using the telephone line!**

Do miracles still happen? YES! We just need to slow down to see God and God's great work around us. My uncle died that afternoon, quietly and peacefully. I was not there at the very moment because my wife had come to take my place.

We shall not forget that Holy Moment, when what could not happen, happened! That experience gave my dear wife and me a rejuvenation of faith and an undeniable sense of God's peace that passes all understanding.

My walk with the Lord has continued to bring, within me, an increase of faith. I take time, as much time as I can each day, to allow myself to focus upon God and the wonder of God's Creation all around us.

Holy Moments, miracles, time alone with God, all continue to be gifts to us—unexpected and unplanned gifts, from our Creator. Thanks, Glenn, for sharing that experience with us. It is now a tool in our journey, as we seek to grow in the Way and Will of God.

Roger Pimm

Roger is a long-time friend. He lives in Riga Center, just five miles or so from Churchville, New York. In high school and college he was an outstanding athlete. If I recall correctly, he was planning to teach physical education and coach in public school.

However, after graduation from college, Roger went into selling real estate. He was very successful in this and now owns his own company and mortgage loan business. Being an only child, Roger's parents were his best friends and vice versa. The family unity and mutual caring and sharing in love was very real and apparent to all who knew them well.

His parents are now deceased. Roger was there to help and care for them until the very end. While chatting with him one day I told him about my writing this book. Sensing his genuine interest, I invited him to share some of his Holy Moments with me that could be used herein.

I found out that this dear man has had many Holy Moments and they have been instrumental in giving him evidence and assurance of God's Presence with us. The experience he shares here came about as he was involved in hiring a new secretary for his business.

For many years I have had a keen interest in observing coincidences or Divine interventions. I have come to agree with the great thinker of the past when he said something like, "There is no such thing as a coincidence." For me, that is so helpful in my acceptance of miracles, of God's wondrous activities, of Holy moments, call it whatever you want.

An example of one such experience happened a few years ago when I needed to hire a secretary and two or three other persons. I was alone without a secretary, and I decided to try to get along with just a part-time person. In my effort to find some candidates, I phoned someone who had interviewed people for a like position. It turned out that he had interviewed someone whom he would have hired, but she could only work part-time and he needed a full-time secretary. He gave me her name and telephone number.

I called the number my friend had given me three or four times that afternoon. Since no one answered the phone, I decided to try and reach her from home that evening. No success. The next morning when I arrived at the office, I thought that I would try to reach her again.

Good thought. Now, mind you, I was the only person to be in this office. I had no employees at the time. But when I looked for the number I had written on a small piece of paper, that I had left on my desk, it was not to be found. So, somewhat disgusted with myself, I called my buddy back and asked for the phone number he had given me the day before. He said, "I'm sorry, but since I was not interested in a part-time person, I threw it away."

By now I was FRUSTRATED! To help me calm down, I decided to take an early lunch. I went to the restaurant in Churchville. An attractive and efficient appearing young woman came to wait on me. As she reached my table, without thinking about it, or intending to do it, I said, "Would you like to be my secretary?" She quickly replied, "I would love to."

The unique part of all this is that she did not know where my office was located, what kind of business I had, what the hours would be, nor what I was going to pay her. Since that most bizarre hiring of a new secretary, we have laughed about it many times. When I left the restaurant that day I said to myself, "What have I done? I've hired someone that I know nothing about. I don't even know her last name! In fact, I do not even know if she can type, file, if she has good telephone skills, comes to work on time or even she is an honest person"!

I went back to my office and there in plain sight, right beside my computer was the scrap of paper with the telephone number of the original person I had planned to call for an interview! How do you explain that? No one had been there and I had searched diligently for that piece of paper before giving up and going to lunch.

I cannot explain this series of events. But I can tell you that the young lady waitress came and she worked part-time for me for three-plus years. We have become real good friends and I am grateful for that Divine Intervention that put me in touch with her. She has been an ideal secretary and a wonderful friend to me. None of this would have happened if that piece of scrap paper with the telephone number on it had stayed where I finally found it, and where it was not, prior to my returning from lunch.

Yes, it has become a Holy Moment, when in frustration I asked an unknown waitress if she would like to be my secretary. She became not only an efficient and knowledgeable secretary; she also became the wonderful caring friend that I so desperately needed at that time.

Roger commented that he did not know how it could have happened as it did. But in essence, he said that he knew God had an important part in it. His remark reminded me of the response made by the man healed from blindness. When the Pharisees asked him who Jesus was, he remarked that he did not know, but this he knew, "Once I was blind, but now I can see"(John 9:25).

That is how we feel when a Holy Moment of Assurance and Peace strikes us. How could it happen; who did that and all such questions become irrelevant, if not inappropriate. God gives us these holy experiences to "grant us wisdom for the living of these days."

Jean Mathews (Mrs. Thomas)

Jean and her husband, Thomas Sr., are our neighbors at the Road Runner Travel Resort, in Ft. Pierce, Florida. We are neighbors during the winter months. During the summer months they live in McVeytown, Pennsylvania. Here they have proved to be good neighbors, and it has been a joy to get to know them a little more each year.

In the Christian Faith, they are Mennonites and thankfully they take their faith seriously. In our home area of New York, there are a number of Mennonites, and we have always felt a kinship in the faith with them. I think of this Christian Group as kind, loving, and caring people. Jean and Tom fit that "mode" without question. Great people.

Jean's experience took place on one side of the experience and her husband on the other, so to speak. Both pertain to the time when Thomas had a heart attack. It is interesting to hear of God's Holy Moment from the patient and the patient's dear wife.

> I am Jean Mathews, my husband Tom and I have been married forty-seven years. We have been blessed with three daughters and one son. In addition to that, we are now blessed with ten grandchildren and three great grandchildren.
>
> It has been sixteen years since Tom had his heart attack. At that time we had three weeks of not knowing if we were going to bring him home or not. His future was questionable; his life was in God's hands. I kept praying that he would recover and that I would be able to bring him home.

Then one day the doctor came to see me with some good news! The doctor, for the first time, told us that Tom was going to be okay. We were elated, to say the least. I sent all of our kids home and went to the motel to get some much needed sleep. Just before I was ready to go to bed, I called the hospital to see how Tom was doing.

I could not believe the words I was hearing, To my horror, they told me that they were just getting ready to call me because he had taken a turn for the worse. They were at that moment taking him to the operating room for emergency surgery. In a near state of shock, the first thing I did was to call our Pastor, Gerald Peachy.

I asked him to pray for Tom and to have the church family praying for him also. I was praying before I called, as I called and after I called. **My prayer was asking the dear Lord to give me the strength to face whatever happened.** My conversing with the Lord helped to give me that strength and the assurance of God's presence with Tom and with me.

We often think of the fact that the Lord works in ways that we cannot understand. Well, I quickly became aware of another truth, God works in ways I did not even think about. I am now so aware of what God was doing to help me. **I believe with all my heart that the Lord was trying to tell me to put my trust in him! God was telling me, "I will take care of you no matter what happens."**

Yes, when I was all alone with God, that personal relationship between God and me gave me strength and afforded me renewed hope and assurance, that I

could attain nowhere else. I live each day with a more real sense of God's Presence and with a Peace that is beyond my ability to explain. And that is because in putting my TRUST in God, I now know that God walks with me, and will care for me, no matter what happens to me, or to anyone else.

What a beautiful Holy Moment it must have been when Jean grasped the revelation God was giving her. Thanks for the sharing, Jean. Her candidly beautiful account of this experience brings to my mind the words of Proverbs 3:5-8

Trust in the Lord with all your heart,
And do not rely on your own insight.
In all your ways acknowledge him,
And he will make straight your paths.
Do not be wise in your own eyes;
Fear the Lord, and turn away from evil.
It will be a healing for your flesh
And a refreshment for your body.

Now, we will turn to Jean's husband and we will interestingly find his Holy Moment of Assurance and Peace that parallels that given to his dear wife.

Thomas G. Mathews Sr.

As I mentioned at the offset of Jean and Tom's "introduction," they are our neighbors at the campsite. Once we got to know one another, he readily agreed to share an important Holy Moment with me for this book. The experience happened to him a number of years ago, but is as fresh to him now as the morning dew.

It was 4:00 o'clock in the morning when I was awakened with terrible chest pains. I thought that I had a bad case of indigestion. Wrong! I was taken to the emergency room at the hospital. There they proved it was a heart attack. I was just forty-eight years old.

I was in one hospital for two days and in another hospital for two weeks. I had angioplasty two times in two days. I was in terrible, horrible pain.

About 10:00 o'clock that night I was taken to the operating room for emergency surgery. While I was on the operating table, and while the doctors were working on me, I heard a voice. I **quickly realized that it was the Lord speaking to me. He said, "The reason I am not taking you now is because of all the prayers for you."** I was completely awake during that time. I felt like I was floating above the table but I returned to the table shortly after I heard those words.

I then heard the doctor say, "I think we have found the problem." They proceeded to repair a clogged vessel to my heart, without having to do open heart surgery. Amazingly, the next morning I felt well enough to go home.

That was sixteen years ago as of February 2006. I praise God for his love and kindness. During those sixteen beautiful years, I have had the blessing of five more of my ten grandchildren and three great grandchildren coming into my life.

God comes in so many ways, His love to display and share. What a blessing and what a Holy Moment of Assurance and Peace that must have been! With thanks for his delightful witness and faith-increasing sharing of that Holy Moment, I would call our attention to some further words found in the passage from Proverbs 3:21-26:

> My child, do not let these escape from your sight:
> Keep sound wisdom and prudence,
> And they will be life for your soul
> And adornment for your neck.
> Then you will walk on your way securely
> And your foot will not stumble.
> If you sit down, you will not be afraid;
> When you lie down, your sleep will be sweet.
> Do not be afraid of sudden panic,
> Or of the storm that strikes the wicked;
> For the Lord will be your confidence
> And will keep your foot from being caught.

Lorraine Hendrickson

I introduced my sister, Lorraine, in Chapter Four. She's the one who flew from Rochester to New York City with her boyfriend to get a cup of coffee! She lives in Colleyville, Texas, with her husband, the guy who took her for coffee! In this shared experience, Lorraine is sharing her Holy Moment while preparing and delivering he daughter, Mona. She, by the way, is a sweetheart, and her two brothers Gabe and Dale are a couple of the nicest young men you could ever meet.

For me "serenity" is a beautiful word. To have this state of being is to possess an ultimate ingredient in living life to the fullest. It can only be achieved by walking closely with God. The spiritual song, "Put your hand in the hand of the man who stilled the water" is the type of relationship of which I speak.

My personal journey was nourished like a fragile flower; like one that needs to be nurtured and grows only with proper care. My spiritual life was certainly nourished by my parents as role models, along with love from family, aunts, uncles, and cousins. There is not a day that goes by that I do not verbalize to God my thankfulness for such a foundation in the faith.

It seems to me that there is a time in life when a situation presents itself, an epiphany—-caused by great joy, by sadness, by fear or something that causes you to be raised to a higher level of consciousness. Then a feeling of thanksgiving and humility before God prompts one to turn to God in total supplication. With such an experience your awareness is truly beginning.

Every day I find myself contemplating some words from scripture, or from a hymn or song that is comforting or helpful. I repeatedly thank God for my many blessings.

Prior to my marriage to the man I loved, I became more aware of God's Presence and my need for God. This was many years ago, and my parents were concerned because this young man was a Roman Catholic. I knew my parents only wanted what they thought was best for me. I also knew that he was the one and only young man I loved and wanted to marry.

During this difficult time, I found myself walking from my work place to a Roman Catholic Church that was close by. I spent many lunch hours there, praying for God's help, guidance, courage and support. I already knew he would be a wonderful husband and father. In this close relationship with God, I found the courage and conviction to accept Jack's wedding proposal.

Seeking and finding that closer relationship not only helped me to have a joyous and blessed wedding, it also enabled me to have a sense of that "serenity" of which I previously wrote.

To be blessed with children is awesome. To think that God has given you the honor, privilege, and love to guide and nourish his creation, is truly a blessing. We have two sons and one daughter. My communication and my walk with our Creator took another big step forward, with the birth of our daughter. It was a breach birth. When she was born she had numerous serious health problems.

I was in bed for several hours after delivery without yet seeing my newborn. Finally, the doctor came to talk to me. He said they were doing everything in their power to take care of our baby. He elaborated on many things, most of which I did not focus on very clearly. But then, as the kind doctor was leaving, his last words to me were, "We are doing all we can do and it is really up to God." Wow, those words got my attention in a hurry!

Once again, I found myself in a place along the walk of life that I could not handle alone. Again, I was truly aware that as always, God is the One we can call out to and ask for help. It was and still is a blessing to be copiously aware of that truth. **I vividly recall talking to God about that doctor's last words to me. I told God that I would accept His Will, and if He did allow her to live, I WOULD DEVOTE MY LIFE TO HER CARE, and WHATEVER IT TOOK.**

I am immensely grateful to be able to say that we were blessed to have our daughter live and be a part of our family. She was a beautiful, talented and intelligent child. I would rate her with the same attributes still today. She now has a devoted and loving husband and they are the parents of two of the best children any grandparents could hope to have.

My daughter's birth, like all experiences in our lives journey on earth, makes us who we are. We had experienced a number of miscarriages before her birth. She has been a rich blessing to all of us in our family unit.

Here is yet another inspiring example of how God touches us and feeds us with the food of increased faith. As I read and reflected upon Lorraine's shared experience, I could not help but feel sincerity in her sharing of her faith journey. Being my little sister, I could hear her speaking as I read her words. What was so special for me was how, in the experiences shared she so candidly put her trust in God, that a Holy Moment of Assurance and Peace engulfed her very being. Jesus said it would be so:

> "So I say to you, Ask, and it will be given you;
> Search, and you will find; knock, and the door will be opened for you. For everyone who asks, receives, and everyone who searches, finds, and for everyone who knocks, the door will be opened" (Luke 11:9-10).

Thanks, Lorraine, for sharing with all who read this book. You are a blessing to us.

Mary S. Reagan

Mary is my youngest of two daughters. Mary was born in Bangor, Maine, in a rather speedy fashion. I took Audrey to the hospital, dropping her off at the front door in the care of nurse who was expecting us. I then parked our car in the hospital lot. As I ran to the main entrance, our obstetrician was just pulling in. He screeched on his brakes, jumped out of the car and said, "Park my car, I have a baby to deliver!"

After that, I hurried to the delivery room, where that same nurse met me with the words, "You have a beautiful baby girl!" I had a momentary thought of being mistaken by the happy appearing nurse. She sensed it, I guess, because she said, "Yes it is your baby, she is the only baby we have in the hospital!"

Poor child. When the nurse first let Audrey see her newborn, Audrey said, "That can't be my baby, she is too big." That nurse used the same words, "Yes, it's your baby, she's the only one we have in the whole hospital!"

Thankfully, our dear Mary had no idea that both her parents had questions as to her actually being their child. I am happy to say, and I suspect a bit proud to say, we have never questioned her being our child since. She is a dear. She has compassion for all people and all creatures as well. (Well, I am not too sure I can say that about snakes.)

In high school Mary played a trumpet and was in the band, marching band and just about any other place where one would blow a horn. In fact, she was part of a group of former students that joined together to play at their old high school, in an effort to give appreciation and honor to their retiring director, C. Edward VanZandt, in March of 2006.

Mary was also very much involved in sports. She played one game on the Junior Varsity basketball team. After her first game, in which, as I remember it, she made eighteen points, she was immediately moved to the varsity level, where she played all four years of high school. She was fast and such a good shot that she was a delight to watch. I did at one time enjoy shooting baskets with her, now I hesitate, not much fun if you can never win!

Following her graduation from the State University of New York at Geneseo, Mary began working for the Department of Social Services for Wyoming County, in Warsaw, New York. She went from there to become a social worker for the Wyoming County Community Hospital, in Warsaw. She was a natural at her work. Her employer and those with whom she worked appreciated her gentle, kind, and effective work.

Mary's sharing of a Holy Moment of Assurance and Peace was an experience she had at home when she was a child.

One of my earliest memories of feeling God's love and all surrounding peace was when I was eight years old. It was shortly before the school year began. I was to be starting the third grade.

My dad returned from a rescue (ambulance) call, which was one of many for him at that time. But this call was so very different. One of my second grade classmates had been hit by a car and killed. Although my dad was always a sensitive man, I am not sure that I had ever seen him so sad and tearful.

I retreated to my bedroom and I sat, looking out the back window at the trees behind our house. With tears streaming down my face, I could only think of one thing, "Why?"

Instantly, **I felt a love and peace filling my entire room and I thought I heard the words, "It will be okay, trust me."**

We had company coming for dinner that night; a minister and his family from out of town. While they were there, when sadness would sweep upon me and **I would feel tears beginning to develop, I would think of the experience I had earlier that day in my bedroom, and I would feel peace and my tears would evaporate.**

God is so intently involved in our lives that it makes your head spin. Here is an example of which I was very much involved. Mary was with all of us that evening, for dinner and thereafter, yet while God was comforting her, and drying her tears, none of us were aware of what was going on between God and her.

I find the words of this hymn, appropriate here and so very true.

"The Wonder of It All" (by George Beverly Shea)

There's the wonder of the sunset at evening,
The wonder as sunrise I see,
But wonder of wonders that thrills my soul
Is the wonder that God loves me.
There's the wonder of springtime and harvest,
The sky, the stars, the sun;
But the wonder of wonders that thrills my soul
Is the wonder that's only begun.
(Refrain): O the wonder of it all! The wonder of it all!
Just to think that God loves me.
O the wonder of it all! The wonder of it all!
Just to think that God loves me.

Thanks, Mary, for your sharing that Holy Moment with us and for your continued sharing of compassion and love each new day.

The Holy Moments of Assurance and Peace that God sends our way are so priceless on our journeys through life on this planet. While those moments are often so very personal, yet as we share them and their meaning for us, they become a very real part of who we really are. Indeed, as we share the fact that "God is still speaking" we are supported in our own experiences, and we become an encouragement for others. Yes, our sharing of and in the faith, is a stimulation for others to take ever more seriously their discipleship to Jesus the Christ.

To one and all, I petition you, keep all this shared love of God in your hearts and minds. And **keep your ears and eyes open to the many moments that you yourself will know as "Holy."** Unquestionably, there will be moments that will give to you an assurance of God's presence and love, along with a peace that is beyond description.

CHAPTER SEVEN

God Prepares Our Path

Like most of the Psalms, the Twenty-Third Psalm is packed full of significant meaning for our lives. In this chapter we are sharing personal experiences that are highlighted by the Psalmist's words found in this familiar Psalm. Verse two includes the words, "He leads me beside still waters" and verse three includes the words, "He leads me in right paths." HE LEADS ME, are words that we will be keeping in mind in this chapter. Those who have so kindly shared these experiences have found them to have had a significant influence in the direction of their lives.

To fully grasp the significant impact of God's leading us in our lives is to have a companionship of love with God that surpasses all relationships, bar none. As the Psalmist writes, "Even though I walk through the darkest valley, I will fear no evil; for You are with me…."

Our Christian friends who share their experiences with us have a renewed appreciation of God's desire and willingness to lead us as we live in this world. I want to begin with a most unexpected experience that happened in a Funeral Home. The experience brought a sense of great joy and appreciation for a loved one's life.

Susan Merriam Koval

Susan is the granddaughter of my mentor, the Reverend Ellwyn Merriam. He was my pastor for most of my elementary and high school days. He not only officiated at our wedding, but some three years later he baptized our first child. Susan is the daughter of two greatly loved people. Her mom, Dodie, and her dad, Zeke, were conduits of joy and laughter. They were living examples of what it means to love and accept all people as sister and brothers in Christ.

Now, Susan is all of that, plus she has her own extraordinary sensitivity to God's presence in all of life. She is a stewardess for one of our major airlines. She often shares with Audrey and me how God's being wherever she is gives her a sense of awe and peace. She is a great person and we love her dearly.

Susan shared this experience with us. We took notes as she talked about this experience. The eventuality only occurred because of a lifetime of shared love and family unity in their home. Sue spoke of how, as they grew up, her brothers would wear each other's clothes. This was especially true of her brother, Paul. He, being the youngest and quite naturally the smallest, was a regular recipient of his older brother's clothes. Paul always had "hand-me-downs" which may have been part of his desire and reasoning for putting on his brothers' clothes before they were handed down! After all, one might wonder how this or that would feel and/or look.

As the family grew up, some words often heard in the family household were, "Mom, Paul has my socks on!" or maybe, "Mom, Paul has my pants on!" That short explanatory sentence was heard frequently. Consequently, in their adulthood they remembered it well.

To help us more fully appreciate this shared experience, Susan explained that her brother Roger was an automobile mechanic. He came naturally by it; his father was one of the best mechanics in our area of the country. Her brother Bobby was a contractor and he basically never wore a suit. But when he was invited to a formal wedding service and reception, Bobby had to buy himself a new suit. He went to K-Mart and grabbed a good-looking suit. It looked really sharp on him.

Following the wedding and reception, Bobby hung the suit in an upstairs closet, expecting it would be quite some time before he put it on again. He also thought that if he ever had an occasion to wear a suit again, it would be hanging right where he put it.

Sometime later, Bobby moved to Georgia. Shortly thereafter, his brother, Paul, tragically left the confines of this world, joining his dearly beloved father in the Eternal Kingdom..

Understandably, the entire family was grief stricken. In their deep sorrow, sense of loss and mourning, they had to plan for Paul's funeral. In all the necessary arrangements, they had not given much thought about what clothes Paul would be buried in.

When it came time to make that decision, someone suggested to Jim, a close family friend, that he run upstairs and get a suit for Paul to wear. Jim looked around, could not find a suitable suit, until he came across Bob's K-Mart suit. He grabbed it and ran down the stairs. He handed it to the undertaker and said, "Here, this will work well."

While all that was going on, Bobby was running a bit behind time. The family was to go to the funeral home, just prior to calling hours. The others in the family had just left for the funeral home when Bob came hurrying in to shower and put on his suit. He looked and looked but there was no K-Mart suit to be found.

Being industrious as he is, Bobby found something to wear and hurried to the funeral home. He arrived just after the others in the family had gone in to see brother Paul's remains. It was tough. Tears were common for all of his family as they gathered together, prior to the public's visitation. Like many a family before them, their faith in God was strong. They knew Paul was at Peace and in God's Eternal Kingdom. In juxtaposition, they mourned his leaving them; they knew they would seriously miss him in the future. The immediate concern shifted as they realized that any minute they would be greeting the general public. Without ever verbalizing it, individually they were concerned as to how they were going to gain their composure. Their brother was loved and so deeply missed. **Well, this is when God took over the lead for the family.**

When Bobby came into the room, he was equally grief stricken as the others. Then, he noticed the clothes his succumbed brother was wearing. There was his missing K-Mart suit! **Without thinking about it, Bob blurted out, "MOM, PAUL HAS MY SUIT ON!"**

Susan knows that was God's leading them in the time of great sorrow. When those words popped out of his

mouth, the whole family burst into joyful laughter. Those impromptu words changed their whole perspective. They went from feeling so devastated and so grief stricken— to remembering Paul's life of joy and love with them. Indeed, in that turn around from centering on Paul's death, to centering on his life, came about by the unrehearsed and unplanned words that were so treasured by the family.

With thanks for God leading them, Paul's family was able to appropriately greet those who came to express their condolences. In that new focus, they were able to be living examples of God's Love and the assurance of God's Presence.

Humor is a very real way to help us refocus. When he unexpectedly came out with those meaningful words for the family, Bobby was an instrument of God, even though he surely did not know it.

God leads us into still waters. God leads us and God prepares a path for us to follow. Wherever we are going, wherever we have been, God seeks to lead us to an ever more meaningful relationship with God and God's Son, Jesus.

Thanks to Susan for sharing this experience. God does work in many ways; some are actually aimed at making us laugh, and in the laughter, to clear our minds to help us refocus!

Dorothy and Wayne Burlingame

I have always felt close to Dorothy. I was the sixth child in our family and she was the seventh. There was a brief time when Dorothy and I, and our younger sister, Lorraine, were the only children who lived at home. I guess that we were drawn closer as we did the family household chores, shared in school events and a variety of family activities.

After I was drafted into the Army, I learned that Dorothy was dating a very nice young man. I responded, "He'd better be nice!" The next thing I heard about Dorothy's friend was during a phone call. Audrey and I were making final plans for our wedding service and Audrey suggested that we should have this guy Dorothy was dating as our soloist. I wasn't too sure about that, until she assured me that he had a voice that was truly beyond belief. Wayne did sing at our wedding. I can still remember his singing of The Lord's Prayer. He had a voice that was beyond description, and so it was all of his days.

Dorothy and Wayne were later married and they have shared some personal experiences of God's involvement in their lives. **It was a few months after I received their typewritten experiences, that Wayne left this world.** He and Dorothy were moving a ladder in their backyard when Wayne simply tripped and fell. The fall caused him to be paralyzed, and he was put on a respirator to keep him alive. His injury and ultimate death left us all in shock.

Dorothy, their two children, Lori and Paul, as well as Paul's wife, Nancy, and their children, and all of us in his extended family felt his departure so profoundly. It was all so unbelievable. Wayne had been a great and loving husband, father, grandfather and friend, all which made the void so huge.

Dorothy and her family are getting along quite well now. Their faith in God, their family togetherness, and the all but unbelievable support of friends, have helped them tremendously.

Lori, their daughter, is now Dr. Lori Burlingame. She teaches at Eastern Michigan University; Paul, their son, is now a police officer in the Albany, New York area.

Wayne typed the sharing that follows. It is a message of God preparing their pathways in the life they lived together.

Dorothy and I were married in September 1955. We, like all young couples, had dreams for the future. We looked forward to having children, having a home of our own, and a successful career of some sort. We were very fortunate in establishing our own home. We settled down in Churchville, New York. Then the great recession of the 1950s became a reality. Jobs were hard to find and as a result, I was unemployed. After much soul searching we decided that I should try to go to college. This decision led to a degree in Music Education from State University of New York (SUNY) at Fredonia and a teaching position in Oriskany High School, near Utica, New York.

In retrospect, we could easily see how, in our married life, God was ever preparing a path for us in the wilderness of life. After a number of years, our concern over not having children brought us to the realization that we would have to choose another path if we were going to have children. We both felt that God was guiding us in that direction. As a result of this, we applied to adopt a child. Several months went by. Our case worker was a lovely lady who worked very hard and she felt that there would be a child who would be perfect for us. All during this effort, we felt that God's hand was at work through her.

One morning in May 1966, I was teaching a class at school when a knock came at the door. Dorothy was outside, (she was employed part-time in our guidance office). There was a wonderful smile on her face. She said, "We have a daughter!" We were to meet her the following day. She was a beautiful baby and we loved her instantly. God had led us down life's path to this point and we were so very grateful.

We loved Lori so much, we wanted another child. Wayne felt that now was the time for us to adopt another child. He thought we should not wait and then miss this certain child. Again, we sensed that God was leading us down this particular path. And we were blessed with our son, Paul. We truly believe that this was God's plan and we rejoice in these two beautiful gifts that God brought into our lives. If we had waited, it might not have been Paul.

Dorothy and Wayne conscientiously followed the path that God was leading them. It is therefore not at all surprising that they know they made the right choices. This is a truth of life that we should all grasp. When we walk down the path set by God and by trying our best to follow God's lead—there is no way that we can fail. It is when we side step the path or take a detour elsewhere that we find ourselves making errors in judgment and not being true to the love God has for us. Lori and Paul were indeed the right choice. They are beautiful people and one would never guess that they were adopted. They and their parents made up a family unit that, as their parents believed, was made in heaven.

It would be perfect to stop here, but life sometimes brings not only joy, but also pain. In 1989, Easter Sunday, after church and a family dinner, we played a round of golf with Paul. He left after this to return to college at Alfred University where he was a junior. At 5:20 the next morning our phone rang. It was a nurse at St. James Hospital in Hornell, New York—Paul had suffered serious burns in a fire at the fraternity house.

When we got the horrific news of Paul's injury, we called a friend. This began the outreach of prayers from our friends and Church family. We called our family in Churchville; prayers were begun throughout the world for Paul. The doctors were outstanding in their efforts to keep him alive. In this short number of words it is hard to express the closeness we felt with our Lord and Savior throughout this time of uncertainty and agonizing suffering. To this day, the miracle God gave still grows and shines."

Paul spent 74 days in the Intensive Care Unit at Strong Memorial Hospital in Rochester, New York. (He was 20 years old on the 21st, the day he woke up from Adult Respiratory Distress Syndrome (ARDS) for the first time.) Our son also spent two weeks in our local hospital, and again, some time in the Intensive Care Unit. God was present with us in this time of trial.

For nearly three months, Paul was in the Intensive Care Unit at Strong Memorial and Dorothy and Wayne were there as well! It was an extremely difficult time for all who knew and loved Paul. It was also an extremely amazing time. Utica is about a two-hour drive on the expensive New York

Thruway. And in spite of the time and money involved, Dorothy and Wayne had friends from their hometown and/or their Church family sitting in the waiting room with them nearly every day. It was so beautiful to witness. God had to have been guiding these dear people down the paths of love and support during this time. For me, it was an intensely powerful display of the Love our Lord called for us to share with one another.

Dorothy and Wayne had another deeply troublesome time in their journey together. They also shared this next experience with me for this book.

> The dreaded words, "You have cancer" happened to us. Wayne had cancer! You feel like your life is gone, that there is so much more to live for, so much more love to give and receive. Our children were there for us from the very beginning. Our Lord and Savior was with us during this time of worry and in the decisions we had to make. We could feel His presence with us. Thankfully, we could also feel His presence in the necessary therapy that was given to combat that invasive malignancy.
>
> **Throughout our lives we feel that God has been there in times of joy, and times of sorrow and pain. Without God, we do not think our lives would have come to this point. We have two wonderful children, a beautiful daughter-in-law, three beautiful grand children, and lives that are filled with love of family and friends. With God's blessing we cherish yesterday, dream of tomorrow, and live today.**

Wayne, as I mentioned earlier, has left our world and has entered the Eternal Kingdom, as our Lord has promised to all who follow Him. **All who truly knew Wayne have been blessed by his uncompromising love for one and all. We have been blessed over and again as he shared his God-given talent by singing and singing and singing. But, as I ponder the beautiful way he lived among us, I feel we have been blessed as well by the way he wore his Faith in God on his sleeves!**

That is who he was and is still. If he were to write the ending words to share his true Love for God, for Jesus the Christ, for Dorothy and his whole family—-I truly suspect that he would rewrite the words with which he summed up his sharing experiences above. He perhaps would add something like, "Remember, I will be waiting and watching 'til we meet again!"

I just loved to hear Wayne sing; one solo that I've heard him sing, that I have never forgotten is so appropriate here. **The words express the faith that Dorothy and he had as they walked down the paths of life, holding each other's hand and clasping their hands in the hand of God. The solo, His Eye Is On the Sparrow** (Author: Charles H. Gabriel), was so beautiful that I can all but hear it still, as I remember when he sang it, and ponder the words, which are:

> "Why should I feel discouraged, Why should the shadows come Why should my heart be lonely and long for heav'n and home When Jesus is my portion? My constant friend is he: His eye is on the sparrow, and I know He watches me; His eye is on the sparrow, and I know He watches me. (Refrain)

(2) Let not your heart be troubled,' His tender word I hear,
And resting on His goodness I lose my doubt and fears;
Though by the path he leadeth But one step I may see: His
eye is on the sparrow, And I know He watches me; His
eye is on the sparrow, And I know He watches me. (Refrain)

(3) Whenever I am tempted, Whenever clouds arise,
When songs give place to sighing, When hope within me dies,
I draw the closer to Him, From care He sets me free; His
eye is on the sparrow, and I know He cares for me; His
eye is on the sparrow, and I know He cares for me.
(Refrain) I sing because I'm happy, I sing because I'm free,
For His eye is on the sparrow, and I know He watches me.

Wayne and Dorothy have shared how vividly they have experienced God's Presence in their lives. They shared how God prepared for their pathway, and enabled them not only to walk in it but to know they never walked without the Presence of God and/or God's Son, Jesus the Christ. I thank them for this positive sharing and I give praise to God that Wayne and Dorothy were able to share this, prior to his departure from this world.

An Anonymous Couple

I have made it a policy to introduce all participates in this book. The reason for that is I want you who read these experiences, to know they are real people. Their experiences are authentic and are shared in this book because of the impact they have had on their lives.

Here, however, I am making an exception. As a clergyman who has been involved in many people's lives, including many who have been referred to me by individuals in groups like Alcoholics Anonymous (AA), I want to share this story and in doing so allow the couple sharing to be anonymous. We will know them as "Jack and Jill" because I realized they had an enormous hill to climb!

Jill was an alcoholic. Jack realized his wife was in a critical situation. Doctors had done surgery and reported to Jack that there was nothing more they could do for her. Jill had been told they could remove the blood vessels from her esophagus to the outside. This would prevent them from hemorrhaging any more when she drank alcohol. **Her doctor told her that surgery might save her life. "It is necessary," said the doctor, "because you cannot quit drinking." When Jill heard that all this horrible surgery was necessary because she could not stop drinking, she responded with, "OH YEAH, WATCH ME!"**

Jill refused to have the surgery and told her husband, "And don't go over my head to get someone else to sign anything either." The medical team required her to sign before they did the surgery. After her refusal to have that operation, the medical team told Jack that her life was in the balance, and she probably would not live for very long.

Jack said that was extremely difficult news for him to hear. Thinking of their many years of married life, the joys of their children, and their hopes and dreams for the future seemed to be blown helter-skelter like dust in a desert storm. Jack decided that since he had been in the hospital all night and since Jill was still heavily sedated, he would go home, take a shower, get a change of clothes, and come back.

On his way out of the hospital, he went to the chapel. Jack says he has no idea how long he might have been there—a half hour, an hour, he just didn't know. But while he was in the chapel, Jack spoke candidly with God, asking God's help for Jill's health. He also prayed for his own ability to be the person that God wanted him to be, in sickness and in health.

When Jack left the chapel, he felt a sense of calmness as he realized that he had now done everything in his power he could do. He was confident that Jill knew he loved her, and treasured their long life together as husband and wife. In his heart, Jack knew he had done everything he could do medically, by getting her the best of care. And now that he had turned her life over to God's tender care, he felt a sense of relief. Jack said it was amazing, the relief he felt after he earnestly and sincerely turned her life and their future over to God.

When asked if she had a sense of God's presence with her during her critical time, when she refused that last surgery, she said that when she heard the words, "Because you can't stop drinking," something happened that made her realize, with confidence, that she could overcome her drinking problem. **It was as if God just put those words in my mouth and at the same time made me aware that His presence would guide my path to overcome.**

Because this couple entwined their lives in God's love and were able to support each other in their distress and great need, they have told me that alcohol is no longer a problem for her. Living in the west, they choose their friends carefully, so as to be sure the "flow of alcohol" does not become a problem.

Jill knows that it was God who helped her, who prepared the path in which she could walk safely and soberly hand in hand with God. I have met with and counseled with many dear people who have been basically crippled with the disease of alcoholism. But I have never known anyone to make such a dramatic turn-around, as did Jill. God's name be praised!

She was at the bottom of the hill, so to speak, when the pathway that God prepares finally became visible. With God's help she took off "up the hill" and never looked back! Today, Jack tells me that they are at the top of the hill, mutually enjoying life and praising God for so clearly preparing the path for them to follow.

I do hear from them at Christmas and sporadically during the year. They tell me, they have never been happier. They also "report" that they are involved in their church and seek to be the disciples, Jesus would have them be. Thanks be to God for preparing the path for them and walking it with them!

Tamara Pardee Burton

I know Tamara as "Tami," the granddaughter of one of my most active members in the church where I was pastor for many years. Tami's grandmother, Gladys Pardee, spoke of Tami so often and so lovingly that my wife and I felt like we knew her before we had the joy of meeting her! She grew up in Buffalo, New York, and now lives with her husband and children in Gaithersburg, Maryland.

We have had the opportunity to be with Tami on a few occasions and I am happy to say that her grandma was not overly exaggerating Tami's attributes. Upon hearing from her after she read my book, I felt humbled. When I asked her to share an experience for this book, she pleasantly agreed. She has a strong faith in God and practices her Christian Faith in the Roman Catholic Church.

Tami now shares a very meaningful experience that she had at a time of deep sorrow.

> This was my closest communication with God. It was certainly when I needed God the most! It was on the drive to Buffalo, to see my father who was in the hospital. I wanted to see him before he died, even though I was told his death was imminent.
>
> I prayed and cried all the way there from Maryland. I made the trip with only one brief stop, but even during that stop I continued to pray as I did all the way. I even enlisted the help of my grandfathers in heaven, petitioning them to hold dad's hand until I got there.
>
> As I traveled, it appeared that every cloud formation had the imprint of God's face. In retrospect, I realize that it was a divine action that kept me cognizant of the fact I did not travel alone.
>
> My father was still alive when I got there, but there was really no hope of his recovery. We agonized over turning off life supports. Knowing his medical condition and being aware of dad's wishes, we made that decision. Once the decision was made, each family member was going to sit and say goodbye. Only my brother, Larry, got to do that—Dad died "on his own" before the nurses came to unhook all the tubes.
>
> Larry was holding Dad's hand and my mother, my other brother Chad and I were in the room. **The next**

thing I saw was a fine white light come out of thin air and surround his body. The light shimmered and then disappeared. It was like his spirit/soul was gone and I knew he had really left us.

It was the first time in my life, that I knew what it really felt like to have my heart break. I mentioned this experience of the light to my cousin, Bev, and she instantly said, "I was in the presence of angels coming to take Dad to heaven." Her words were both amazing and comforting, as was the experience, knowing that God prepared the path on which the angels tread.

Thank you, Tami, for sharing that sacred moment with us. God is so good. Again, how wonderful are the ways that God prepares the paths for us to walk. God is still speaking to us in all sorts of ways. Tami's experience reminds me of the occurrence that the disciples experienced after Jesus' death.

As they were watching Jesus, he was lifted up and a cloud took him out of their sight. While he was going and they were gazing up toward heaven, suddenly two men in white robes stood by them. They said, "Men of Galilee why do you stand looking up toward heaven? This Jesus, who has been taken up from you into heaven, will come in the same way as you saw him go into heaven."

Evelyn Page

If my memory serves me correctly, the first time I met Evelyn and her husband, Gordon, was at their home where a couples group gathered for a tureen dinner. They were great hosts and my wife and I still remember the group singing, led by Gordon on the guitar.

Evelyn and Gordon were energetic members of our church. At the time of his untimely death, Gordon was the Historian of the church. Evelyn was my secretary and held the title of Administrative Coordinator. Evelyn was my secretary for over twenty-five years. She was such a valuable helper, always cheerful, totally confidential when her position gained her privileged information about others. It mattered not, whether she gained information about those who were in counseling with me or from people who may have discussed personal problems or concerns with her. I was never concerned that confidential matters would not remain confidential. That is a most valuable attribute for any secretary, but especially so for secretaries of pastors and counselors.

I would be hard pressed to try and list all of her areas of activity in the church. Evelyn had at one time or another done everything from directing vocal and hand bell choirs to being Church Organist; from teaching Sunday School to being the Financial Secretary for the church family.

Evelyn shares with us how she has felt God' presence with her, day after day and year after year.

> Fortunately, I was born in the United States of America, into a Christian family. And, thanks be to God, God's presence has been with me all of my life. Sometimes I have wondered why I am thus blessed, when so many others in the world deal with such poverty, inhumanity, diseases and hunger.

I remember it so well. When I was a child playing in a neighborhood barn haymow with other children, we would climb up a ladder into the mow and then jump off into loose hay on the barn floor below. As we were joyfully doing this, some of the kids started turning summersaults on the way down.

It looked like fun, so without much thought or concern about anything, I tried it. However, my summersault was not a success and I landed on the back of my neck. Needless to say, I did not try a repeat of that stunt!

Fortunately, I was not injured. I thank God that I did not break my neck and end up with paralysis of some kind. **Looking back at this experience, I am sure God was there protecting me even then, although I was oblivious of God's presence.**

In my adulthood, I continue to be cognizant of God's involvement in my life. God has often prepared a path for me to follow, even though I have the choice to walk in it or not. I have tried to take the path God has planned for me. Being blessed with a good husband, we lived together in devoted love and were blessed day after day in a joyful, faithful, and committed marriage.

After years of marriage, Gordon was diagnosed with Alzheimer's disease. Doing all I could to help him with his disease was increasingly difficult as the disease progressed. It took all of my faith and the aid of my pastor, my church family, friends and family to see me through the years dealing with his Alzheimer problems.

Here again, I thank God for preparing the path for our journey. It was a path on which we journeyed together; a path where I knew God's love and compassion. Whether my dear husband remained cognizant of that presence or not, I cannot be sure.

There are other times when God's presence has been more strongly felt. One of those times was when I underwent a triple by-pass surgery. God kept me calm and serenely ready for any outcome during and following the surgery. God did the same thing again, when I had a car accident, saving me from any serious injuries, while at the same time, my car was completely destroyed.

In our journey through life, God is always with us. In her first experience, Evelyn indicated that she was thankful for God's protecting presence, even though she was not aware of that presence at the moment. That is part of the glory of God's love. It is never absent from us, be we jumping from a haymow or casually walking in an evening's twilight. We can be oblivious to God's love and presence or fully aware of it, but, praise be to God, our awareness has no bearing on God's reality with us.

Evelyn, thank you for sharing with us. Your overview of God's presence in your life is a positive attribute for us all to strive to attain, and improve upon. Evelyn also wrote that her favorite hymn was, "God Will Take Care of You." Anyone who can sing the words of that hymn with a depth of assurance, knows God's Love never diminishes nor does

God's presence ever wander away from whatever path we may find ourselves.

Ruth Broughton

I have known Ruth for over forty years. She is a member of our church in Castile. Ruth is simply a dear, dear person. She has, over the years, made more beautifully decorated cakes than I could begin to tabulate; weddings, anniversaries, birthdays, celebrations, are among the kinds of occasions when she would appear at our door with a cake, marvelously decorated and a mouth watering taste.

Ruth has what is known as a "green thumb," the results of which are seen in an array of magnificent flowers. Those flowers have been seen on the church altar, as well as in the gardens that grace her home. She is sharing an experience that reminds me that God not only prepares our individual paths, but God also prepares the path for those who might come our way in times of need.

> I live in a trailer that has a small back porch. It is thirty-six inches from the railing on each side and twenty-eight inches from the door to the edge of the first step. On the last Sunday of March 2000, I came home from church as usual. I then went to open the storm door that goes to that back porch.
>
> The wind was very strong and as I opened the door, the wind caught the door and threw it open. I don't leave the safety spring attached to the door because I have

repeatedly had the door close so quickly that it caught my heels with a painful slap!

In the process, because I was hanging on to the door, the force of the wind and the quick moving door, I was picked up and thrown ten feet past the porch and onto the ground. It all happened so fast, that I flew past the railing without ever touching it and landed on my left shoulder.

I was almost eighty-six years old at that time. I was not able to get up from the ground without someone to help me or without something to hang on to. The only choice I had was to call for help. My son lives in the house that is on the other side of the garage and barn. I realized no one could hear me with all the noise of the blowing wind. But, I kept calling and trying to get up.

At this time my son started out to the garage and when he got out there, he had no idea for what it was that he came out. But as he got closer he found out. When he was between the barn and the house he could hear me calling. He came running like a deer and got me up and into the trailer.

My left shoulder was hurting very badly. Consequently, Bill took me to the hospital where I was given an x-ray. Thankfully, I did not have any broken bones. I had a light blue suit on that morning and I unbelievably could not find any dirt on it, even after landing in the dirt, and all that struggling I did trying to get up.

As I contemplate all of the above experiences and many others similar, I thank God for walking the paths of life with me. I know that in the last few years I have experienced several of God's miracles. I am sure that I have a guardian angel watching over me. I am so very thankful to God, for he prepares my path, be it when blown in the wind or riding other highways of life.

What a blessing her experiences are to us. Over and over again Ruth has experienced the presence of God in her life. For her to recognize that God does prepare a way for us has to be a blessing not to be taken lightly.

It is significant that Ruth's son, Bill, could not think of any reason that took him out of his comfortable house and into the blowing wind. Numerous times we have heard of such experiences. So often, when we walk where we think God points us, we later find out that it must have been God's path for us, because of the events that took place on the journey.

Thanks, Ruth for your sharing. May it help us all to be ever more aware that we never travel alone. And may we also be enriched as we recall that God prepares paths for us to follow, and by following, we are blessed beyond all belief.

Doris and Norman Dubie

I first introduced the Reverend Dubie in Chapter One) When Audrey and I first arrived in Bangor, Maine for me to attend Seminary, we lived across the city from the Seminary. In familiarizing ourselves with the area, we came upon a small church. On our first Sunday in Bangor, we attended that church named the Forest Avenue Congregational Church (United Church of Christ).

I particularly wanted to worship there because I learned that a student from the Bangor Theological Seminary was the pastor. Following a most meaningful and worshipful service, I was more than impressed! I quickly gave myself a reality check. Norm was a student at the seminary. He preached like a pro. My real concern became, how far I had to go before I could preach like that. Thankfully, I soon realized that God only asked for our best effort, whatever that might be.

Norm and Doris and their children and our family became good friends. We lived in the same apartment complex and had many good times together. After he graduated, we kept in contact.

The experience that they sent me to share in this book includes me. From phone conversations and notes I was asked to write up their experience. Here it is:

> I was still a student in seminary when my family and I traveled to Manchester, New Hampshire to visit the Dubies. Our stay was planned to be from about Wednesday through Sunday. I looked forward to hearing Norm preach, once again.
>
> Very soon after our arrival, Norm had to go to a dentist. He found out that an infected tooth that rendered him almost unable to talk caused his pain. He immediately began an effort to find a clergy person to lead Sunday's service and to preach the sermon.
>
> At that point in his ministry at that church, he had not yet been able to train or prepare a layperson to step in. The same thing happened to me once. On a Saturday a disc in my back slipped (or whatever they do) which

found me confined to complete bed rest for ten days. I had my sermon all prepared and to make a long story short, I had no one I could ask to fill in for me. I had always promised Audrey, she would not have to get up in front of a congregation, if she did not want to.

Well, she did and she was very good at it. I have not asked her to do that since…. you know, job security? Norman was in about the same situation. As he began his search for a 'stand in' he pondered the choices before him. He did not have many choices, which I suspect, caused him to look at me and say, "There's my preacher, sent by God!"

I was shocked into it, because, I could see that Norman meant it. I had not been to visit them since he had graduated, a year or so before then. I was a student who just decided to "take off" a few days for some rest and relaxation.

I spent the rest of the week trying to come up with a sermon and on Sunday I did my best. I did not feel like someone "sent by God," but I did have to agree that it was quite uncanny that I just happened to be where Norman, that devoted man of God, needed me to be.

Thanks, Norm and Doris for sharing that experience and for reminding me about it. As we consider that experience, we ought to be reminded that God often prepares a path for us, upon which we can walk before we realize it. Likewise, we should be truly aware that as we go to and fro, we might be traveling on a path so designed by God, that we become "one sent by God" to another.

In the Acts of the Apostles 26:15-18 we find these words that the risen Jesus spoke to Paul.

"I am Jesus whom you are persecuting. But get up and stand on your feet; for I have appeared to you for this purpose, to appoint

you to serve and testify to the things in which you have seen me and to those in which I will appear to you. I will rescue you from your people and from the Gentiles—to whom I am sending you to open their eyes so that they may turn from darkness to light...."

Yes, God uses us to help in the effort to prepare paths for others that they may more specifically walk in God's chosen path for them.

Kay Nadeau

I first met Kay when I became pastor of the Federated Church of New Sharon, Maine. She was one of my parishioners. Kay was a young widow. Her husband had been killed when a heavy bulldozer crushed him while he was working in the woods.

This left Kay alone, to raise their three small children. The family was involved in our church, to the degree they could, and as their pastor I enjoyed having them around. As I remember it, Kay was the local town librarian. All who knew her loved her for her compassion and willingness to be helpful to the children as well as the adults.

I am sure that God has always walked with me. My mother began teaching us to pray at an early age. She taught us in the beginning, by having us use that popular children's prayer, "Now I Lay Me Down to Sleep."

As we grew and became older, she taught us the Lord's Prayer. My mother also read to us from the Bible every Sunday. It did not matter our age, we all would gather around her rocking chair and she would read to us. We had good parents and a great bringing up.

When my husband was killed in 1947, my children were three, five, and ten months. At that point in my life, I moved back to New Sharon from Lewiston. Being back closer to home, my family and many friends helped me so much. Some of the help came from people I didn't even know.

There were times when we did not have very much. But I am so thankful that we always got by and were able to stay together. Without any doubt, God prepared paths for my children and me during those difficult, financially burdened days.

Later in my life, my doctor told me that I had cancer and needed to have surgery. For some reason or other I did not worry. I knew God was with me and I totally expected to get well. That was over forty years ago and I am still going strong.

My thankful heart finds me expressing thanks to God for being with me on the paths I have had to walk. Each day when I awake, the first thing that I do is to thank God for another day. I am so thankful that I am as healthy as I am. And I am so grateful my mother taught me that there is a God who cares and loves me. And that is ultimately why I have always known that God has walked

> beside me. I could never have walked the path I had to walk, without the guidance, support and compassionate presence of God with me.

Thanks, Kay, for that affirmation of faith. As we mull over Kay's living experience with God, let it remind us of God's continued presence and guidance as we journey down the paths of life. May her words also inspire us to teach or train up a child in the way he/she should go. As Kay confessed, the training of a child can be a source of strength and faith for life.

Roger Pimm

I introduced Roger to you in Chapter Six. You remember that Roger is in real estate and shared with us how he hired his secretary. He has an experience to share now that helps us to know God's activity is often beyond our comprehension.

> A number of years ago my father had a stroke. He did not recognize me when I went to the hospital to see him. We had no idea what sort of recovery my dad might have in the days or even years ahead.
>
> At that time my mother was still alive, but her physical condition was such that she could not be left alone. I hired a woman to stay with her. Dad had been Mother's main caregiver. Now with his stroke, it was truly an appalling situation. I felt simply terrible with both my parents in such physical condition and both so needy at the same time. With that, of course, I was concerned over how I could meet the needs of both my parents.

One evening I could not believe my ears. I was beginning to wonder if my mother was having problems thinking clearly. I went over to her bed to tell her how Dad was doing and to see how she was making out herself. As I was about to go sit down she said, "Don't worry about your dad, he has made a good turnabout and he'll be okay!" Trying to stay calm so as not to upset her, I simply turned toward her and said, "Oh good." I then went out to our living room.

I sat there wondering if Mom was just having a moment of "wishful thinking" or if we had another problem on the horizon. Within ten or fifteen minutes the phone rang. I heard some man talking. I finally figured out it was my father! He, indeed, had a turnaround. His speech was slurred but he was able to dial the phone and communicate to me that he would be okay. By the next day he was speaking clearly and I realized that my mom had been given a message.

God had given Mom a message, even though she herself was bedridden, in pain and basically helpless. As close as I could tell, it seems that Mom's message came at the same time Dad was given more time and healed from his stroke. God prepared the path for me to walk. God cleared out the debris that was filling me with despair. How could it happen; how could God send that message to my Mom without anyone hearing it or knowing it? The only answer seems to be; it was all the product of God's Love.

God is always preparing paths for us. The paths are truly the walkways of our lives. God knows that our walking in the paths he prepares, will lead us to greater joy, fulfillment and peace. A well-known hymn helps to express this aspect of God's love:

> All the way my Savior leads me,
> Oh, the fullness of His love!
> Perfect rest to me is promised
> In my Father's house above;
> When my spirit, cloth'd immortal,
> Wings it flight to realms of day,
> This my song thru endless ages;
> Jesus led me all the way.

Lolly Webster

I had the privilege of being pastor to Lolly and her husband, Bev, for a number of years. Lolly worked for Wyoming County Social Services Department. Since their retirement, and their move to Smartt, Tennessee, we have kept in close contact and we are the best of friends. Bev was diagnosed with cancer, and a year of so thereafter, he died. Both Lolly and Bev had a strong faith in God. That became an important and valuable fact in their journey together here on earth.

Lolly shares some events or true happenings that truly were blessings from God. This is her forthright sharing of how God prepared their path as they journeyed together in this world.

> Being where we were, when we were, proved to be very important. Bev had a pain in his side when we were in Huntsville, Alabama, at our daughter's. We were at

Lori's because her apartment had been broken into, and we went to see if we could be supportive.

Because we were there when Bev had the pain, we went to a walk-in clinic where he had x-rays, and was sent to the hospital for further testing. If we had been at our own home, they would have sent Bev to Nashville Hospital. This would have been very inconvenient and much more expensive, because there would have been no free place for us to stay.

Being able to stay with Lori in Huntsville when Bev had to have treatments was indeed much more pleasant. Instead of being in a city far from home and staying in a motel, we had the close-by apartment in which to live. Perhaps, more importantly, being with Lori meant we had support from family which was more helpful than anything money can buy.

A second aspect of wonder and blessing was how God had prepared our pathway. Because I turned sixty-two in May, and Bev was diagnosed in June, we had that extra Social Security check to help pay his medical bills. Without the extra income it would have been very very difficult, if not impossible, to pay for the extensive and expensive medical care. If it had to be, God made it so much more bearable, once again. This time helping us to not have bills that would have severely depressed us. God not only prepared the path, but God also set the time on which we would walk it.

This third experience continues to amaze me, as do the two above. Lori had moved to Huntsville a year and a half prior to Bev's becoming ill. Her house in Shortt,

Tennessee, was on the market for sale all that time. She just could not get anyone to show any interest in it. The Realtor was trying, but it was a time when the market was in a slump.

Living in the same town as was her house, we were happy to look after it; caring for the inside, watching for broken windows, water leaks, and outside taking care of the grounds, mowing and whatever may have needed to be done. We tried to keep it looking at its best so any potential buyer would be encouraged.

When Bev was no longer able to care for Lori's place, it sold immediately. Selling on a Monday, and as impossible as it may seem, closing on Thursday! Neither Lori nor Bev and I saw any angels during that time, but there surely must have been keeping a close eye on things. God again, cleared a mountain that loomed in our path.

The last marvelous happening that I want to share is something that still keeps me giving praise to God. In this event I became eternally enriched for God did what only God could do.

To this day I praise God for providing me with the help I needed, and is still hard to believe. At the same time as I say that, I want all to know that the experience was so vital and instrumental to my faith in God that my faith is strengthened each time I recall the experience.

When I first started working in Warsaw for Social Services of Wyoming County, New York, I was driving up the hill out of Varysburg. It is a long winding hill that can become and often is, very treacherous in the winter.

Wet pavement can quickly become black ice and a swirling blanket of snow can gather more quickly than a cat can climb a tree.

It was on that hill that I was ascending on my travels to Cowlesville to pick up a client for an appointment. I was meeting cars and trucks coming down as I drove upward. In a flash, these vehicles began skidding in all directions as they came down the hill. I was very frightened. Visibility was not the best, road conditions were at their worst and I wondered what I should or could do. **All of a sudden, there was a cleared driveway for me to turn into. I quickly drove in it, turned around, and was promptly headed back to the office.**

The storm was so bad that a few days later I wanted to show my husband where I had turned around. I knew exactly were it was on that hill. **But I was flabbergasted; there was no driveway anywhere near that area!** I know now that God once again prepared a path for me. I was so desperately frantic that the Good Lord provided me with a place to turn around. I'm sure of it!

Thanks, Lolly, for sharing those-ever-to-be sacred times in your life. As is the case with all who share "holy moments," I thank God that your faith is strong enough and your relationship with Christ close enough to recognize the dynamic presence of God in your midst. Your shared experiences have been and continue to be a real blessing to you. And now they are a blessing to us, as we gain from your witness.

Allison M. Hadley

Allison is our eldest grandchild. We remember well the day she was born. She was a beautiful baby, and has become an adorable young lady. Audrey and I were blessed when Allison was a child. She was born in Buffalo, at the time when her mother was in medical school. Because of the nature of her mother's intense schooling, we offered and often would keep Allison with us. I remember that one time we kept her nearly a month. Her mother was in contact daily and needless to say, she missed her daughter more than words can describe.

I think that Allison became closer to us, as grandparents, due to the fact that her mother was so busy; she spent more time with us than she might have otherwise. In an e-mail to us she wrote about living in Seattle, Washington. She went on to speak of how happy she was to be back in the area where her family and we live. Being the young lady that she is, it was not totally surprising to read these words as part of her cause for being so happy now that she is in the area: "That's because we are near the greatest grandparents ever – YOU GUYS !"

Allison wrote me about what she wanted to accomplish in her sharing. What she hoped to get across was that at a point in her life when she thought she could never be happy again, she began to pray. She wrote me about how prayer gave her a new pathway upon which to walk and a joy that she never thought was possible.

Do you ever feel that you cannot go on anymore; that you just can't deal with the stress of life and all that goes along with it? I have been there before. And I have figured out a way to beat it! Put your trust in God and fall head over heels in love.

At one point in my life I was devastated beyond belief. I felt that there was nothing anyone could do about my sadness; like there was no way that anyone would understand how I felt. That was at about the same time I was taking a Bible as Literature class. Our assignments were to read certain chapters and write down what we thought it meant, for a discussion during the next class.

That was at about the same time I started praying regularly. That was also the same time I was dumped and soon met the man of my dreams. A man who not only understood the sadness in my life and how I felt, but also knew how to make it all go away. Yes, I met a man who put a smile on my face.

I truly believe that when you are at a point in your life where you have loved God, the best that you thought you could, God jumps right in and says, "Hey, you can do better than that!"

Rudy and I began dating in November of 2002. We have prayed together every day. We were married by my grandfather on June 10, 2006. On that day, God and all who were present were able to see the true happiness that we have found in each other. As we said our vows before God and all present, joy and love shown brightly. It is because of Rudy that I have found God to be a pure source of hope and inspiration in my life. It is, for me, a pure fact that God brought Rudy to me.

When Rudy and I were dating, we would walk onto our balcony overlooking Puget Sound and watch the sunrise each morning. That was our time together, in which we would focus on God. We would hold hands and pray together; asking God to watch over and be with us and our family and friends.

God answered the heart-felt prayers of Rudy and me and also of our families and friends. God made it clear to us, once again, that when the going gets tough, there is always a way around it. Neither of us were really fond of our jobs in Seattle and we both missed our families.

We prayed about it and with God's help and guidance we picked up and moved back to New York. We bought a house and live within forty minutes of our parents. I can now see my little sister grow into a mature adult. I can now see my parents edge toward retirement. I can now see our families when we get together and spend evenings just sitting around talking.

We knew that we needed to be near our families to be completely happy. And, just like God showed me Rudy, God has shown us that love and happiness is the most precious gift of all.

Thank you, Allison. Your sincere appraisal of how God has prepared the pathway for you over the years is a testimony of the faith that we never walk alone. And, the fact that you are aware of God's continued involvement in your life has to be a rich blessing. It is something that many people just don't seem to comprehend. You and Rudy are beautiful people, and that portrayal will parallel your faith and activities throughout your lives.

Hopefully, reading Allison's contribution will remind all of us of God's desire, to prepare our pathways, and to walk them with us.

Colin Peter Brown Reagan

Colin is my favorite grandson—albeit he is my only one! If you read my first book, you will remember that his father was killed in a tragic automobile accident when Colin was only seven months old. He was hit head-on by a careless driver who passed a snowplow in a blinding snowstorm. I haven't asked, but I often wonder if Colin's dedication to police work has its roots in his Dad's untimely and catastrophic death.

Colin attended the University of Buffalo for one year, and then transferred to Erie Community College where he received his Emergency Medical Technician (EMT) certificate and his certification as a Paramedic. In 2004, Colin received his Associate Degree from Erie Community College.

He is an ambitious young man. In 2006 he worked part-time as a Warsaw Village Police Officer and as a Wyoming County Sheriff's Deputy. He did that while attending Genesee Community College; graduating from their Police Academy. He is now a full-time Deputy Sheriff for Wyoming County.

Colin is a tall (over 6 feet), very trim and in good physical shape. He has a very interesting experience to share with us. When he was six years old, his mother was married to J. Thomas Reagan, and it is this new family unit of which he speaks.

My family has a place in the Adirondacks at Olmstedville, New York. We have gone there for vacations since before I started school. It was there that we did a variety of things, such as skating, snowshoeing, or skiing in the winter, as well as hiking up mountains as the weather and time permitted.

It was in the summer of 1996 when I was about thirteen years old that we were spending a few days there relaxing and swimming. The water was always cool, and I use that word to mean not warm! That first toe in the water was always a shocker for me. My dad just seemed to think it was perfect for swimming. Of course, he grew up spending most every summer at that place and evidently his skin must have toughened to the challenge. While we were there in that beautiful mountain area, it was quite a normal event to take a hike up one of the nearby mountains.

On one particular day something happened on our hike, that still lingers in my mind, and makes me smile in utter amazement. We, my sister Beth, my mom and dad and I, climbed Big Slide mountain. Beth was only age six or seven and her little legs would only go so far before Dad would give her a "horseback ride" as we journeyed steadily upward. Of course, our family dog, Buffy, went along with us. She just loved the woods and was always ready to climb a mountain, regardless of the weather, be it hot or cold.

That day it was beautiful and the views were breathtaking, as usual. But all that has been pushed aside in respect to how I remember that particular outing. As we started our descent, I asked Dad if I could run ahead. He agreed, and I took off down the mountain. Our home in Warsaw, New York. is a quarter of a mile off the highway; it is a slight uphill walk, which had helped to keep me in good shape physically.

Buffy and I were quickly out of sight, but my dad was not concerned because I was accustomed to hiking. I was quite some distance from the top and the bottom, when I unintentionally took the wrong path. There was a place where the path split off in two directions and I took the wrong way.

Before long I was beginning to think things looked different than I had remembered them, but I just kept going. The further I went, the more confused I became. **All of a sudden I realized that I was LOST.** I did not have a compass, nor could I have used it correctly if I did. I walked, and then ran here and there, until I became so frightened that tears began to roll down my cheeks. In desperation I sat down on a very large rock amidst the huge expanse of that Adirondack Mountain.

I was there, when Buffy appeared a short ways up the path. She barked twice at me and then disappeared. I ran back in her direction, which brought me back to the path's split. I was, however, still lost and I did not know what to do. **In my confused turmoil, I did not hear him approaching but I was not startled when a man's voice spoke to me. "What is wrong?" he asked. I said, "I am lost." And he said, "Follow me."**

My mind is a blur from that moment until I remember reaching near the base of the mountain and seeing my dad and sister. I ran that ten or twenty yards like an Olympic sprinter. At this point, the three of us went down and met my mom, who had not climbed the whole way.

A tremendous relief came over me as we were all together once again. **Seeing that I had been crying, they asked what had happened. "I got lost." I said. Then my mom asked, "How did you find your way?" I spoke as I turned around saying, "That man helped me." Mom and Dad had a puzzled look on their faces as they questioned, "WHAT MAN?" There was no man there; nor had they ever seen anyone!**

I have thought about that day a lot. Thinking about it and that particular experience has brought me to the realization that the **one who said "Follow me" and helped guide me was either my biological father who was killed in an automobile accident when I was only seven months old, or it was Jesus.** Somehow, I suspect it was actually both.

Wow. What a powerful faith-expanding experience! Thanks, Colin, for sharing that with all who read this book, and for all whom the readers' themselves share it.

This is a vivid example of just how far God's love extends into the deep woods of our life's journey. Our Lord not only prepares a path for us to find our way, but He walks with us every step that we take, as He calls, "Follow Me."

As this chapter comes to its close we have been made aware of so many people and so many ways that people are guided to walk the paths of God. I want to underscore the importance of keeping a watchful eye for the paths made for you by God. They may be everyday places that God would prefer you go, as opposed to walking helter-skelter without thought. It may be a path that leads you to a needy neighbor, a lonely friend or in fact to any place or person. It may be for you, an urge to take a step in faith and go ahead and accept the position of service in your church or in your community. Yes, God's paths go all over the hills and valleys of our lives

I am reminded of the Reverend Larry Brodie's experience when he felt a compulsion to visit the gravesite of a former parishioner. Although he was tired, he took that path, believing it was a path God wanted him to take at that time. When he reached the cemetery, it was not the grave that was primary, but the man whom God had guided there—-in the hope that Rev. Larry would "touch" him with the Love of Jesus. Either one could have refused to follow the particular path somehow pointed out to them, but how sad it would have been. Think of how much help would not have been given and how much help would not have been received and accepted.

As we consider how paths are offered to us. We will do well to strive to decipher between those prepared for us by God, and those other path-makers that seek to incite our travel their way. It may not always be easy to know which way to go—which path to walk. The words contributed to Yogi Barre may suggest just how difficult the path choice may be when he said: "When you get to a fork in the road, TAKE IT!"

Well, to endeavor to walk the path prepared by God, we need only to intently follow God's Son, Jesus.

In the Old Testament we read that Joshua sought to show the path to travel: "Now therefore, revere the Lord, and serve him in sincerity and in faithfulness…choose this day whom you will serve…but as for me and my household, we will serve the Lord" (Joshua 24:14-15).

The Yogi Barre words may have more validity than we may possibly have thought. Think about it. If we walk hand-in-hand with God, as Jesus has called us to walk, then any path in the road that we find ourselves on is still a valid path. Walking with our Lord can never be anything but the right way to go!

Praise be to God, for God has "marked" the right paths for us to take, we need only to walk where Jesus would walk.

CHAPTER EIGHT

God Comforts Us in a Variety of Ways

In reading all of the experiences given me for this book, I have been all but overwhelmed by the multiplicity of those experiences. In this chapter I want to present you with a sample of how diversely God speaks to us. Just like all the others throughout this entire book, these are experiences that have had a powerful effect on those who have shared them.

The idea that we can ever tabulate all the ways that God shares love and compassion with us is foolhardy. The Psalmist who wrote Psalm 106 expressed this thought. In verse three he writes: "Who can utter the mighty doings of the Lord, or declare all his praise?" No one is the answer, save Jesus the Christ. For this truth we should rejoice! God's ways are not our ways. True also is the fact that God's ways are endless. The ways God makes himself known to you and to me may be exactly the same, or they may be totally and completely different. What should be of most importance, is that God does continue to love and travel with us. With all that, we can be assured that **when we keep our eyes and ears open, we will experience the very presence of God's comfort in endless ways, endlessly.**

Vickie and Courtney Bly

Courtney is Vickie's daughter. They are two dear people. I have known Vickie since her birth and I can say the same for her daughter. The Blys are members of our church family in Castile. Vickie teaches in our Sunday School; is involved in Youth programs and music among other things. Courtney attends our local central school. I'm quite sure she's in the ninth grade, and I see her name on the honor roll, so I am sure she is an excellent student. Like her mother, Courtney is a kind, loveable, and compassionate person.

Their experience is a beautiful example of how God can make such an impact on us, using the most unexpected way of accomplishing the task. Vickie and Courtney shared the experience together. Vickie now shares their comforting experience that only God could explain.

> This is a miracle my daughter shared with me. My grandmother died in the summer of 2001. Grandmother loved my daughter, Courtney. She was always so pleased to look after Courtney when I had to work, if my daughter was ill. Whenever we would stop in to see Grandma, she would always have something to give to her and to me.
>
> The miracle happened a few weeks following Grandma's death and burial. Courtney and I were coming home from church one Sunday, when I noticed something. I was a bit taken back because there was a flower growing right where I had just yesterday sprayed grass and weed killer. But, there it was, a beautiful flower standing tall and shining as if it belonged there.

I called Courtney to come and see the flower. As we looked at it, I realized the flower was a portulaca. A portulaca is a plant with rose-like blossoms, cultivated for its showy flowers. I knew what it was, because it was Grandma's favorite flower. She would grow these in pots outside her trailer in the summer. I told my daughter that the flower had to be a sign from God that Grandmother was being well taken care of by God.

Courtney then told me that she had prayed last night, asking God to show her a sign that Grandma was okay. What a beautiful miracle given by God, to support and aid my daughter and me in our grieving.

The portulaca grew through the summer, giving us fifteen or more blossoms on it at times. After that summer that plant has not returned. It only came the summer when Courtney had asked for a sign. I was very concerned that the weed killer that I had used would eventually kill it, but it didn't.

My daughter, age ten at the time, made a cross of wood and put it next to the flowers. My grandmother was a wonderful caring person, and she would not have wanted Courtney to worry about her.

Grandma would not have wanted Courtney to worry and the same is true with God. God gives us comfort in so many different ways. To make an attempt to tabulate them would be foolhardy, at best. Without question, in a plot of land recently sprayed to get rid of grass and weeds——there was a beautiful flower, but not just any flower, Grandma's favorite flower! On top of all that, Courtney, a ten year old, prayed to God for a sign that her dearly loved and grievously missed grandma was in God's care.

It is really a beautiful experience for two people to be so blessed with the assurance that God's love is actively involved in the lives of those who have left this earth. God, is marvelous, not only did God somehow have the flower bloom in their yard, God also made sure the path they walked would bisect with that flower of flowers. And, how much more meaningful and beautiful it is that God knew exactly what kind of flower to choose!

Thanks, Courtney and Vickie, for sharing with us. Your experience will surely help others to gain a growing appreciation of God's love and the assurance that love does span the world in which we now live and the Eternal Kingdom of God.

Agnes Remsen

I have known Agnes for many years. Her husband, the Reverend Gerald Remsen, was at the Bangor Theological Seminary in Bangor, Maine, part of the time that I was also there. Being students, we actually did not get to know each other as well as I wished we had. However, once he began serving a church in Rochester, New York, we were able to cross paths much more frequently. We were only some forty-five miles apart at that time.

Agnes is a dear person. She has a dynamic faith and a great sense of humor. I am not sure if she always had that sense of humor or whether it simply developed from living with her husband all these years! Regardless, Agnes and Gerry are a great couple who have worked hard in the Christian Church. They have always been involved in the community where they resided. They also worked tirelessly for justice and peace, for all sorts and conditions of people who live in this world.

Agnes knits beautifully, with a very relaxed manner; just seems to be no effort on her part. The results are amazing, be it a sweater, baby blanket or whatever. What a fortunate grandson they have. He will never know what it's like to be without a sweater!

Agnes shares with us an experience that was a tremendous gift at a time when only a gift from God would suffice. The paths that God prepares are always the paths to take. My friend, Agnes, seeks to walk those paths day after day.

> It was 11:00 p.m. on a cool Saturday night in early fall of 1989. My husband, Gerry, was putting finishing touches on his sermon for Sunday morning and I was reading an article from Good Housekeeping Magazine. The radio was playing classical music, which is a favorite of ours; it is both invigorating and restful for us. However, the calm peacefulness of the evening was interrupted when the telephone rang.
>
> It was our son Larry's commanding officer calling from Eakers Air Force Base in Blytheville, Arkansas. Larry had been in the Air Force for ten years. Previously, he had been stationed for three years, at Griffith Air Force Base in Rome, New York. After that he was at Eakers Air Force Base for seven years, where he was the Crew Chief on a B-52.

The Commander told us that there had been a motor vehicle accident and Larry was not expected to live. He asked if we could fly down to Memphis, Tennessee, where Larry was hospitalized.

After making numerous arrangements to cover an indefinite period of time that we would be gone, we were on a flight in the early morning hours. We stayed on hospital grounds for two weeks with wonderful support from Air Force, co-workers and friends of Larry. Gerry's sister and my sister flew from New Jersey to give us additional support along with our other two sons, our oldest, Gerry III, and Dan, our youngest.

After two harrowing weeks we flew home with the expectation that Larry would be transferred to a Veterans Administrative Hospital near us. This was not to be. Once again the Air Force had other plans. He was transported to Kessler Air Force Base Hospital in Biloxi, Mississippi.

After three weeks of talking with his nurses and doctors at the hospital, it was decided that our son be allowed to die with dignity. He was disconnected from artificial support, having been in a deep coma from which he could not recover.

The memorial service in which my husband participated went very well. Shortly thereafter, all of Larry's belongings were shipped to us. We went through everything, kept some and parted with others. We then needed to put our lives back in order.

Anyone who has had to face a child's death, or who has lost a cherished loved one, knows there are many ups and downs when going through the grieving process.

On April 15, 1992 our grandson, Neil Lawrence Remsen, was born. When Neil was about ten or eleven months old he and his parents, our son Gerry and his wife, Kathy, were visiting us. One afternoon during their visit, Neil was trying to walk with the help of his mom and dad.

That same night after I had fallen asleep I had a dream. The dream took me back to Neil learning to walk when LARRY CAME INTO THE ROOM. I went to hug him and he said, "You can't hug me, I'm not really here." He was balancing very well on his crutches after having lost a leg. **He then said, "I just want you to know I'm happy. I'm in heaven with Grandma and Grandpa Remsen and Grandma and Grandpa Bridgeman and I don't want you to worry or be sad. I'm helping Jesus and that keeps us all busy and content."**

As Larry spoke and faded away, the door opened and our youngest son, Dan came in. I turned to give him a hug and started to back off fearing he wasn't really there. He said, "I'm fine, Mom. I'm here," and he got the biggest hug ever.

When I woke up the next morning a tremendous peace came over me. I COULD LAUGH AND SMILE AGAIN!"

What an incredible gift. My surveillance of that striking experience makes me want to point out two different expressions of love. First is God's great love and compassion on those who suffer. God's love for Agnes and Gerry poured out in that experience. And let me add that because these two tried to walk the paths of life with God—it made it so much easier for them to see and accept the Holy Presence of God in that experience.

By all that, I am simply reminded of Jesus speaking about His sheep knowing His voice and thus following Him. "The one who enters by the gate is the shepherd of the sheep. The gatekeeper opens the gate for him, and the sheep hear his voice... and the sheep follow him because they know his voice" (John 10:2f). As we involve ourselves in a meaningful relationship with God, we are more ready to see with our eyes and hear with our ears. Jesus went on to affirm, "They will not follow a stranger, but they will run from him because they do not know the voice of strangers"(John 10:5). Dear people, remember that the closer you walk with God and His Son, Jesus—the more you will be able to recognize God's voice no matter who or what instrument God uses to speak!

And quite naturally, the experience also demonstrates a dear and abiding love that Larry continues to have for his mom and dad. "I don't want you to worry or be sad; I want you to know I'm happy."

In a way, Larry gave a reaffirmation of Jesus' words in the Gospel of John 16:33 "I have told you these things, so that in me you may have peace. In this world you will have trouble. But take heart! I have overcome the world." I can almost hear Larry saying, "Mom and Dad, don't fret anymore, Jesus' words are still true today, the Eternal Kingdom is the best!"

No wonder Agnes woke up to "a tremendous peace" and as she said, "I could laugh and smile again." Thanks for sharing this holy experience. It is obvious, that as God's Son promised, walking with Him enabled Agnes and Jerry to find God's Peace.

With that Peace they also experienced "mountains" of grief being removed from their path, as they walked hand in hand with God.

Ellen LaCroix

I introduced Larry LaCroix to you in Chapter Three. The introduction included some information about Ellen, and I will try not to duplicate any of that here. Like her husband, Ellen has a strong faith in God. She has served on many of the official boards of the church and no matter where, she is a creative thinker and promoter of action.

Ellen would come up with ideas that seemed all but undoable, and with planning and leadership, it would be smoothly accomplished to the Glory of God. One example was her suggestion that we as a church adopt a Bosnian family. We did this, which meant our being involved, to help them get settled, find employment, housing, doctors, dentist, English lessons, and on an on. Thanks to her and the great support and leadership of the Rev. Stephen Slakovits, who was our pastor then, we brought to the United States a lovable family. We as a church were richly blessed for the time and expense of giving to help others.

Another example of Ellen's forward thinking and creativity is seen in the youth group that she began called the GBO Group. That stands for "Going Beyond Ourselves." That group has been a tremendous blessing to the youth involved. As they seek ways to give help to others, they have traveled to Washington, D.C. to help in soup kitchens and other church programs there. They went to South Carolina one summer to teach a Vacation Bible School for a week, in a predominately black church. And in Rochester, close to home, they have led worship at a Soup Kitchen and helped to serve meals. They have helped others in our own church and community as well.

With that, I will turn this over to Ellen who will share a very intense experience. She was on a journey to help others and it became obvious that God was with her on that pathway.

In my middle years, I decided to study for a new career. Events had been leading me toward this change for quite a while. After teaching elementary students for over twenty years, I obtained my Masters Degree in Counseling. I made a vow to myself that I would be a counselor who was totally committed to the job.

My education had prepared me well for any type of counseling. I jumped into situations if I thought there was a chance that I could help someone. With personal counseling, one must listen effectively to determine the main concerns of the client. More difficult is family counseling, where the dynamics between every participant and the counselor can be overwhelming.

Tempers can be explosive in a dysfunctional family. In each and every situation, I let my clients know that I was available in times of crisis, regardless of the hour. Fine, I had the commitment, but often more is needed. The ramification of making a wrong "call" while counseling is frightening. We counselors try to determine how a client will react, but that can certainly backfire when emotions flare.

I asked God to help me make the right calls, so that I would not do harm during counseling, but hopefully, help. Naturally, I learned from each client and group what reactions were soothing and those that were less than helpful. A prison group helped me learn, as they were not concerned with the polite thing to say, only responses from the heart (as politically incorrect as they may have been).

After retirement, I only counseled people as a way of giving back to God for all my blessings. My counseling was only people who "by word of mouth" heard about me. Many of my clients were from church, or neighbors, or just acquaintances. I charged no fee and if the case was beyond my expertise, I would refer the client to a full-time therapist.

Many of the people with whom I met over the retirement years were grown children of friends. It was interesting to me, to counsel people that I had known since they were toddlers. We could get right to the point a little faster, as the rapport-building phase was easier. Surely, I still needed God's help to make those right calls, so that progress could be made.

God was especially close to me on a spring evening, when a middle-of-the-night phone call awakened me. I was still telling clients that I was available at anytime during crises. The agitated voice on the other end of the line told me that we were smack in the middle of a crisis. The man, who had come to me previously with marital problem and anger management needs, was calling from a car phone. He was in the next village about eight miles away. He was out of control and crying. His wife, who did not come home that evening, apparently was at the home of a male friend. He had spotted her car parked there.

The husband's anger toward her and her male friend was at a peak. Before I left home to go to his aid, I tried to enlist a promise from him that he would take no action whatsoever until I arrived. He could only say, "I'll try." Not a comforting reply!

As I drove the eight miles, I prayed that God would be with this soul and keep him from doing anything foolish out of his anger. I argued with myself each and every mile whether my first stop in town should be to the police station to get back-up help with this situation. I imagined gunshots. I felt that there was a possibility of suicide. I was frankly scared.

There would be negative consequences to involving the police for my client and I knew that he would lose all faith in our relationship if I made that choice. We were just beginning to progress and I did not want to hinder that progress. But, I was well aware that I bore responsibility for their lives. **I needed an answer to the predicament and I needed it quickly.**

The darkness of the night made all of this even more painful for my client. In daylight, it seems easier to focus on what is important and gives one more confidence that an answer will be found. But the night—it's scary.

I was traveling fast, but thankfully God's answer was faster! God told me to trust in the ability of my client to maintain some control during this painful situation. When I arrived at the address of the wife's lover, my client was in his car in front of the house awaiting my arrival. We sat in the darkness while his emotions ran the gamut of disbelief, anger, betrayal, and hopelessness.

In time, he calmed down to the point where he agreed that I would go into the house to speak to his wife. I entered and had a conversation with her about her husband's feelings. She had, by her actions of that evening, made a decision that their marriage was over and she had no interest in working the misunderstandings out.

Her husband, for the first time in a long, long while had fought his inner demons and controlled his actions. He was able to control his long-feared temper. Through his pain, he saw this change and appreciated his growth. **Was God only walking with me? No, I believe God helped this man—for the first time he was able to deal with his anger responsibly!**

Through the long evening (make that morning) God, once again walked with me as I dealt with the responsibility I had for three lives. God helped me to make the right decision that terror filled night. Now, several years later, I know that God also walked with my friend. His reworked personality has changed and he is a vision of calm and control. He has not lost his temper in a very long time. And for the first time, he can look at himself in a mirror and say, 'I am a good person.'

I did not do any of that for the client who called in such distress. My Shepherd did that. And for that

continued and constant support, I am thankful. Praise be to God.

Yes, God does give us aid in a variety of ways; in this experience, Ellen found again that God also walks and helps a variety of people. To ask, or be concerned about how God accomplishes all this meaningful support is imprudent. To ask why, is the appropriate question to ask. The answer is made known to us in God's Son, Jesus. In Jesus, **love, compassionate love for all God's sons and daughters is the impetus.**

Stephen Hadley

Steve is my son-in-law. He is married to my daughter, Cindy, who has also shared with us in this book. Steve is a teacher in Letchworth Central School, Gainesville, New York. He consistently gets the "highest rating" from his students whenever I ask about him! More importantly, I seldom ask any such question, but I regularly receive glowing remarks from students and others when they come to realize that he is my son-in-law.

Steve teaches in high school, but he has "hooked up" with the State University of New York at Geneseo and is offering a few classes that give the students college credit. This has proven very popular.

When it comes to his teaching, I think it speaks volumes that although he has the education to be in administration, he tells me that he would miss teaching too much to make that move! Steve has traveled all over the world and enjoys the arts, with a special appreciation, I think, for the paintings by the great artists of yesteryear.

Steve and Cindy have two children, Allison, a college graduate writes for a newspaper and is married to a very nice young man, Rudy Diedreck. Their younger daughter, Kristen, a high school student, excels in music, playing the violin, piano, and flute, as well as having a solo voice. Kristen is also a top student academically and in sports. (I suspect she gets it from her grandpa!)

Steve is sharing an experience that touched his whole being.

The summer of 1995 was a difficult one. My daughter, Kristen, was just beginning to form a bond with her grandmother, who unfortunately was dying of throat cancer. Mom had just recently begun to live again after many years of sickness and unhappiness. We spent many hours at the hospital as she endured the pain of the cancer and an unsuccessful operation to arrest it. It was with a heavy heart that I drove home to begin my school year.

On a beautiful September day as I was driving home from work, my mind was typically cluttered with thoughts of the day and plans for the next. I often chide myself for failing to turn off my brain and just enjoy the pleasant country drive. On this particular day, as I approached a magnificent tree in full color on the outskirts of Castile, something truly remarkable happened.

For what seemed like one or two minutes, I began to experience "snapshots" of my mother's life. They were especially of her when she was younger. They were photos like: Mom and I playing tennis, Mom hanging up the sheets to dry on a breezy afternoon, Mom and I reading a long-forgotten book. There must have been hundreds of these pictures, but they were orderly, coherent and crystal clear.

As I "awoke" from this altered state, I was not confused in the least. I felt love in a way I had never felt it before—a calm reassuring love for my mother and a gentle reminder that she had always loved me very much.

A half-hour after I entered the house that afternoon, my brother called to tell me that Mom had died. It was certainly a blessing, given her suffering. I felt very sad that Mom was no longer with us, and that Allison and Kristen could never spend Christmas with her again, but I also felt happy.

I had been prepared by God for her death, and in the course of that preparation, I had been privileged to experience the love that can truly exist between people—the very love of God.

Yes, God does prepare the paths upon which we walk and drive. What an experience to have been given on the day of your dear mother's death. Thanks, Steve, for sharing this holy enriching experience. Your sharing surely will be a supportive instrument for an increase of faith for all who read and/or hear about this holy God-given experience.

Stephen Hadley said that in the whole overwhelming experience, dealing with his grief, "he had been privileged to experience the love that can truly exist between people—the very love of God." That had to be an elevating, inspiring experience. It is one, let us not forget, that God would have us experience again and again. St. Paul writes in Romans 13:8 "Owe no one anything, except to love one another; for the one who loves another has fulfilled the law."

And Paul was voicing the message of Jesus who is recorded in Mark 12:29-31 as saying, "The first [commandment] is, 'Hear, O Israel: the Lord our God, the Lord is one; you shall love the Lord with all you heart…soul…mind…and strength.' And the second commandment is this: 'you shall love your neighbor as yourself. There is no other commandment greater than these.'"

God continues to use a variety of ways to support us as we experience the ups and downs, the realities of life here on earth. . Though there are a variety of ways, all are consistently supported by the love Jesus taught us; all the love of which Paul spoke—and the love experienced in his grief, and now in his joy and peace.

Tricia Holzwarth

Tricia is new to me as she probably is to you. In corresponding with her cousin, Rachel Waterbury, in regards to this book, Rachel forwarded Tricia's experience. Upon reading it and checking with her for permission to use it, I am pleased to share this with you. Tricia lives in Davison, Michigan, and she begins writing with a note to her cousin after reading Rachel's experience.

> Wow! What a story. You made me cry. Is it not amazing how things like that come about to let you know that everything will be okay? I remember when my

grandfather passed away. It was a warm July night and I was sitting on the floor in my den with the slider door opened, just crying like a baby. I was crying so hard that my head felt as if it was going to pop, so I got up and went into the bathroom and looked in the mirror only to see that I looked like a raccoon.

I had mascara all over my face. I started laughing and said to my grandfather, "Grandpa, you must think I look like a darn raccoon." I cleaned my eyes and went back to sit on the floor by the slider door and you would not believe what came up to the screen. It was a raccoon! It came right up to the screen, stood up on its back legs and put its front paws on the screen. It was making a very light chirping sound as if it was talking to me.

Then came another, so now I have two raccoons standing at my screen. I absolutely could not believe it! I have lived here in the city for five years and I had never seen coons around here.

All of a sudden, I felt an overwhelming peace come over me as soon as I thought it was Grandpa's way of saying it was going to be okay. Those raccoons gracefully got down, turned and walked to the side of the deck. There they stopped and looked back at me and then they were gone. I have never seen them again.

So, I do believe that there can be signs from the other side that come to us, to comfort us, and to let us know it really is going to be okay.

God gives aid, support, and encouragement, in so many different ways. Who would think that God would use a raccoon to speak to Tricia like that? Just try to put it all together. First, in order for the raccoons to have any meaning at all for Tricia, she had to have her tears mess up her mascara. She then had to look in the mirror and think, "I look like a raccoon!" Joking about it with her deceased grandpa made it all the more significant. In five years she had never seen raccoons around there; but right then, two came, not a hour later or a minute sooner! They waited until, in her mind, she thought it was a message from her grandpa. Then they begin to leave, look back at her, and disappear, never to be seen again.

God uses such a variety of ways to give us messages. It is so vital for us that we take time to listen and to see. Her experience was so powerful for her, but yet so very calm and peaceful. In Matthew's Gospel account we find these words that seem to be so pertinent to her sharing. Jesus is speaking: "Come to me, all of you that are weary and carrying heavy burdens, and I will give you rest. Take my yoke upon you, and learn from me; for I am gentle and humble in heart, and you will find rest for your souls" (Matthew 11:28-29).

Thank you, Tricia. Do continue to share this and future experiences, as God's Presence is known to you!

Rachel Waterbury

Rachel is Tricia's cousin. I got in touch with her after she had read my first book. She is a dear friend of my sister, Lorraine, who may have twisted Rachel's arm to get her to read it! My sister wrote me about Rachel saying, "She is such a down-to-earth lady, and she has my admiration."

Rachel lives in Wichita, Kansas, and shares an experience that has helped her deal with the untimely death of her husband.

My beloved husband, Carl, and I were married for over thirty years. We had a wonderful married life, and raised two children, Shelley and Eric. When the children left home for college, we decided to return to our home state of Michigan for a short while. Carl could then work and add time to his roofers union pension fund, which he started when we were married.

Carl could not read a single word. He had dyslexia, as did other members of his family. With nine children in the family, his parents did not have time or financial resources to get them the proper schooling. Carl picked up the trade of roofing and he loved his work.

One snowy December day in the year 2000, Carl went to work in downtown Detroit. A crew of twelve men was anxious to get started, knowing that Christmas was coming up. The safety lines were not yet attached to the roof but the foreman ordered his men on the roof. Carl slipped off the roof, and four days later died of his injuries.

My life's dreams with Carl were shattered. I lived for a while with my children in Colorado then moved to Wichita, Kansas. In September of 2003, I had to make one last trip to Detroit for a court appearance. After almost three years, my court settlement over Carl's death was coming to an end. I felt a tremendous relief when the judge used his gavel to conclude the case.

I stayed at Ada's that night. About midnight, I was awakened by the hard downpour of rain…and a tap-tap,.tap-tap-tap. Again, for several minutes, that went on. It was the familiar sound of a hammer, like it was someone starting a nail with the first tap-tap, and then driving it in with the tap-tap-tap.

The rain and tapping also woke Ada. We met in her kitchen, lights still off, as we looked out to see what was happening. When we stepped out on to her covered porch, we saw her neighbor on his roof, apparently repairing a leak. He was there with a flashlight in his mouth, lighting the way!

Returning to the kitchen, we both agreed that the experience was Carl's way of telling us he is with us, even through the difficult times I had that day. **I came home to Wichita early the next morning, relieved that this terrible accident and court case was behind me. With all that, I thank God that I came home with something much more valuable** and long lasting than that for which I went to Detroit. I came **home revived in faith, knowing that Carl's love and the Love of God was strong and real and would always and forever be with me.**

The Love of God some times seems to "wiggle" its way in and around us in order to make itself known. Thankfully, God uses a variety of ways to speak to us; numerous instruments already in our midst, to drive a nail of faith and love into our hearts and minds. As I thank Rachel for this sharing, I lead you to another significant experience she had while driving her car. It must have almost caused her to toot her horn!

> My dear daughter Shelley, as I followed you out onto the freeway, I noticed your license plate number on the back of your big pretty truck. I know that Dad would be happy with you, for buying something for yourself that you have always wanted. But what a wonderful surprise, to see that when you got your plates you got the number 108 and the initials CLW. After I thought about it for a minute I thought that maybe Dad had his hand in that, too.
>
> The number 108 came through you and your dad's life twice. The very first house you came to after you were born was your grandma's home; the address was 10898. We moved to Hall Road in Hamburg where we had many happy years together. The address was 10828. And with your license plate number, 108, you have your dad's initials—CLW –for Carl Louis Waterbury.
>
> So, if you read all those *Angel* magazines I ordered for you and believe as I do, you will realize your license plate was no coincidence, but a gift from your father…. God bless you Shelly-Belly, Love you so very much. Mom.

The instruments that God uses to comfort and give us support are so diverse in nature. As we keep a close relationship with our Lord, we will recognize more and more that God seeks to comfort and encourage us, as we live our lives each new day. Thanks Rachel (a beautiful Mom), for seeing, and for your sharing. God is so good.

Jack Hendrickson

I first introduced Jack to you in Chapter Six. As you remember, he is my brother-in-law who flies airplanes as comfortably as I drive a car. I was going to say he flies airplanes as comfortably and as capably as I drive a car—but I can't compare my capability to the capability that Jack has with aircraft of any size.

To help you appreciate his sharing, I remind you that our brother-in-law, Wayne Burlingame, died after tripping in his back yard and falling to the ground, which unbelievably caused paralysis and ultimate death.

> About the time Wayne fell, either before or after I am not sure, but I had a most vivid dream. In the dream I saw myself lying in a gray casket. Standing at the end of the casket stood Dad Embling. [Dad Embling had died many years prior to this.] He was shaking his head back and forth indicating I was not supposed to be there.
>
> That dream left me with a strong conviction that someone in our family was going to die. There was no doubt in my mind about it. Since Wayne was in the hospital with a serious condition, I can only wonder if this is what Dad meant.

Thanks, Jack, for being used as an instrument of God. Your sharing is another example of God's Compassionate-Eternal Love. On the question you left us to ponder, I can only speculate after more than seventy years on my faith journey. I have heard tell and personally I have had experiences where God has used experiences reminiscent of yours, to give aid and/or support to the loved ones of one who would soon leave this world.

Now, in all cases that I am familiar with, the message of coming demise was not shared with the one expected to expire. The real support from our loving God is given, as the recipient of the message later becomes an instrument of God. How? By sharing the experience with those closest to the loved one who had died. It helps the bereaved to know God is intimately aware and infinitely involved in the life and death of their loved one. And it also is a reaffirmation of their faith as Jesus shared in John 3:16.

Lori Burlingame, Ph.D.

Lori Burlingame is my niece. Her parents are my sister, Dorothy, and her husband, Wayne Burlingame. Lori was adopted as an infant and has been a part of a most loving and caring family. She was very close to her dad, Wayne, whom you met earlier in this book. He died as the result of a freak accident.

Lori received her Ph.D. from the University of Rochester in Rochester, New York.

Dr. Burlingame is a professor at Eastern Michigan University in Ypsilanti. She has two very meaningful experiences to share. One comes from her cousin, whom she introduces to you and shares a very comforting and amazing experience.

> This account comes from my cousin, Brian Frisby; it has brought great comfort to me and my family in the

wake of my father's passing. Brian's mother is my father's sister, Joyce Frisby, and Brian and I corresponded after Joyce passed away in January of 2006.

Brian tells me that his mother strongly felt the presence of her departed loved ones before she passed away. He says, "I have no doubt that our family members, who have passed on are on the other side of the great 'veil' together." In March of 2005, my father, Wayne Burlingame, passed away. These are Brian's words about what happened at his mother's funeral:

"My Mom had always said that your dad was to sing at her funeral. Obviously, that couldn't happen since he died some months earlier. However, my daughter Carisa decided to sing, "How Great Thou Art" at the funeral, in place of your dad. After she sang, several people in the congregation (some family and some not) asked, **'Who was the man standing next to her as she sang?'**

"Members of the family knew who it was. It was your dad, and he was smiling. I didn't see this, but Purdy [Brian's wife] did, as well as my brother Kevin, and at least three others who didn't know your dad."

What a moving and comforting experience. Here again, we find a most unusual and unexpected way in which God endeavors to touch the very core of our being. Being so touched, the essence of God's Love and Presence becomes ever more real to us, to whom we are, and shall be. Thanks, Brian, for sharing this special experience with Lori, and ultimately with us.

On April 22, 2006, I turned forty. That was about a year after my beloved father, Wayne Burlingame, passed away on March 23, 2005 in Livingston, New Jersey. My mother, Dorothy, came out to Michigan to be with me for that week. On my birthday, Mom and I went out to dinner. It was a relaxing time for us, and the food was very tasty. For dinner, we had driven to a restaurant near Saline, Michigan.

As we were enjoying dinner, we noticed that it had begun to rain very hard. We commented on how pleased we were that we made it inside before the cloud burst! When we came out of Ruby Tuesday's restaurant, my mother noted that the rain had stopped. As we approached the car, we were again so thankful that the torrential onslaught was over. **And then we were awestruck; we saw the most beautiful double rainbow we had ever seen.**

It was a very wide rainbow with many colors in it; the first rainbow could be seen in its entirety at points, and the second rainbow could be seen on one side. We dróve to my home in Ypsilanti, about a twenty-minute drive, and the rainbow was visible to us the whole time. **I told my mother that I thought my father sent it as a birthday gift because the last time we had seen a rainbow was when we were taking my father to Kessler Institute for Rehabilitation in West Orange, New Jersey.** (That was after he had had that terrible accident.)

The rainbow was visible until we were in sight of my home, and then, it entirely disappeared. When we got inside the house, I looked at my watch and it read 6:20 p.m., the exact time I was born forty years ago. I will always be thankful to God for this gift, because I see it as a sign from my father, assuring us that he is well and always with us.

God indeed uses all avenues of approach, to give us comfort and assurance. Lori, thanks for your sharing with us. It is, once again, mindboggling to read of such miraculous events happening around us, over and over again!

Cynthia Embling Hadley, M.D.

I introduced you to my dear daughter, Cindy, in Chapter Five. There, she shared an experience she had after bringing back a patient who had stop breathing. This sharing, is also a powerful experience, that shows God gives us support, that is dreamed of, but most likely not expected.

God's Gifts

Every parent knows how special their children are. In 1991, in rural New York State, we were a young family with an infant who cried almost continuously her first ten weeks of life. We endured many long, fretful nights and prayed for the patience to make it three months—when we were sure the "colic" would resolve. That tenth week, however, Kristen ran a fever and we discovered that she had a urinary tract infection. Once treated for infection, her crying stopped!

Further testing by a pediatric urologist revealed one kidney to be much smaller than the other, and we were concerned that our dear baby had a serious problem. The three months between tests were long but prayer filled. A repeat test three months later showed two perfect, symmetrical kidneys that functioned normally. Her specialist smiled, shrugged his shoulders, and sent Kristen home with a clean bill of health. We couldn't understand this turn of events, but we were elated at our good fortune and didn't ask questions.

As Kristen advanced to toddler hood, she quickly met all her milestones. She started walking at eight months, spoke clearly and in full sentences early, and by age eleven months, at her first Christmas, she was entertaining the family by singing carols in their entirety. In spite of these achievements, she came to me one Saturday morning with a story that brought tears to my eyes and made my jaw hit the floor! Imagine my surprise as I was fixing breakfast and Kristen, age eighteen months, stated nonchalantly, "I went to Jesus' house to play last night."

"You did?" I replied noncommittaly.

"Yes," Kristen spoke matter-of-factly. "He told me that when I was a little baby I was very sick, but He made me better."

Silence. Disbelief. But, of course! "What else did Jesus say?"

"Nothing. Then I came home."

We ate our breakfast and life was as usual. I decided to say nothing to anyone and see what happened. Kristen attended church with us and spent time in the nursery, but at her age she had not received any other Christian education.

Later that same day, Kristen had a similar conversation with her father. I happened to be within earshot, but around the corner in another room. I peered around the corner at my husband just about the time his jaw hit the floor! And the instant our eyes met we understood the significance of her message to us. It was not a fluke. Our unanswered questions from her infancy were brilliantly clear. Now we knew how special our little girl really was, and how fortunate we were that she was healthy. Then came our delayed fears. Why were we told? Was Jesus going to come and take our little girl to His house again? Was this a preparation for unthinkable tragedy?

We knew our child was in God's hands, and after our weak fearfulness abated, we came to the conclusion that God had a plan for Kristen yet unknown to us, and our faith would guide us to enjoy her and nurture her the way He intended. Today, Kristen is fifteen years old, and no longer remembers her trip to Jesus' house. She is a very spiritual young lady and has had experiences with God that are uplifting and enviable. She and her older sister, Allison, have been gifts from above, and we always remember the responsibility God has given us to raise His children and to never forget how each child is so special, not only to us, but to God.

God is so wonderful. What a gift you have been given. God does indeed use a variety of ways, His love, to proclaim. Here we encounter God's Love in at least two ways. One, a child is restored to complete physical health, and her parents—people who have a strong faith, were at the same time knowingly blessed by the Almighty. In Kristen's "trip to Jesus" a double portion of God's presence is also made aware. Kristen accepting the experience so calmly and assuredly; her parents, humbled before the God of Love and Peace and Life—with the intense reminder of the depth of God's Love!

This chapter hopefully reminded us all of the many ways in which God endeavors to comfort us, as we live the life God has given us. Let us keep close to our Lord, and to His Creator and our Creator, that we may also be increasingly aware of God's presence and desire to comfort us, in so very many and different ways.

CHAPTER NINE

Occurrences Intensify Faith and Discipleship

There is any number of ways that God seems to channel our experiences in order that they may be used to intensify our faith. And if one's faith is increased, then the natural by-product is a greater degree of discipleship. Many occurrences that happen to us can be said to be miraculous. There are also divine relationships, or guidance, or support that goes unrecognized. Yet, in retrospect, they may be "seen" to have had divine involvement; miraculously understood, once our focus is on the scene in its entirety.

Jesus' followers had been sent out into the world to proclaim, or to share the truth of Jesus with them. Upon their return and their report of the exciting things that took place, Jesus said to them in private. "Blessed are the eyes that see what you see! For I tell you that many prophets and kings desired to see what you see, but did not see, and to hear what you hear, but did not hear it" (Luke 10:23-24).

As it was when Jesus walked the roads of this world, so it continues to be in the world today. The more we involve ourselves in discipleship, the more clearly we are able to "see" the Divine in our midst, both concurrently and in retrospect. In this chapter we will see how the wonder of God's involvement blesses us day after day, time and again.

Henry Snyder

Henry is a long-time friend of mine. He resides in Churchville, where I grew up. We sang in our church choir together during high school days. The primary difference between his singing and mine was that he sang on key! Henry has always been a joyful person, one who can "give you a lift" just by sharing a few minutes with him. That is not to say that he has not had to contend with sadness, heartache, and pain. Henry has a dynamic faith that he carries with him, and he knows the feeling of having that faith, carry him!

Henry has a number of occurrences to share; occurrences that could not help but intensify his faith and give new impetus to his discipleship.

> A couple of years after we were married, Gloria left work in the middle of the morning. She worked at the Jewish Home in Rochester. She did not know why she left, but she just felt something was wrong. She had no idea what might be wrong.
>
> It turned out that my son Greg had wrapped her Chevette around an electric pole on his way to work. When my brother notified me of my son's accident, I was told that he had tried to call Gloria but she had already left work. This made my brother think that she already knew of the accident and so that thinking was passed on to me.

Gloria knew something was terribly wrong, but she did not know what. It is significant that Gloria had never left early before this, nor did she after.

Here is an example of a message being sent and/or received without a cell phone. It is all the more mind boggling, when one has no sender identification. Of course, we could ask, until we are blue in the face, "How could this really happen?" But even then, we would have no answer.

Thanks be to God, we know the One who enables this to happen and who gives us the eyes to see and ears to hear even though we do not know HOW.

My good friend, Henry, has more to share with us. You will probably remember when that TWA Flight 800 blow up just after take off in the New York City area. Well, Henry's brother, Captain Steven Snyder, was the pilot of that aircraft. Henry has two totally different happenings associated with that tragic air catastrophe. Both speak to occurrences that had to be faith building.

In July of 1996, my wife, who then worked as an associate at Kaufman's Clothing Store, had a most unusual occurrence. I was driving truck over the road and gone for weeks at a time. One evening, just prior to closing, Gloria said for some reason she absolutely could not count the money in the register. As she was preparing for closing for the day, she struggled with it until she finally had to ask for help to do that simple task.

From past experiences she knew something terribly wrong had happened but she did not know what. She was immediately concerned for me. In her near stupor she got herself to her car, said a quick prayer and took several deep breaths, intent on being able to drive home safely. She had left the radio turned on and when she started the car it came on. That was when she heard a news report of a plane crash off Long Island. **She knew it had to be Steve's plane, even though she did not know then what airline owned the plane. It was not until the next day that we finally learned that indeed, Steve was one of the pilots on TWA 800.**

My intent upon writing this book is not to explain how these various events take place. My objective is to help people to know that these occurrences are plentiful and they become an ingrained cause for intensifying a person's faith and ultimately, a more entrenched reason for discipleship of God's Son, Jesus.

This is an age-long factor in the ongoing truth that **God is still speaking. Miracles, Holy Experiences, Divine Occurrences all speak the language of people in every place—and to those most touched, they become "fuel" for the engines of Faith and Discipleship.**

Henry shares another astounding, almost unbelievable occurrence, that took place before hundreds gathered at his brother's memorial service.

Several similar things have happened in our family that we have taken to be signs from God that our deceased loved one was okay. At my mother's memorial service, during the service a picture of her on a stand in front of the church turned without any known cause. At the funeral of Peter, my niece's husband, who was killed in a farm accident, a flower vase turned, again, for no apparent reason.

When my brother, Steve, was killed on that flight 800, we held a memorial service in our high school in order to accommodate the multitude of family, work associates, friends and all who planned to attend. It is a good thing that we did. Prior to the service, his captain's hat was placed on a pedestal on the stage near the speaker's podium. Those who put the hat on the stand took special care to fasten it so it would stay put during the sacred service.

The beautiful and meaningful service proceeded without incident, until a soloist, Steve Valvano was singing a song, that was making a devotional impact upon all in attendance. During that high-moment in the service, Steve's captain's hat, fastened as it was, fell to the floor.

We all gasped when that happened, a sign to all that Steve was in God' care. It was a shocking surprise to all, except for some of his family, who were not totally surprised that something of that nature took place.

That was a heart warming, faith-intensifying occurrence. I was not personally in attendance, but I know many of my extended family and friends who were there. One after another spoke of the event and how it was so meaningfully moving.

The Power, the Love, the Presence of God is so great that it behooves us to acknowledge God in our midst. God speaks and speaks to all humanity, sometimes through music, other times through occurrences that are miraculous before us, and in every other thinkable experience.

Henry shares another contact made by God, as in God's own way, God still speaks.

> Things that some people might say are coincidences, are no doubt God's Will being worked out. Our dear friend, Elaine Page, has been my brother Tom and Carol's close friend since their college days. Elaine has nursing and ministerial training. (She is a registered nurse and an Ordained Minister in the United Church of Christ.)
>
> She was for several months the Interim Pastor at our church in Churchville. It was during her time there that brother Steve's airplane blew up. Rev. Elaine was there for us in a very significant way; as a dear friend whom we all loved, as a clergy person who communicated with us in a deep spiritual way that gave us support and reassurance of God's Eternal Love and Life, and she prepared and conducted a most meaningful Memorial Service for Steve. Yes, she was an inspiration for us, before, during, and after the Memorial Service. Soon after that Rev. Elaine went on to another position at Nazareth College from which she retired in May of 2003.
>
> After that, she set herself up in a one-person care-giving business. It was about then that I needed someone to help me care for Gloria. We became Elaine's first clients in her new venture. She was literally a godsend to us. It had to be more than just happenstance that this

dear, compassionate lady would become so important to our family in such desperate times in our lives. "To me and my house," God has been the administrator of the many blessings we have received. Not just in sorrow, but in day after day occurrences that have enabled us to "hold the course" in faith, and continue our desire to serve our Lord and Master.

Without discussion, I want to lead you right into an experience that could have been tragic if somehow God did not "protect" Henry from some particular thoughts!

Many years ago, I was very busy farming, along with my brother, Tom. I was married and raising our two wonderful children. I had two goals in those days; I wanted to leave the farm a better one than what we had inherited. My second goal was simply to stay married to the same lady for life. The farm was having financial difficulties, and my marriage was in trouble.

I viewed myself as a total failure, not coming close to achieving either of my two goals. I actually thought the world would be better off without me, and I tried to figure out a way to accomplish that. The thought of screwing up and becoming just disabled kept me from doing anything.

I never said a word of this to anyone at the time, so it wasn't a cry for help. As time passed, the marriage ended and I met and married Gloria. I left the farm and realized that there was life after farming, and that we were not the only farmers in financial trouble. As the years went on, I realized that some folks had ended their lives by driving into trains, and other such foolproof ways.

Today I am utterly convinced that God kept those thoughts out of my head, because God knew if I thought of them, I most likely would have followed through.

The experiences and/or occurrences shared in this chapter by Henry have truly been diverse. In each case, the very presence of God was recognized, as the experience took place or came into light thereafter. God speaks in many ways and when we become aware of that dialogue, our view of life and our goals in life are put to question. Indeed, as faith is made more real and stronger, we most generally put our whole being under scrutiny, as we look for ways to better serve the God of all life.

Henry has one last experience to share with us. It pertains to an assurance he received that his deceased wife was alive and doing well.

Late this fall, my wife's niece's husband—who is really much closer than the "title" might indicate—wanted to look up something like "Heavenly Sightings." Keep in mind my wife, Gloria, passed away a year ago in September. As he logged on he had to establish a password.

As he started to type his first name, Gary, the name "Gloria Snyder" with the appropriate capital letters popped up on the computer screen. According to knowledgeable people he knows, the only way that name would have been there is if someone had typed it in on that particular computer.

Gary is not a practical joker and he was astonished when he saw it pop up. I know Gloria had not used any computer in fifteen years. That was back in the dark ages before the Internet, computer wise. The only explanation is hard to believe, but somehow my dear wife Gloria gave us a beautiful message that she loved us and was doing well.

It is a miraculous, mysterious, comforting and reassuring occurrence when we are shown that neither God's love, nor our life, is terminated when our life on this planet meets its demise.

Nancy Glidden Maier

Nancy is a dear friend of my sister, Lorraine and her husband, Jack. Nancy was a high school classmate of Lorraine and they have kept in touch over the years. She shared her experience with my sister, who was so engulfed in it that she requested her to send it to me. Her experience is so truly supportive of God's Love and Presence that it will "lift you up" as you read her sharing of it with us.

In September of 1977 I kept having the same dream night after night. I had it so often that it was like a part of me and I knew just about every detail of it. In the dream, the Lord was leading me to the hospital to witness to doctors and nurses. I was on the operating table singing, "Bless the Lord, O My Soul" and also "All That Is In Me, Bless His Holy Name." In the dream, in addition to the singing, I was to tell the doctors and nurses, "The Lord loved them and wants to be their Savior and Lord of their lives." (I was not going to say the name of Jesus so I would not offend anyone who was Jewish.)

After having that repeated dream, I went to my doctor for a check up for a fibroid tumor. He told me to come back in six months. When I went back we found that the tumor had been growing rapidly. There now was more than one, and one of them was the size of a three-month pregnancy. As the doctor was talking about surgery, I said, "I was thankful for medicine and doctors and nurses, but I also believed that God could heal me." He went on to explain that he would do a complete hysterectomy and remove a lot of scar tissue, which had my uterus and bladder, stuck together. Continuing on, the doctor said, "I will also take care of several scar tissues in your intestines resulting from past caesarian section surgeries."

When he took a breath, I blurted out, "Can't you just scrape them out?" He responded, "No, you have to have the surgery." I went home and I prayed, asking the Lord what I should do. I did not know if I should tell the doctor, "I will trust the Lord to heal me and refuse the operation," or if I should have the surgery and trust the Lord that it would be to His glory.

As I was praying, it was as if He was sitting at the table with me. I had my Bible and opened and my eyes focused on Ezekiel 2:4-8: "Go where I am sending you and do not be afraid of their faces. They will know they have heard a message of the Lord." That was pretty clear. But when I turned the page and there it was again. "Go where I am sending you and do not be afraid of their faces. They will know they have heard a message of the Lord." With that, what else could I do but go?

As a result, I started writing scriptural verses on little homemade bookmarks. I put them in some small red Bibles. I made them so that I could give them to whoever came in my hospital room.

My surgery was scheduled for May 6, 1977. I had to be in the hospital the day prior to my surgery. Once I arrived there and got a bit settled, I took a bath and **I was no longer in pain.** When the house doctor came in and checked me, I said, "Are you sure the tumors are still in there? I am out of pain!" He took some life history and I gave him a little red Bible, with one of the scripture bookmarks. The doctor said, "O, a Bible, I'll pray for you." With that I responded, "I'll be praying for you, it appears that you know the Lord." The doctor got up and left and then came back and said, "I believe in God."

"Later, my doctor came in and I asked him the same question. "Are you sure the tumors are still in there?" He replied, "Yes, they're still there and progressing." I was all ready for surgery, with IV's and all necessary preparation.

"They took me to the operating room. The first thing the anesthesiologist told me was that once he put the medication in my IV, I would go right to sleep. I said, "You mean I won't even have time to sing?" He said,

"You won't even be able to talk." I did not get to sing it but I did at least say, 'Bless the Lord.'

"My doctor came over to me and he appeared to me as if he were a messenger of the Lord. It turns out he was! I knew that the Lord was with us and that He was in complete control of everything and everyone in that room.

The next thing I knew, the anesthesiologist and a nurse were trying to wake me up. Then they told me, "The tumors are gone and you did not have to have surgery." I raised my hands to the Lord and said, "Praise the Lord! Bless the Lord! Alleluia!" At that a nurse said, "She's Pentecostal." To which I responded, "No, I'm just a Christian, I love Jesus and He healed me."

After I was taken back up to my room, my doctor came in and sat on the window sill and said, "I don't know what happened." I said, "The Lord healed me." And then he looked at me and said, "I guess so." I had made my doctor a plaque with the scripture in calligraphy: "Walk worthy of the vocation wherewith you are called." I gave it to him and he was pleased.

We have been sharing "Occurrences that Intensify Faith and Discipleship." I have not seen Nancy in quite some time but with that miraculous experience, I am confident that her strong faith has been enhanced and her discipleship intensified. Thank you, Nancy, for sharing this, and allowing us to include your experience in the libraries of our minds, and faith.

Harold Hart

I introduced you to Harold in Chapter Five, at the same time that I wrote of his wife, Alvah. They are a happily married couple who have been very active in the Christian Church wherever they have lived. Their love of God, their consistent good will and compassion for others has endeared them to me (and Audrey). Harold's sharing, like Alvah's, was given to us at their home when we visited them on one of our trips. With a depth of faith and deep appreciation for a miraculous occurrence he had, Harold now shares with us as his wife speaks for him.

After Harold sold their grocery store in Castile, New York, he worked at different places to keep busy and have some time to make plans for the future. Eventually he put in an application for work at Tops Market. He enjoyed his work in his own store; had a special knack for cutting meat and preparing it for sale. On his way home from Tops, he stopped by Gowanda State Hospital and there he also filled out an application.

He said that he did not know why he had stopped at Gowanda, because he absolutely had no plans to do that. **Two weeks later he was awakened during the night hearing a real rough, gruff voice saying, 'No, Not Tops! No, Not Tops! He was dumbfounded as to why that happened to him, but his faith and past experiences made him take it seriously.**

The next day about ten o'clock, Tops Market called Harold and asked him to come to work. Remembering the tough and rough voice he had heard in the night, he said no to the offer.

About one o'clock that same afternoon, the hospital at Gowanda called and asked him to come to work. He accepted that position and stayed with them for fourteen years and ten months as a therapist aide. (His wife, Alvah, had worked there for twenty-one years prior to and after they owned the Red and White Store in Castile.)

Harold is convinced—in fact he says "he knows" that God wanted him to work there in the Gowanda Hospital. His dark night experience with that clear but rough and tough voice was a message sent by God.

God speaks to us in so many different ways. The variety of instruments that God makes use of, ought to keep us alert to that Divine Presence as God calls us, directs us, enables us, and in any other way, seeks to influence our lives to the glory and purpose he intends for us.

Harold is a calm man of great faith in God and God's Son, Jesus. An overview of his life and his wife, Alvah brought these words in the Thirty-Seventh Psalm to come to my mind.

"Do not fret because of the wicked;
Do not be envious of wrongdoers,
For they will soon fade like the grass,
And wither like the green herb.
"Trust in the Lord and do good,
So you will live in the land and enjoy security.
Take delight in the Lord
And He will give you the desires of your heart."
(Psalm 37:1-4)

Mary S. Reagan

I introduced you to Mary in Chapter Six. She is our second child and she is about to share with us an occurrence that had to speak volumes for her faith, for her continued love of God, and her discipleship.

Mary was married during her college days and she lived with her husband, Donald Brown, in a small basement apartment that we put together for them. Don was an artist. He worked for Champion Products of Perry, New York, and he did a small amount of artwork for hire, for individuals who realized his tremendous talent.

On or about their third anniversary, they purchased a fix-up house in the village of Castile. It was there that they lived when Colin, their son, was born. It is also where they lived when Don was killed in a head-on automobile crash. Another person driving as if he were suicidal passed a snowplow in a blinding snowstorm, hitting Don head-on, killing him instantly. It was devastating to all who loved him. It is in reference to that fatal accident and its aftermath that Mary shares with us.

> It was 10:15 in the morning. I was a case worker for the Wyoming County Social Services Department. I was sitting at my desk when my chair seemed to turn by itself, so that I could see the clock on the wall on the opposite side of the office. I felt an unsettled feeling all morning. A few hours later, my parents arrived at my workplace to tell me my husband, Don, had been killed in an automobile accident earlier that day. (Since I was not home to be notified by the police, the police had gone to my parents' home to try to locate me.)

My first question was really a statement. "It happened at 10:15." Yes, it did. Don had come to me to say goodbye on his way to heaven.

When I was in the fourth grade, my Grandpa Embling died.

During gym class, while waiting for my turn in kick-ball, **I doubled over in pain—-looked at the clock and the pain was gone. Later that day I found out that Grandpa had died at the same time as my gym class incident.** I always felt that Grandpa had stopped to tell me good-bye on his way to heaven. It was, for me, a Holy Moment that I have never forgotten.

My first husband, Don, disagreed with me. He stated that such encounters were imaginary. Well, about two weeks after Don's death I had an experience when I was sitting on the sofa in our home. I was tired, but unable to sleep. Suddenly, Don came walking across the room toward me.

He looked different only in that he looked totally relaxed and elated. He communicated with me, but without really speaking. He told me he felt no pain when he died. He was driving down the road and suddenly he was face-to-face with Saint Peter and the Pearly Gates. He let me know that he had argued that he could not just leave Colin and me, so he was allowed to visit us at the time he died.

Now he was allowed to see me! Don wanted me to remember a conversation we had had on several occasions about his desire if he died. It was that I remarry and Colin be adopted by his new dad, **"because a picture can't raise him."**

I told Don "I don't want someone else—I want you." At that a tear slipped down his cheek. He told me he had to go. He couldn't stay any longer, because he was not ever to be in a situation where he was unhappy. As he faded from my vision, he told me, "I've gotten to see you and Colin (in the picture) and you are going to be so happy."

Then he also said to me, "Remember, I told you these visits couldn't happen. Well, you were right, and (in a disbelieving tone) I was wrong."

After all that, I want only to say, Holy Moments, Sacred Occurrences and Miracles are happening all around us. When we become aware of them, they give us a peace that comes from God, not to be found in any other place. For those who are a part of or who see these experiences, recognize them as Holy, Sacred and forever to be treasured moments—because they know that they are truly one way in which God speaks to us.

Thanks for reading this book. I hope you have gained as much as I have in writing, reading over contributions from others, editing, and sharing so many experiences by so many wonderful people. And may God's Love continue to touch you and yours and all God's people.

Now then, please:

BE HAPPY, GOD LOVES YOU, AND ALWAYS WILL.